Hockey Chicago Style:
The History of the Chicago Blackhawks

by

Paul Greenland

SAGAMORE PUBLISHING

Champaign, IL 61820

Interior design: Mary Jane Harshbarger
Editor: Susan M. McKinney
Jacket design: Michelle R. Dressen
Proofreader: Phyllis L. Bannon

ISBN:1-57167-021-1
Library of Congress catalog card number: 95-71923

We have made every effort to trace the ownership of copyrighted photos. If we have failed to give adequate credit, we will be pleased to make changes in future printings.

The name Blackhawks is spelled as one word throughout this book. The author acknowledges that the name was spelled as Black Hawks until it was changed in the late 1970s.

Printed in the United States.

70 Years of Hawks Experience.

This book is dedicated to:

All the men who have donned the Indianhead sweater with pride;
and to Scott M. Fisher, author of *The Ironmen: The 1939 Hawkeyes*;
and in loving memory of Frank A. Isabelli, Jr., cousin and friend. You will never be forgotten.

————————————————————————

ACKNOWLEDGMENTS

A book such as this requires the cooperation and insight of many individuals. Without all the cooperation received from the many players, officials, and individuals associated with the Chicago Blackhawks it would have never been possible. To the Chicago Blackhawks and all of the many individuals who have helped me over the past five years, I will be forever grateful. I would like to acknowledge the following people for their special contributions to the book:

George Allen
George H. Bathje, III
Jim Belushi
Mrs. Max Bentley
Chris Chelios
Vince Chiaramonte
Cully Dahlstrom
Barbara Davidson
Jeff Davis
Ron Elkins
Scott M. Fisher
Jack Fitzsimmons
Bill Gadsby
Billy Gardner
David Greenland
The Greenland Family
Glenn Hall
Mary Jane Harshbarger
William "Red" Hay
Dennis Hull
Dick Irvin, Jr.
Thomas Ivan
Cliff Koroll
Ed Litzenberger
Chico Maki

Harold "Mush" March
Robert Markus
Pit Martin
Stan Mikita
Billy Mosienko
Harris G. Mosley
Grant Mulvey
Joe Murphy
Jim Pappin
Pierre Pilote
Rudy Pilous
Cliff "Fido" Purpur
Billy Reay
John Robertson
Jeremy Roenick
Terry Ruskowski
Cam Russell
Al Secord
Steve Smith
Pat Stapleton
Bill Stewart
The Sunday Family
Gary Suter
Sammy Taft
Brian Thomas
Andy vanHellemond

The radio home of Chicago Blackhawk Hockey.

Cold Steel On Us.

Chicago's Sports Leader

CONTENTS

FOREWORD

BY BILL GADSBY

The year was 1946, I was 18 years old—the event—training camp for the Chicago Blackhawks. To say I was excited would be an understatement, a dream come true is more like it. Skating with Doug and Max Bentley, Billy Mosienko, Johnny Mariucci, Red Hamill, names I had listened to on Foster Hewitt's hockey night in Canada while growing up in Calgary, Alberta. Hockey was my first love. I played other sports, but hockey was my favorite. My dad would help flood the neighborhood rink and often I'd come in for lunch without taking my skates off.

It's true our team in Chicago was not doing well in my rookie year, but I got a lot of ice time and improved my game watching the older players in practice. Detroit also had a rookie in 1946 who was to become my teammate and friend—Gordie Howe—he was a few months younger, he never lets me forget it, and I never let him forget that I out-scored him in our rookie year. From then on he took off in the goal scoring department.

The old Chicago Stadium was an exciting place to play, with the big organ and eager fans, I mean EAGER and loud.

From Calgary, a city of 180,000 in 1946 to a great metropolis like Chicago—from a crowd of 2,500 to a record of 20,000 fans in the Stadium, it was awesome!

Major McLaughlin, owner, Bill Tobin, president and general manager, Johnny Gottselig, coach, and Joe Farrell in publicity were all instrumental to me in my eight years as a Blackhawk. I have many happy memories.

The Blackhawk organization, with owners' names like the Norris family and the Wirtz family, has been a stalwart and successful hockey franchise. I am proud to have been a small part of their great history.

– Bill Gadsby #4

PROLOGUE

As I sat there in an empty Chicago Stadium, waiting for the athletes to emerge from their locker room for practice, everything around me was dark and quiet. Above me, attached to the rafters, were the banners commemorating various Chicago Blackhawk achievements and the numbers of retired athletes. The only sound was the ghostly movement of air circulating through the cavernous area.

Sitting alone in an arena with 17,317 empty seats, except yours, is quite an experience. I took a minute to reflect upon all of the great athletes and achievements that have been witnessed in this empty arena, and the project that I had undertaken in trying to write about them.

Before long, the players began to emerge one by one into the unlit rink. Donned in red-and-black practice jerseys they gracefully circled about the rink in true hawk-like fashion. Eventually, after hundreds of pucks were brought on the ice, and the main lights had come on, the rest of the players emerged and the grueling practice began. As pucks and men crashed into the plexiglas near my seat and the players began to look exhausted, I realized that the season that lay ahead of them was in a certain sense symbolic of the long road ahead of me in completing this book. As far as my performance is concerned, I hope that I won't let you, the reader, down.

This book is written out of the deepest respect and honor for the Chicago Blackhawk tradition. Many men have made sacrifices, physical and otherwise, to make it the great tradition it is today. In a February 12, 1995 *Chicago Sun Times* article by Brian Hanley, Chicago Blackhawk defenseman Gary Suter said: "Chicago traditionally has been a hard-working team. That's what the Blackhawks emblem is all about. With the Chicago Blackhawks, it doesn't matter if the players change, it's still the system. You're pushed to play hard every night. That's what the Hawks are all about."

A professor of mine used to tell me "writing is an imperfectable skill." There is always something more to be said, something that could be said differently or in a better light. As a writer, I have pushed myself hard to get the information that was available and to get the interviews from those individuals associated with the team who were willing to share their stories with me. Many of the players themselves have proofread chapters pertaining to the eras in which they played. For this help, I will be forever thankful. Jeff Davis and the staff at the Hockey Hall of Fame in Toronto, Ontario, have also been an invaluable resource from the very beginning in myriad ways. I have strived for accuracy and a variety of perspectives as much as possible. With that in mind, I hope that you, the reader, will find enjoyment in the following pages that will take you on a journey through Chicago Blackhawk history.

"What color should I paint the nursery, home or away?"

THE BUILDERS

The Chicago Blackhawks are a franchise rich with history. Several men have been influential in the development of the team since its inception in 1926. Major Frederic McLaughlin, Bill Tobin, James D. Norris, James D. Norris, Jr., Arthur Wirtz, and William Wirtz have all contributed in a myriad of ways, financial and otherwise, to bring a dynamic hockey club to the Windy City. The Chicago Blackhawks' extraordinarily colorful past began with a 1901 Harvard graduate and coffee millionaire whose name was Major Frederic McLaughlin.

Born on June 28, 1877, in Chicago, Illinois, "The Major" served as secretary-treasurer of his father's coffee business before becoming involved in the world of hockey. They produced the well-known brand of McLaughlin's Manor House Coffee. After his father passed away and his brother George was killed in a car crash, Frederic McLaughlin stepped up to become company president.

Later, in 1917, McLaughlin served as a sergeant with the First Illinois Field Artillery on the Mexican border. He then went overseas to command the 333rd Machine Gun Battalion of the 8th (Blackhawk) Division of the U.S. Army during World War I.

A skillful polo player, The Major was responsible for bringing big-time polo to the city of Chicago. The board of directors of the American National Jockey Club elected him to head their organization in 1927. He also belonged to both the

Major Frederic McLaughlin founder of the Blackhawks. (Photo courtesy of the Hockey Hall of Fame/Ernie Fitzsimmons Collection.)

Onwentsia Club and the International Team. As a member of Chicago society, The Major also belonged to many clubs, such as the Saddle and Cycle, Shoreacres, Old Elm, and the Chicago Club.

Longtime off-ice official Jack Fitzsimmons recalled The Major:

"He was a nice man, he was a gentleman but he wasn't the sportsman that [later owner Jim] Norris was. Norris used to go into the dressing room and talk to the guys, which was important and is important. Major McLaughlin didn't have that technique, or maybe he didn't think it was important. But in all fairness, at that time hockey was just getting off the ground and you must give Major McLaughlin credit for reestablishing the franchise from Portland, Oregon to the Chicago area."

John Robertson, who has been with the Blackhawks since the late 1930s, recalls The Major in a colorful light. Said Robertson:

"[It's because of him that] I started to learn how to drink coffee. In those days, they kept the equipment over at 666 North LaSalle Street, which was the coffee warehouse. The Blackhawk office was on the first floor. On the second floor they had coffee testing, and that was one of the things that Major McLaughlin [had us do]. He had us come up to the testing room and test the coffee. The Major thought that hockey players should be like polo players. I now remember one time, he was one of the first to stress fitness, and he sent the club down to Tim Howard's Gym on Randolph Street, where the Civic Center is now. Earl Seibert, one of the defensemen, and in my opinion one of the strongest men I ever saw, was working out in the gym. He was pulling those rubber stretchers, and he'd go 'one-two, one-two-three,' and break it. So he said to Major McLaughlin, 'we can't go to the gym anymore.'"

Thinking back, George Allen, former defenseman of the early forties, gave his impression of the Chicago-born McLaughlin:

"He was Sergeant major, ya know, and he was tough. When I knew him, one time you'd talk to him and he'd be like your mother, and the next time he'd be like a bloody wall cat! He treated us not too bad because we were cleaning up in Chicago, averaging crowds of 17,000 to 18,000."

Cully Dahlstrom, who played center for the Blackhawks during the thirties and forties, remembered The Major as all business.

"I thought he was a boss, ya know, he was number one. He was the money behind it [the Blackhawks]. But, I always found him to be pleasant with me and I thought he was fair."

Cliff "Fido" Purpur remembers The Major this way:

"I don't know if he was English or what, but he was great for horse racing. He always said, "Well, you take a horse...," and tell me about a horse. Oh, I loved the guy! He owned the Manor House Coffee Company. Hell, we went to the Manor House Company to pick our checks up. One time, he started tellin' me about a goalie he had from Winnipeg, ya know. He said, 'He'd leave you only so much room,' and I said, 'I'll have to pick the puck up and put it in sideways!'"

It was Tex Rickard, a well-known New York boxing promoter, who got The Major interested in ice hockey and in placing an NHL franchise in Chicago. Tex, who had placed a franchise in New York, thought a rival team in the city of Chicago would be an excellent idea. So did The Major. By September 25, 1926, he had received an NHL franchise for $12,000 and purchased the entire Portland (Oregon) Rosebuds hockey team of the Western Canadian Hockey League for $200,000. The Rosebuds were one of six WCHL teams being sold by Lester and Frank Patrick. The Major headed a group of businessmen to buy the team. The group included R.H. "Tack" Hardwick (former Harvard football player), R.A. Gardner (famous golfer), C.F. Clere, I.N. Perry, L.P. Ordway, and John F. Mitchell, Jr.

One of The Major's business deals took him into the Federal courts shortly after his newly-formed Blackhawk team had taken to the ice. A Canadian sports promoter by the name of Edward J. Livingstone charged that The Major had stolen four of his star players and his Chicago franchise in 1925, while trying to establish the yet-to-be Blackhawks. According to Livingstone, The Major and two business associates by the names of William J. Foster and John S. Kellog went up to Canada where his America Hockey Association franchise, the Chicago Cardinals, were playing. They persuaded his four best players—Edward Graham, Marvin Wentworth, Robert Burns, and Ralph Taylor—to break their contracts and sign with the New NHL Chicago Blackhawks. He attempted to sue The Major for $700,000 ($500,000 for damages and the remainder for malicious practices), claiming that this had cost him his franchise. Livingstone had also made arrangements to lease the Chicago Coliseum, but as it turned out, the always-shrewd major ended up getting that as well. The rest is history!

McLaughlin's originality was a major force in making hockey a more exciting game for the fan by speeding up the action. Reportedly, it was he who, along with his managers, began using three sets of forward lines for three-minute intervals. This move reduced the fatigue experienced by the players.

In 1923, The Major surprised Chicago society when he married Irene Castle, the famous dancer and movie star of the 1920s who invented the "Castle Walk" with her brother Vernon, who was also quite a dancer, and a former heroic World War I fighter pilot. After The Major became Castle's third husband, they took a lengthy honeymoon in the Orient. "She was at all of 'em [the games]," said George Allen, "she'd put on a new shoe and was always strutting around." Slightly eccentric, her name was always in the newspapers. Perhaps she was most famous for her crusade to save all of Chicago's homeless dogs. Teaming up with the Chicago Police Department, she had a three-building facility built to house the stray animals. She was famous for protesting tail sets at horse shows, and advocating the adoption of stray dogs rather than pedigreed ones by people wanting pets.

Unfortunately, her Orphans of the Storm dog haven was set on fire and, according to the police, it was no accident. With the help of nearby neigh- bors, she saved 35 dogs but lost the remaining 90. Exhausted and covered with soot, she exclaimed to a *New York Times* reporter: "I got notes saying the place was a nuisance and the dogs howled at night, but it wasn't true." Whatever the case, she continued serving as director of the Anti-Cruelty Society. Castle also spent time in New York, trying her luck as a fashion consultant. She designed the Blackhawks' first uniforms and failed (fortunately) to place tassels on them.

The Major passed away on December 17, 1944, leaving two children, William and Barbara. In 1963, he was inducted into the Hockey Hall of Fame as a builder.

BILL TOBIN

Born in Ottawa, Ontario, where he played amateur hockey, Bill Tobin became involved with the Blackhawks in the late 1920s. He supposedly was en route to Ottawa from a goaltending stint in Edmonton when he stopped to visit some friends who were playing for the Hawks. It was then that he met The Major and became his right-hand man.

William (Bill) Tobin became The Major's right-hand man. (Photo from the Hockey Hall of Fame/Ernie Fitzsimmons Collection.)

He remained in Chicago, and worked his way up in the organization to serve as manager, alternate governor, and eventually team owner when The Major passed away and he, along with a syndicate of businessmen, purchased controlling interest. Tobin was the owner of the Chicago Blackhawks until September 11, 1952, when he sold his controlling interest to the men who owned the Stadium: James D. Norris, James D. Norris, Jr., and Arthur M. Wirtz. During his association with the team, Tobin was pressed into coaching for The Major for half a season after coach Tom Shaughnessy was fired. He also went on to share half a season behind the bench with Dick Irvin in 1931.

During his association with the Hawks, in 1941, Tobin operated the Kansas City Americans of the U.S. Hockey League. He did so for ten years, until the independent club became part of the Blackhawks' organization. Tobin passed away from emphysema on May 8, 1963, in Chicago.

"Bill Tobin was a terrific General Manager," recalled John Robertson. "He operated the club on a shoestring for Major McLaughlin. He was a very shrewd business man, and a good fellow to work for. I know that was one of the things that Bill Tobin wanted to do [was] to share the gates. In those days, as it is now, your team depended on all of their money from [them], and paid all of their own expenses. He was voted down. But he was very progressive for his day, due to the fact that he wanted to give bonuses to escalate play. They [the players] were lucky if they made seven thousand a year. Thirty-five-hundred was the going salary. One thing that Mr. Tobin used to do was give ya four thousand, or if you got so many goals or so many assists, give ya eight thousand."

James D. Norris, Sr.

Born in Montreal, James D. Norris was a true lover of the sport of hockey. While in Montreal, he attended both McGill University and the Montreal Collegiate Institute. At the latter institution, he was known for his ability in both hockey and lacrosse.

Known among his business associates as "Big Jim," Norris came to Chicago in 1907 and became a wealthy grain broker and international businessman after starting the Norris Grain Company. He later held business interests in different hotels, railroads, banks, transportation companies, and arenas such as Chicago Stadium, Madison Square Garden, and Detroit's Olympia Arena. Once he was established in the grain business, he invested portions of his fortune in sports, especially hockey teams.

At one time, Norris attempted to gain a second NHL franchise in Chicago, but The Major wouldn't allow it. So, Norris formed the Chicago Shamrocks of the American Hockey Association and later became owner of the Detroit Red Wings. He relished it whenever the Red Wings beat the Blackhawks because of his rivalry with The Major.

Unlike his son, James, Jr., the elder Norris was well respected by many players. Recalling a fond memory of Norris, Ed Litzenberger, former Team Captain of the 1961 Stanley Cup champion Blackhawks, said:

"I really admired the guy. I had a problem in Chicago and I used to wake up in the hospital and he would be standing at the foot of my bed. He was a powerful man and he either liked you or he didn't like you, and if he didn't like you, then get out of the way. I really thought Mr. James Norris was my kind of guy, and for some reason or another he took a liking to me and I really admired him. He did a lot of things, but he never ever bitched or criticized or swore, even when we had our bad years. At least I can't remember. I like a tough guy because at least I know where I stand. I knew what I expected, and I knew what he expected of me. It made it easy for everybody."

On December 4, 1952, at the age of 73, Norris died of a heart attack in Chicago's Passavant Hospital. A short while before his death, Norris withdrew his controlling interest in the Stadium, and a syndicate composed of his sons, James Jr., and Bruce Norris, as well as Arthur Wirtz took over. At the time of his death, his son, James D. Norris, Jr. was co-owner and vice-president of the Blackhawks. In

1958, Norris was inducted into the Hockey Hall of Fame as a builder. He also was awarded the Lester Patrick Trophy (outstanding service to hockey in the U.S.) in 1967.

JAMES D. NORRIS, JR.

A very wealthy man, James D. Norris, Jr. inherited his fortune from his father. While involved with the team, he was both co-owner and president of the Chicago Blackhawks. He was said to have been more comfortable around sports and sporting figures than the society crowd into which he was born.

Norris controlled the world of boxing from 1949-58, while serving as president of the International Boxing Club. Controlling arenas in Chicago, New York, Detroit, Omaha, and St. Louis, a federal court eventually declared the operation a monopoly. Two of his associates, underworld figures Frankie Carbo and Frank (Blinky) Palermo, went to jail for conspiracy. In the February 26, 1966 issue of the *New York Times*, he was quoted as saying his relationship with Carbo had embarrassed his business associates, and, as he said, "embarrassed me with my horses, which after hockey are my greatest love."

In 1962, Norris was inducted into the Hockey Hall of Fame as a builder. He was also awarded the Lester Patrick Trophy (outstanding service to hockey in the U.S.) posthumously in 1972. Norris died of a heart attack at St. Luke's Presbyterian Hospital on February 25, 1966. He had experienced two previous heart attacks, as well as a disturbed heart rhythm condition. When he passed away, he had about $250 million in personal wealth, including three homes, one in Chicago, and the others in Coral Gables, Florida, and Mattituck, Louisiana. After Norris' death, William Wirtz became president of the team.

ARTHUR M. WIRTZ

Born January 23, 1901 to Chicago policeman Frederick Wirtz, Arthur Wirtz became involved in the sports world when he and the elder Norris purchased Detroit's Olympia Arena in 1933, and later the Chicago Stadium in 1935. During the thirties, they brought the Hollywood Ice Revue to the Stadium, which featured four-time Olympic medal winner Sonja Henie. The event was so successful, it allowed the two to pay off the Stadium, and ac-

James Norris, Jr. preferred sports and sporting events to the society crowd into which he was born. (Photo courtesy of the Blackhawks.)

quire both the St. Louis Arena and Madison Square Garden.

The two men had formed a business partnership in 1929 when Norris purchased land at Randolph and Michigan Avenue through Wirtz. After that, the two were partners in many different ventures for 37 years. After Norris died, his son James, Jr. continued the partnership until his death in 1966.

Known by business associates as the "Baron of the Bottom Line," Wirtz graduated from the University of Michigan and then began a successful career as a commercial leasing broker. He made his fortune through real estate, which was always his primary business interest. A very brilliant man who kept a relatively low profile, Wirtz was well liked by the community and was named the Chicagoan of the year by the Chicago Boys Club in 1977.

Wirtz died in Henrotin Hospital on July 21, 1983, after spending almost eight months in the hospital. His wife of 57 years had passed away the year before. At the time of his death, he left behind a great fortune and was the owner and chairman of

Arthur Wirtz was known in the business world as the "Baron of the Bottom Line". (Photo courtesy of the Blackhawks.)

ventures, he is involved with both the Maryville Academy and the Rehabilitation Institute of Chicago, as well as the Prairie State Games (past Chairman, 1984/85). He also served on both the 1980 and 1984 Winter Olympic Committees. Currently, he is a trustee for the Chicago Latin School Foundation, and is very much involved with the new United Center, along with Chicago Bulls owner Jerry Reinsdorf, Wirtz's partner in the venture.

In 1976, Wirtz was inducted in the Hockey Hall of Fame as a builder. In 1985, he was inducted in the U.S. Hockey Hall of Fame as an administrator. In addition to these honors, Wirtz was also awarded the Lester Patrick Trophy (outstanding service to hockey in the U.S.) in 1978.

the board of the Blackhawks. In 1971, Wirtz was inducted into the Hockey Hall of Fame as a builder. He was also awarded the Lester Patrick Trophy (for outstanding service to hockey in the U.S.) in 1985.

WILLIAM W. WIRTZ

William Wirtz is the President and owner of the Chicago Blackhawks today. The son of Arthur Wirtz, William graduated from Brown University in 1950. He is currently a member of the NHL Executive Committee. Prior to the 1991-92 season, when he chose to step down, Wirtz had been elected as Chairman of the NHL Board of Governors nine times, serving a total of 18 years in that capacity. During his years on The Board of Governors, Wirtz successfully faced many challenges. Among them were such endeavors as the merger of the WHA with the NHL and League expansion.

Wirtz has been, and still is, actively involved in pursuits aside from the Blackhawks. In addition to responsibilities related to his family's business

William W. Wirtz is the current president and owner of the Blackhawks. (Photo courtesy of the Blackhawks.)

6

THE EARLY YEARS

1926—1930

The game of hockey was a totally different game during this era. Teams skated with seven men per side, utilizing one skater as a "rover," and goals were but two poles mounted on a moveable base. Dick Irvin explained these conditions from a player's perspective in a February 13, 1956 *Sports Illustrated* article by Whitney Tower. "Hockey, in my day as a player, may have been dirtier—but it was not tougher to play," he explained. "By dirtier I mean plain brutal. The butt end of a stick could break off in a man's ribs and the referee would never call it. Today the refereeing is better and the hockey is better too. A man does more skating now than he used to in a whole game. It was the total legalizing of the forward pass in 1929 that opened up hockey. In my [day they had] board-checking, but the game was so slow that if you tried it today, you'd put 15,000 people to sleep—or else they'd walk out on you."

Chicago Blackhawks First Team 1926-27, left to right: Hugh Lehman, Bob Trapp, Duke Dukowski, Gord Fraser, Dick Irvin, George Hay, Mickey MacKay, Babe Dye, Cully Wilson, Eddie Rodden, Rabbit McVeigh. (Photo from the Hockey Hall of Fame/Ernie Fitzsimmons Collection.)

The players who donned the earliest Chicago Blackhawk sweaters were a tough breed for sure. This was doubly true for the net-minders. While playing without the masks and protective equipment players wear today, they were often subject to abuse from rowdy fans in the different leagues in which they played. In a press advance, one Canadian sportswriter of years past once commented that "they were …prime targets of fans who hurled empty spirit bottles, pieces of boards and even chairs in their direction. On outdoor rinks, where tobacco-chewing spectators perched on adjoining snow banks, goalies had to contend with another hazard: A squirt in the eye at the most crucial moments."

The newly-formed Chicago Blackhawks, named after the army division The Major commanded during World War I, contained greats like Cecil "Babe" Dye who led them in goals with 25. Dye went on to secure fourth place for scoring that season in the American Division. They also had Dick Irvin, the Team's first captain, who led them in points during their first season with 36. Others included Duncan "Mickey" MacKay, Hugh Lehman, George Hay, who was one of the League's smallest players, as well as several other men The Major acquired through different deals. Such men played a major role in laying the cornerstone of professional hockey.

CECIL HENRY "BABE" DYE

Born on May 13, 1898, in Hamilton, Ontario, Cecil Henry "Babe" Dye's professional career spanned from 1919-20 to 1930-31. His father died when he was a baby. He learned to play hockey from his mother. Obviously, she must have done something right.

Before officially turning pro with the Toronto Aura Lee (OHA Junior Champions) in 1917, and later the St. Pat's Hockey Club (which won the Stanley Cup in 1922) in 1919-20, Dye was a star halfback for the Toronto Argonauts. He was an incredible baseball player as well, hence the nickname "Babe." He played professional baseball with Buffalo and Toronto of the International League. He played part of the 1926 season with Dan Howley's championship team. After turning pro in hockey, Connie Mack offered Dye a $25,000 bonus to come and play with the Philadelphia Athletics. However, Dye remained true to the sport of hockey.

A short and stocky right-winger, Dye developed a reputation for his blazing shots. While play-

Babe Dye had a reputation for "blazing" shots on goal. (Photo from the Hockey Hall of Fame/Ernie Fitzsimmons Collection.)

ing for Toronto, Dye once scored a famous goal in a Stanley Cup game against Vancouver. As it happened, he executed a shot that was so hard, neither the Vancouver net-minder nor the crowd saw where the puck had gone. A while later, the puck was found inside the Vancouver net. Toronto went on to win the game and the Stanley Cup, with Dye scoring nine goals in the five-game series. Popular stories about Dye have him smashing a clock on the wall of Toronto's old Mutual Street Arena with one of his shots from center ice, and smashing the boards out of the ends of rinks with others!

Dye led the league in scoring three times, in 1921 with 35 goals, in 1923 with 26 goals and in 1925 with 38 goals. Twice, he scored goals in eleven consecutive games. He also has the honor of being the first NHL player to score 200 career goals. Twice during his career, he had five-goal games, one of them, on December 16, 1922, occurred against Montreal with the legendary Georges Vezina between the pipes. Altogether, including the play-offs, Dye scored 213 goals for 256 points in 285 games.

Dye came to the Blackhawks with the League expansion that occurred in 1926-27, leading the team in goals with 25 in 41 games. The next season, Dye broke his leg at the Hawks' training camp in Winnipeg, taking him out for most of that season. He tried to make a comeback the following season with the New York Americans, but was only able to score one goal in 42 games. Before retiring, he played for the Toronto Maple Leafs in 1930-31 and briefly for New Haven of the AHL before turning to coaching in 1931-32 with the Chicago Shamrocks. He later refereed in the NHL for five seasons in the mid-thirties.

After hockey, Dye worked with a large paving contract firm as a foreman until his death from a lengthy illness on January 2, 1962. He was inducted into the Hockey Hall of Fame in 1970.

DICK IRVIN

Dick Irvin, who was born in Limestone Ridge, Ontario, on July 19, 1892, was the son of a star-caliber hockey player of days long ago. The fourth of ten children, Dick played his first hockey in Winnipeg, Manitoba, when his family moved there in 1899. He played wearing an old pair of overshoes until he earned enough money from his job in a butcher shop to buy a pair of ice skates.

In a February 13, 1956 *Sports Illustrated* article by Whitney Tower, Irvin recalled those early days, saying:

> *"We moved to Winnipeg where I saw a pair of skates and the game of hockey for the first time. I think it must have fascinated me because I can remember staying out in the backyard practicing shooting a puck at a spot on the wall until my mother would have to come and drag me indoors for dinner.*
>
> *There were commercial leagues in Winnipeg and naturally I wanted to get on the team sponsored by the butchers [his father was a butcher]. I was 15 before I got my chance. One of the regular forwards was taken sick and a friend of my father's suggested that I be given a chance to play. The man came to the rink before the game and said he'd give me a dollar for every goal I scored. Under the circumstances I suppose I was as excited and nervous as any boy of 15 can be. But I was confident too. I had developed a good wrist shot and somehow I always knew how to score. In that game I got five goals—and five dollars—and I know I've had few thrills like it since."*

After playing for the McDougall Lion Methodist Church team in 1908, and the Machray school team in 1909, he played for the Winnipeg Monarchs, then one of Canada's top amateur teams. Irvin played his first real competitive hockey with the Winnipeg Strathconas, an independent junior team. Then, in 1912, he was in the crowd at a Winnipeg Monarchs game when Dolly Gray broke his shoulder in the first period. Via a megaphone, the announcer Mike O'Connor, who knew Dick was out there, called for him to report to the dressing room to take Dolly's place. Once on the ice, he scored five goals in the team's 8-3 victory over Winnipeg Varsity.

Dick Irvin was known as "the silver haired fox" of hockey. (Photo from the Hockey Hall of Fame/Ernie Fitzsimmons Collection.)

His first season there (1913), the Monarchs won the Allen Cup, repeating the feat in 1915. Once, in the fourth game of an exhibition series between the Monarchs and the Toronto Rugby and Athletic Association, Irvin scored nine goals in his team's 9-1 victory! The Toronto team was champion of the Ontario Hockey Association, which at the time was probably Canada's best amateur league. The feat earned Irvin a spot in Ripley's *Believe It or Not* magazine as one of the wonders of the sports world!

Besides hockey, Irvin was quite a baseball player as well. Along with his brothers Alex and George "Chum," he played for the Winnipeg Dominion Express of the Winnipeg Amateur Baseball Association at a time when the league's clubs were outdrawing pro clubs in the old Western Canada League.

Dick frequently received offers from professional clubs as an amateur, but, like his brother Alex, turned them down. He finally turned pro in 1914-15 with the Portland (Oregon) Rosebuds for $700 (the highest salary in the league at the time was $1,250). In 1917, World War I called and Irvin went, but he returned to hockey with the Regina Caps in 1921, where he remained for four seasons. In 1925-26, Irvin returned to the Rosebuds and led them in scoring with 30 goals in 30 games. He was considered by many to be the best player on that team, possessing a blazing shot and exceptional stickhandling ability.

Acquired by Chicago when The Major bought the Portland franchise, Irvin was known among fans as the "silver-haired fox of the hockey game." He could shoot either right- or left-handed, and could play center or wing equally well. He was well-known for his legendary wrist shot.

After suffering a skull fracture, Irvin hung up his skates and turned to a distinguished 26-season coaching career, during which his teams failed to make the play-offs only four times. He developed a reputation for being a strict disciplinarian, and never smoked or drank in his life, something he was very proud of. He had a stinging tongue, and while with the Maple Leafs, his spats with Conn Smythe were classics.

His coaching career began first with Chicago for a year-and-a-half, and then with Toronto in 1931-32, when the Leafs won the Stanley Cup. After leaving Toronto in 1940, he coached the Montreal Ca-nadiens until 1955, where his team won three Stanley Cups. He finished his coaching career in 1955-56 with the Blackhawks when illness forced him to retire at their training camp in St. Catharines, Ontario.

Hall of Famer Charles "Newsy" LaLonde, whose NHL career spanned six seasons between 1917-18 and 1926-27 with Montreal and the New York Americans, once commented about Irvin in Stan Fischler's book *Those Were the Days:*

"I remember when (Cully) Wilson played for Calgary in 1925 and hit Dick Irvin so hard in the mouth that Dick's teeth were practically embedded in his tongue. Irvin was with Regina at the time—the mid-twenties I'd say—and he wasn't the type to take that stuff from anyone. The referee gave Wilson a five-minute major penalty for high sticking but this didn't satisfy Irvin at all. He skated over to Wilson, who was on his way to the penalty box and smashed Cully right over the head with his stick. Knocked him out cold; in fact, Cully took enough stitches in him to weave an Indian blanket. We were a different breed then because life was a lot tougher than it is now."

Another memorable story about Irvin concerns a battle he had with Spunk Sparrow in Regina, after returning from World War I. As the story goes, Spunk hooked Irvin under the chin. The blow happened to cause Dick to bite through his tongue (he had a habit of playing with his tongue between his teeth). Instead of heading for the dressing room, Irvin faced off, won the draw, and skated past the penalty box where Spunk was sitting. He let Sparrow have it on his way past, causing Sparrow to need 16 stitches. Irvin then proceeded to skate off the ice and have his tongue sewn back together.

Finally, one of the more popular tales concerning Irvin surrounds his bell-ringing feats. As the story goes, some "rail birds" from a Toronto arena shouted to him that he could not hit the goalkeeper's gong, which was suspended over the goal at the other end of the rink from Irvin. Without stopping to make estimations, Irvin supposedly skated down the ice and rang the bell

Duncan "Mickey" MacKay played for the Blackhawks only two seasons. (Photo from the Hockey Hall of Fame/Ernie Fitzsimmons Collection.)

on his first try. Reports have it that Irvin would often do this to amuse crowds before games.

Sadly, Irvin died of cancer in Montreal during May of 1957. He was inducted into the Hockey Hall of Fame posthumously the following year.

MICKEY "WEE SCOT" MACKAY

Born in Chesley, Ontario, on May 21, 1894, Mickey MacKay learned to skate on frozen ponds and the Saugeen River near his home. He played amateur hockey for the Chesley Colts of the Northern Hockey League, as well as senior hockey for Edmonton and Grand Forks of the Kootenay League.

In 1913-14, MacKay turned pro with Edmonton and quickly rose to prominence in the Pacific Coast League. From 1914-19 he played for the Vancouver Millionaires, who won the Stanley Cup in 1915. Skating with him were such legendary players as Jack Adams, "Cyclone" Taylor, and Smokey Joe Harris. Due to injuries, he missed the 1919-20 season, but returned to the Millionaires for the following season. When the Millionaires switched leagues (WCHL in 1924-25 and WHL in

1925-26), Mickey remained with them until the league eventually folded.

After that, Mickey came to the Blackhawks for two seasons (1926-27 and 1927-28), where he led them in scoring during the former season, and was second in scoring to Dick Irvin the following year. After the Windy City, MacKay split the 1928-29 season with the Pittsburgh Pirates and Boston Bruins. The Bruins took home Lord Stanley's Cup that season. Midway through the following season, he hung up his skates and served as an assistant coach to Art Ross.

As a rookie with Vancouver, he led the PCHA in scoring with 33 goals, and repeated that accomplishment twice before coming to Chicago. The feat was quite an accomplishment during his rookie season, however, as he beat out his teammate "Cyclone" Taylor by ten goals. Known as one of hockey's greatest centers, many argued over which of the two was the better hockey player. During his entire career, MacKay scored 202 goals in 242 games. For five years, he posted 20 or more goals during seasons of 20 to 22 games.

MacKay was an excellent defensive forward, and was an extremely popular player. He had exceptional skating ability, a great sense of timing and judgment, and a true team spirit. Lester Patrick, who discovered MacKay after receiving a letter from him regarding how he might break into pro hockey, described him this way in a May 31, 1940 *Canadian Press* article:

> *"He was perhaps the greatest centre we ever had on the coast; an equal favorite with Fred (Cyclone) Taylor in the minds of the masses. I always held to the theory that Taylor was the best all-rounder, but many differed.*
>
> *MacKay was a great crowd pleaser. He was clean, splendidly courageous, a happy player with a stylish way of going. He was sensational in making quick breakaways. He was a sure shot alone with the goalie. He could handle his stick and was almost as good a hook-check as Frank Neighbor. MacKay was one of those who helped make pro hockey a great game. He was outstanding in every way."*

An interesting story about the "Wee Scot" involves an incident between him and Cully Wilson. During a game against Seattle, Wilson broke MacKay's jaw in three places with his stick. For this, the Patricks cast Wilson out of the Pacific Coast League for life.

After retiring from play, Mickey returned to Grand Forks, North Dakota, married, and went into the mining business. However, he remained interested in the game and continued to contribute by coaching local teams. On May 30, 1940, he died while driving through Ymir, British Columbia. On the highway, he experienced a heart attack and crashed into a telephone pole.

FREDERICK HUGH (HUGHIE) "EAGLE EYE" LEHMAN

Between the pipes, the Hawks first acquired a net-minder by the name of Hughie Lehman. Born in Pembroke, Ontario, on October 27, 1885, Lehman was one of the great goaltenders of his time, and a fierce competitor. Small, thin, and dark-complexioned, Lehman was among the smallest players in the NHL during his stint with the Blackhawks.

Lehman first played hockey in his hometown, with the Pembroke Hockey Team, who won the Citizen Shield in 1905-06. His first professional hockey was played with Sault Ste. Marie (Soo, Michigan) of the old International League the following season. After that, he played in the Trolley League (OPHL) for Berlin from 1908 to 1911. In 1909-10, he became only the second player to play for two Stanley Cup Challengers within a two-month period when, after losing 7-3 with Berlin in a game against the Montreal Wanderers, he went to play for Galt in the same league in a game against Ottawa, losing there as well. When the Patricks formed the PCHA, Frank Patrick signed Lehman to play for the New Westminster Royals, where he served as their net-minder from 1911-14. From 1914 to 1926 he played for the Vancouver Millionaires, who took home the Stanley Cup in 1915. Future Chicago Blackhawk teammate Mickey MacKay skated with Lehman on that Cup-winning team.

Lehman played goal for the Blackhawks in 1926-27, and for part of the 1927-28 season, when he shared coaching duties with Barney Stanley. Over the course of his lengthy professional career, Hughie led the PCHA in goals against six times, and

played in eight Stanley Cup Finals. He was one of the first goalies to rush the puck around his net. One story has it that Lehman carried the puck halfway up the ice and scored a goal on the opposition. The stories are unclear as to exactly when the feat occurred, with most sources indicating that it happened while he was playing for either Vancouver or Berlin.

After hockey, Hughie went into the road construction business with Warren Bituminous Paving Company, where he served as company president during his 50-year tenure with the company. He was a member of both the Granite Club and the Deer Park United Church. He passed away in Toronto, Ontario, at the age of 75 on April 8, 1961, shortly before the Blackhawks took home their third Stanley Cup. He was inducted into the Hockey Hall of Fame in 1958.

GEORGE HAY

Born in Listowel, Ontario, on January 10, 1898, George Hay learned to play the game in Winnipeg. He played with Dick Irvin for the Monarchs in 1915 and 1916, and later played senior hockey for the Regina Vics in 1920 and 1921. He turned pro with the Regina Caps, along with future Hawk teammate Dick Irvin, where he played for four seasons, scoring 87 goals and 58 assists. Along with Irvin, he then played with the Portland Rosebuds before being acquired by the Blackhawks.

Once in the NHL, Hay lasted only one season with Chicago (14 goals, 8 assists), before being traded to Jack Adams' Detroit Cougars (later named the Red Wings) with teammate Percy "Puss" Traub in a joint $15,000 deal. Blackhawk management had been advised that Hay was too fragile and not aggressive enough to cut it anymore. The reason for his poor debut with Chicago (compared to his professional success in the old Western Canada Hockey League), however, could be attributed to the fact that he played that season after coming back from a torn ligament in his left shoulder. In his first season with Detroit, he was their leading scorer with 22 goals and 13 assists. He spent the remainder of his five-year career with Detroit, scoring a career total 74 goals and 60 assists. In 1927, he played left-wing in the All-Star Game on a line with legendary center Howie Morenz and Bill Cook at right-wing.

Hay was an exceptionally fluid stick handler, a good skater, and possessed abundant hockey intelligence. He had the reputation for being a superb back checker and had an accurate shot from almost anywhere on the ice. He was known for his good temperament and disposition. He was famous for his cool head, being able to contain himself and stay out of the penalty box, even when being roughed around badly by the opposition.

Hay left the Red Wings in 1934 to coach one of their farm teams in London, Ontario for two seasons. After that, he moved to Stratford, Ontario and went into the insurance business, retiring in 1965. During World War II, Hay served as a flight lieutenant and instructor with the Royal Canadian Air Force. He passed away in July of 1975 at the age of 77 and was inducted into the Hockey Hall of Fame on April 27, 1958.

CHICAGO COLISEUM

When The Major's newly-formed Blackhawks took to the ice for their first game, it wasn't at Chicago Stadium. The Blackhawks played their first game ever against the Toronto St. Pat's at the Chicago Coliseum on November 17, 1926, winning 4-1.

The Chicago Coliseum was located in the area of 16th and Wabash Street but was built overseas, in Europe. Later, it was disassembled and transported in pieces to Chicago where it served as a Union prison during the Civil War. After leasing the Coliseum (capacity crowd of 5,000), The Major and his boys moved into their new home at 1800 West Madison Street.

The Coliseum was not the best place for hockey. Due to higher temperatures, ice conditions at the Chicago Coliseum were quite poor in comparison to those found at the Chicago Stadium. Also, fans were not comfortable there. As a result, attendance started dropping and, before long, many of the team's stockholders lost interest. The Major did not lose faith, however. Soon, he had acquired the majority of stock in the team, a move that paid off in the future. After several seasons, plans were made for the team to move to the Old Gray Lady on West Madison Street: Chicago Stadium. However, because the construction of Chicago Stadium was behind schedule and the team's lease at the Coli-

seum was about to expire, the Blackhawks ended up having to play some of their games in Fort Erie and Windsor, Ontario.

THE FIRST COACHES

In the first ten years of the team's existence, The Major hired and fired 13 coaches. Six of these gentlemen were behind the Chicago bench from the beginning until 1930. Among them were Pete Muldoon, Barney Stanley, Hugh Lehman, Herb Gardiner, Tom Shaughnessy, and Bill Tobin.

PETE MULDOON

Coach and general manager of the Seattle Metropolitans before coming to Chicago, Pete Muldoon is likely one of the most interesting men in Blackhawk history. Although he did coach the Metropolitans to a 1917 Stanley Cup victory, that is not the event for which he is most famous.

In his first and only season as coach in Chicago, Muldoon brought the Blackhawks to a respectable third-place finish. The Major, who thought his team was certainly good enough to finish first, called Muldoon into his office, told him so and then fired him.

According to George Vass' book *The Chicago Blackhawk Story, Toronto Globe and Mail* columnist James X. Coleman, who wrote an article about it 15 years after it happened, claimed that Muldoon supposedly said (in his Irish accent): "Fire me, Major, and you'll never finish first! I'll put a curse on this team that will hoodoo it till the end of time." And so, it was to be that the Curse of Muldoon would haunt the Blackhawks until they finally reached first place in the 1966-67 season.

DICK IRVIN, JR.

Son of the original Blackhawk captain and longtime sportscaster for the Montreal Canadiens, Dick Irvin, Jr. commented on his father: "He coached the Blackhawks in 30-31 and they got to the finals. They lost the fifth game against Montreal, (final score) 2-0, Canadiens."

True to The Major's habit of playing musical coaches, Irvin's stay behind the Chicago bench was a short one indeed. "My father was getting ready to go down to Chicago and he got a telegram from

Major McLaughlin saying that 'your services are no longer required,'" commented Irvin's son, who was awarded the Foster Hewitt Memorial Award for making outstanding contributions in hockey broadcasting. "When he went to Toronto, they [the Maple Leafs] hired him the following year and they beat Chicago in the finals. He ended up coaching Chicago again the last year that he coached, in 1955-56." Sadly, Irvin passed away from cancer shortly after that season.

An interesting story surrounds Irvin at the time the Blackhawks fired him in the early thirties. As it happened, he felt he had been the victim of unfair treatment in Chicago. The Toronto Maple Leafs had just hired him as their coach. His new team was scheduled to face-off against the Hawks and Irvin not only wanted the Leafs to win, he wanted a huge lopsided victory. History has it that Irvin pestered his squad constantly about the upcoming game to the point the players were fed up. They decided to let the Blackhawks score a few goals to make Irvin mad and then come back to beat the Windy City later in the game.

The next time the two teams met, the Leafs slaughtered the Hawks 11-3. One shot from a Toronto player even beaned Chuck Gardiner in the forehead, cutting it open. He later returned to the ice and finished the game. The good-natured Gardiner picked up a derby hat a fan threw onto the ice and wore it while playing for good luck, but it didn't work.

Years ago, goalie Bill Durnan who played for Irvin in Montreal, commented on Irvin in Stan Fischler's book *Those Were the Days*:

"The guy who kept us all in line was Irvin. He considered coaching a real profession and it showed through his actions; he lived it. Irvin was proud of what he did and refused to be known as just a guy who looked after a bunch of weekend revelers.

Dick was a tremendous psychologist. It always amazed me that he never swore—anybody associated with a bunch of dodos who'd go hairy now and then would have to curse once and a while. But Dick never drank and he never swore but he could dress you down and make you crawl. He never played favorites either, and that went for The Rocket [Maurice Richard] too."

JOSEPH CHESTERFIELD FARRELL

Although not a coach, Joseph Chesterfield Farrell was an important figure in the team's early years. Said to have resembled Abraham Lincoln, Farrell was the Blackhawks' first publicity man, and was with the team approximately 30 years. During his lifetime, he climbed the pyramids of Egypt and sang with John Philip Sousa's "The March King" band. Throughout his career he worked wonders for the team in the publicity department, sometimes giving away as many as 3,000 tickets for one game in the early years. In the end his efforts, which included meeting with the heads of companies to persuade them to bring family and friends to games, paid off. When the 1930s arrived, the crowds exploded in size as the Blackhawks embarked on a journey through one of the most memorable decades in their 70-year history.

A Place to Call Home

The city of Chicago owes its thanks to a man named Paddy Harmon for the existence of Chicago Stadium. Often considered a "bullheaded Irishman," Paddy was a sports promoter who invested $2.5 million of his own money into its construction. He borrowed the remainder of the $7 million construction cost from "friends" who later forced him out of the operation and left him penniless. At the 1926 NHL expansion meeting in Montreal, Paddy offered $50,000 for a Chicago franchise, but The Major had already been given one for $12,000!

The Stadium opened to the public on March 28, 1929 with a boxing match between world light heavyweight champion Tommy Loughran of Philadelphia and world middleweight champion Mickey Walker of New Jersey. According to the newspapers around the time of the event, Chicago residents hadn't been ecstatic about a fight since Jack Dempsey fought Gene Tunney at Soldier's Field in 1927.

A large amount of excitement surrounded the opening of what, at the time, was the largest indoor sporting arena in the entire world. Preparations for the fight cost Paddy Harmon about

An artist's rendition of the Chicago Stadium. (Photo courtesy of the Blackhawks.)

$50,000. Veteran fight broadcaster Quin Ryan was rushed into Chicago from New York where he had been doing another fight the night before and the event was broadcast over WGN Radio. Ringside microphones that Paddy had installed added to the excitement.

"There are 6,000 ringside seats," commented Paddy in the March 28, 1929 issue of the *Chicago Tribune* as opening day grew closer. "Right over them will be 7,000 arena seats. And the two balcony tiers each have 4,600. And, if that isn't enough, we've got standing room for 7,000." Division chief of the fire prevention bureau, John H. Touhey felt differently about the matter and set about to make sure that no standing room tickets were sold. "We are not going to permit anyone to enter the Stadium who does not possess a ticket calling for a seat," commented the fire chief in the same fight night article. "A city ordinance in effect since 1913 provides there shall be no standing in the aisles or any other place in houses of amusement."

Nevertheless, this "house of amusement" opened its doors with 138 ushers donned in white flannel trousers and jackets patrolling the aisles. In addition to these persons, Paddy had employed 38 ticket takers and 38 ticket checkers to help things move right along.

Before the fight, the two fighters expressed their feelings in the same *Chicago Tribune* article. "I will be fit to fight ten rounds at any pace that Walker wants to set," exclaimed Loughran. "If he does not set a fast clip I will...Mickey may not know it, but I have a far better chance to flatten him than he has to stop me. I am proud of the opportunity to be one of the headlines on the opening bill of the world's greatest indoor sport center."

Walker, on the other hand, had a different view of the bout: "I am in far better shape than ever before for a Chicago fight and you know I have won eight battles in a row in this neighborhood...I will weigh in at 166 pounds and will be the real bulldog they call me...Tommy is a good man and will have a pull in height, reach, and weight. But those disadvantages will not annoy me. I like to fight bigger men. Watch my smoke once I get warmed to my work." In the end, it was Loughran who would reign victorious after ten rounds.

On December 16, 1929, the Blackhawks played their first game in the building on West Madison Street that would become one of the toughest places to play in for enemy teams. After playing in front of thin crowds at the Coliseum, the Hawks experienced a boom in attendance, the largest of all teams in the United States and Canada according to former publicity man Johnny Gottselig. In their debut, in front of a crowd of 14,212 they gave the Windy City crowd a good show, beating the Pittsburgh Pirates 3-1. At the time, it was their fifth consecutive win. Many important people were present for the Hawks' debut. Besides department store king Marshall Field, the NHL governors were also in attendance, due to the fact they had a meeting scheduled for the next day in Chicago. Because of the better ice conditions at the Stadium, the largest hockey crowd that had ever assembled in Chicago witnessed some of the fastest hockey ever seen in the Windy City at that time.

The first period of the game was scoreless. Mush March and Tom Cook managed to make some close shots on goal, but Pittsburgh's defense, combined with its powerful offense, proved to be too much for the Hawks to do much of anything else. Chuck Gardiner, the Hawks' star goaltender, held the team together.

With the second period came a strengthened effort by the Blackhawks. Chicago's Vic Ripley scored two goals in 35 seconds (at 8:15 and 8:50), assisted by Ernest Arbour and Marvin Wentworth. Then, three minutes before the period's end, Frank "The Regina Bullet" Ingram scored on a pass from Wentworth. All three goals were scored on the power play for the Blackhawks.

In the third period, which was filled with much hard body checking, Tex White scored on a Pittsburgh power play for the Pirates, but it was the Blackhawks who skated away with a 3-1 victory when the game was over.

Later, the Stadium was host to a myriad of events. Among them were cycling races, political conventions (Franklin D. Roosevelt was nominated there in 1940 and 1944), mayoral fundraisers, ice shows—even Elvis Presley performed there—and the very first NFL title game between the Chicago Bears and the Portsmouth Ohio Spartans on December 18, 1932. Playing on an 80-yard dirt field, the Bears beat the Spartans 9-0.

Perhaps the most intriguing thing in Chicago Stadium was the antique Barton organ. As stated in the *Chicago Blackhawks 1991/92 Official Yearbook,* it was designed by the late Daniel Barton of

Ice sculpture of the Stadium for its 60th anniversary. (Photo courtesy of the Blackhawks.)

Oshkosh, Wisconsin, and to this day remains the largest theater organ in the United States. It can attain a volume level comparable to 25 100-piece brass bands, all playing at the same time. It was built at the cost of $120,000 in 1929 and installed as the Stadium was constructed. When it was installed, the organ consisted of 4,000 pipes housed near the rafters, 6 keyboards, 32 pedals, and 850 stops. Also quite amazing was the fact that it took 20 minutes to walk from the organ console to the nearest loft. After it was constructed, it had to be transported in 24 railroad cars from Wisconsin to Chicago.

Al Melgard was the first organist at Chicago Stadium and remained so until his death in 1972. In Jay Greenberg, Frank Orr, and Gary Ronberg's book *NHL—The World of Professional Ice Hockey*, Robert Gammie, a construction worker who supervised the bricklaying of Chicago Stadium once commented: "That thing is powerful. One time some fans started a fight and it was getting way out of hand. Melgard pounded the organ so hard he smashed the windows in the

place. He stopped the fight, but he was afraid he was going to lose his job."

Aside from being the NHL's loudest and most electrifying arena, Chicago Stadium was also one of the best places to witness a sporting event. Because the posts that supported the roof were far in back, they didn't block the view of most spectators. It was also built steep, so that fans were above, and not back from the ice surface.

Chicago Stadium truly was an architectural wonder in its day. In the same book by Greenberg, Orr, and Ronberg, Robert Gammie once commented on its construction: "We worked round the clock, two 12-hour shifts a day. If you knew something about construction, you'd appreciate just how much care went into it."

Before its demise, when asked what comes to mind when someone said the words "Chicago Stadium," actor Jim Belushi said: "Loud (with a laugh). There's no stadium like that. It's close in. It's a smaller rink. You're right on top of 'em (the players). You can feel the energy on the ice and the crowd. It's like when you walk in, it's alive!"

Commenting on what it felt like to play under the influence of the crowds in Chicago Stadium, former Hawk forward Eric Nesterenko, in Studs Terkel's book *Working*, states:

"I can remember games with 20,000 people and the place going crazy with sound and action and color. The enormous energy the crowd produces all coming in on the ice, all focusing on you. It's pretty hard to resist that. I remember one game: it was in the semifinals, the year we won the Stanley Cup. It was the sixth game against Montreal. They were the big club and we were the Cinderella team. It was 3-0, for us, with five minutes left to go. As a spontaneous gesture 20,000 people stood up. I was on the ice. I remember seeing that whole stadium, just solid, row on row, from the balcony to the boxes, standing up. These people were turned on by us. We came off, three feet off the ice…(softly)…spring of '61."

Blackhawk legend Bobby Hull in a September 11, 1988, *Chicago Tribune* article with Mike Kiley gave his feelings on the building in which he played for so many years:

"I spent 15 years of the greatest time of my life playing in this building," he explained. "You can't erase those times from your mind, even if you wanted to. And I don't want to erase any of the memories. The Stadium is still the place to play hockey. We had a love affair with the fans. Some people say they don't hear the fans when they play. But they're full of crap. Every time I picked up that puck behind the net I could hear them and feel the electricity. The faster I went, the further up ice I skated, the louder it got—and the more exciting it was."

Former Hawk coach Mike Keenan, in a June 1, 1992 *Sports Illustrated* article by Rick Telander, once gave his impression of Chicago Stadium:

"There is no other building like this. In the locker room you can feel the energy of the crowd. The shape of the stands, the steep seats, the audience interacts with the players, and the sound just reverberates. It [the noise] can be painful, especially when it bounces off the glass behind you. Nobody can hear you, and sometimes I have to go down and grab, pinch, or shake a player to let him know I want him on the ice."

In the January 8, 1993 issue of *The Hockey News*, former Hawk coach Darryl Sutter commented: "The fans are a big part of it. A lot of times the emotion takes over when you've got players not as sharp as they should be."

With a reminiscent laugh, legendary goalkeeper Glenn Hall gave his "from the net" view of playing for Chicago fans in the Stadium: "Well, they're always interesting," he explained. "I'll tell you right now, even more so I think than when we played, they were always noisy. But, in the early years when I went there, there were four, five, six thousand people [in the crowd]. That changed primarily when Bobby [Hull] came in. Like somebody said, the offense sells tickets and the defense wins games…Bobby was probably the most entertaining hockey player that has ever played. When he grabbed the puck and went behind the net, why, you knew something was going to happen."

Bill Hay, a Chicago Blackhawk forward from 1959 to 1967, commented on what it was like playing in Chicago Stadium during the years that he was there. "It was very exciting because they hadn't had too many winning teams prior to that," he said…It's a great building [with] good people. I think they miss that building, but as the game changes, so do the people and the buildings."

Hall of Famer Bill Gadsby, who played for Chicago during the forties and fifties commented on the Chicago fans who gave the Stadium its electric atmosphere: "Chicago, I thought it was a great place to play. It's a hell of a sporting city…I think Chicago and Detroit are the best cities in North America. I can't pick either one because they're both great. I've played in each of them and I think that if you give the fans a contender, a half-assed contender, then they just pack the building and cheer ya crazy, ya know. They go wild."

When asked how he felt about how critical Chicago fans can be, Gadsby stated: "They're allowed to do that [be critical] if you're not playing good. But if you're playing half-assed they're pretty good and if you're winning they're extremely good. I went back to Chicago Stadium last winter for a game. I hadn't been back in there for 25 years. It brought back some great memories...they're louder than they used to be!"

Many years ago, Hall of Fame referee Bill Chadwick recalled some of his most "memorable" experiences in the Stadium in Stan Fischler's book *Those Were the Days.*

"(A) funny thing took place in Chicago when Johnny Mariucci was on defense for the Blackhawks. In the early forties, in Chicago Stadium, the gallery gods had a habit of playing cards before the game started. Once the action began, these fans would wrap up their deck of cards with a rubber band and keep them handy just in case they didn't like the referee's decision. Midway in the game I gave Mariucci a misconduct penalty and suddenly all those damn cards flew out of the balcony onto the ice. Meanwhile, Mariucci kept giving me the business from the penalty box. I leaned over, picked up a bunch of cards, skated in the penalty box, and handed them to Mariucci. 'John,' I said, 'you're gonna be here a while. You might as well play.'"

Another one of Chadwick's favorite experiences in the Stadium happened to be a tied game between Montreal and the Hawks back in 1944. Said Chadwick:

"George Allen felt that Elmer Lach of the Canadiens was holding him. Instead of waiting for a whistle to see whether I thought so or not, Allen started arguing with me and Elmer put the puck in the Chicago net. The Blackhawk fans went wild, tossing debris all over the ice. It must have been twenty minutes before they stopped throwing things at us. I had Ed Nepham and Jim Primeau as my linesmen and we stood in the center of the ice to avoid the litter. Finally, I sent Primeau over to the bench saying, 'Get Dutton [NHL President present at the game] in the corner there and ask him what the hell I should do.' Primeau came back to me about five minutes later. He reported Red's answer: 'You got yourself into it, now get yourself out of it!' That didn't help me very much and from then on I had to have a police escort into as well as out of the Chicago rink."

Prior to the 1994-95 season, veteran referee Andy vanHellemond recalled Chicago Stadium:

"I'll probably end up doing the most league games of any referee ever. I've done 1,373 now. That's 1,373 league games only. My very first game was at Chicago with Vancouver playing Chicago back in 1972. I think [it was in] November of 1972. I did the finals that year with Pittsburgh, and the noise in the Stadium was always loud at a lot of games, but those particular couple of games, when they played at home seemed so much [louder]. Like everybody would say, it gives you goosebumps. And if you can't get yourself motivated to play a game in that type of circumstance, then there is something wrong.

The ice conditions were always very good [at the Stadium]. They always had a fast sheet of ice and I haven't been to the new one, so I truly hope they kept or captured some from the old building. The closeness of the people, with somebody up against a back wall, [when] one of those fellas yells down you hear every word, it carried so well. It felt so much closer than most buildings. They don't build them like that anymore. You always felt like the crowd was right in it with you."

vanHellemond also remembered one of the more colorful moments he experienced while officiating there. He explains:

"I was there one day when some nut threw a whisky bottle half full. It was an afternoon game. Detroit was playing and

Matt Ravlich was standing at the face-off spot where the Blackhawks come out waiting for the players to change. It landed maybe four or five feet beside him and it hit and just exploded and went all the way across to the penalty box. It came at that angle and it was a scary moment. I had a game there where there weren't many people, and they weren't winning many games. There was a fight in the first balcony and the next thing you know, they were right on the edge and it looked like they were going to go over it. That was kind of a crazy moment.

I guess at another game one guy had fallen off one balcony onto the next level. I don't know if that's true or not, but I could see it easily happening when they get going at it right up front. I had a couple of games I was standby. In the play-offs we always watch one game before we work, and I've been standby at a lot of buildings. You know, being in the crowd, the people [were] real fans. I don't know whether it's the organ or the anthem that really starts them getting into it. It's just the Chicago fan, who is just a great fan which is a great sort of thing they have. They get into supporting their team. [They are] so much more vocal and get into it more than [in] other cities."

Many novelties existed within the confines of Chicago Stadium. Included were a cat—named Kat—who roamed the building, except during games, and who today is cared for by the Zamboni driver. Others included a staircase in the Hawks weight room that led nowhere, and a seat in the arena that was completely blocked by a support beam. Another novelty was the foghorn the Wirtzes had installed in 1983, which used to be on their yacht, The Blackhawk. It was so loud that when it was first installed, it stunned some of the players when it went off.

UNITED THEY STAND

With the 1994-95 season, Chicago fans began cheering the Blackhawks on to victory in the new, $175 million United Center, located on Madison Street across from the old Stadium. The Old Barn was demolished and the new, plush building, a partnership between Bulls owner Jerry Reinsdorf and Hawks owner Bill Wirtz, opened for business. The United Center has three levels of sky boxes, and 20,500 seats for hockey. At 960,000 square feet (three times the size of Chicago Stadium), it is truly a remarkable facility.

The modern United Center is a more comfortable facility for the fan, with nine elevators, three times the restroom space, and twice the number of concession stands that the Old Barn had. The eight-sided, color instant-replay scoreboard hanging over the ice is the size of a two-story building, and requires 13 people to operate. Additionally, television monitors pepper the concourses, and fans can hear radio play-by-play of the game in the restrooms.

United Center is not the same as the Stadium, and only time will tell if the unique atmosphere found in the old building will live on in the new one. Unfortunately, the organ is not a part of the new structure, due to an estimated moving cost of $11 million. The new arena has an Allen organ, three times as powerful as the old one (60,000 watts). A club record was set on April 14, 1995 when 22,279 packed the United Center for a regular season game with Detroit.

Betty Bentley, wife of former Chicago Blackhawk and Hall of Famer Max Bentley commented: "You know what, it's the organ that makes that place. I've been to the Edmonton Oilers' rink and other rinks all over, and the way they play those records, along with the singing and carrying on, just isn't like [the Stadium and] how it was in those days long ago. That organ made the game. It really got people excited. Old Al Melgard, he was something else. I've been a Blackhawks fan ever since, ya know."

Prior to the 1994-95 season, current Blackhawk forward Jeremy Roenick commented:

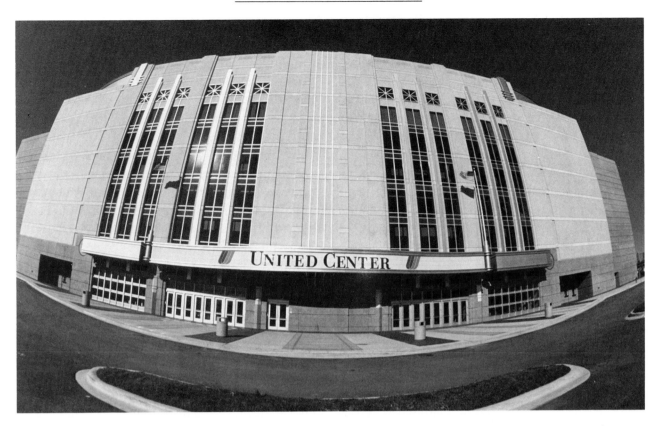

A wide-angled view of the new United Center, located on Madison Street across from the old Stadium. (Photo courtesy of the Blackhawks.)

"I just know it's a spectacular building. It has the makings of being the best building in the world. I think its bigger ice will give us a lot more room to move. We have a speedy team, it could make us a more offensive team. But again, we've only been there for a short time. Our locker room is great. All the side stuff is great, but how it will affect us as a team or how it will affect the fans as fans is something that is yet to be discovered."

Bill Gadsby also expressed his feelings concerning the construction of the new United Center: "It's progress," he said. "The older buildings are fine, but they get unsafe. People want new facilities and you've got to give'em to them. Like the new Comiskey Park. People don't demand it but they like it."

Humorously, the Dallas Star's Shane Churla gave his feelings on the move across Madison Street in the January 5, 1994, issue of the *Chicago Sun Times,* in an article by Herb Gould. "I love playing there—the fans and the noise. Some guy once threw a trailer hitch at me there," he said. "They're a different breed of fan, but that gets me going. I won't miss the cockroaches, though. I wonder how long it'll take before they cross the street."

The final regular season game on April 14, 1994 was an emotional one for the Hawks, one that they lost to the Toronto Maple Leafs. Bill Wirtz allowed this historic game to be televised locally. In a special pre-game ceremony, the banners signifying the retired numbers of four Chicago Blackhawk legends: Bobby Hull; Stan Mikita; Glenn Hall, and Tony Esposito, were lowered from the rafters and presented to them along with Tiffany crystal stars from Bill Wirtz. It was an intensely emotional moment for all who had invested so many years and achieved so many great things in the Gray Lady on West Madison Street.

Even more emotional was the fact that Wayne Messmer, former anthem singer at the Stadium for fourteen years, was absent after being shot in the neck outside a near west side restaurant on April 9, 1994. The Blackhawks played a tape-recorded version of Messmer singing it during the final game, as his wife Kathleen stood in the organ loft with tears streaming down her cheeks.

THE FIRST GAME

Messmer returned from his tragic experience to sing the anthem for the last time when the United Center hosted its first hockey game on Wednesday, January 26, 1995. The Executive Vice President of the Chicago Wolves, Chicago's IHL team, Messmer was released by the Hawks due to a conflict of interest. So ended a distinguished association between Messmer and their hockey club. According to statements made by the Blackhawks, Messmer left by mutual consent. However, in a Thursday, January 26, 1995 *Chicago Sun Times* article by Daryl Van Schouwen, Messmer said otherwise. "[The parting] was not a mutual agreement," he said. "I feel sad and disappointed, because there's a special bond I feel with the fans that's so unique for me and the fans…More than anything else right now, I feel sadness. Sadness because a tradition has come to an end."

Even though Messmer's parting was a low note, the game before which he sang was the complete opposite. The standing-room-only-crowd of 20, 536 at the United Center witnessed a 5 to 1 victory over the Edmonton Oilers, with Joe Murphy scoring the historic first goal against Bill Ranford on the power play at 11:33 of the second period.

The Oilers only managed to get by with 18 shots during the entire game, with 12 of them coming in the third period. The other Hawks that scored in this historic game were Keith Carney, Chris Chelios, Jeff Shantz, and Bernie Nicholls. The Oilers' lone goal was scored at 16:14 of the third period by Roman Oksiuta.

Even though the United Center will have a chance to grow on Windy City fans as the years progress, one thing is for sure—Chicago Stadium will live on in memory as one of the greatest arenas in the history of professional sports. "[Chicago is] a city that has so much history and tradition and I appreciate it so much," said NHL referee Paul Stewart, grandson of former Blackhawk coach Bill Stewart. "It's so important to the family and especially me because I look up at that [1938 Stanley Cup] banner and it gives me a little bit of something to work hard for. I don't want that family tradition to decline because of me, so I always tried a little harder. I always tried to find an empty seat figuring my grandfather was up there helping me. Boston Garden was a new rink once, and the Stadium was new. Everything takes time and [the United Center] will get worn in and it will get its creases and it will feel homey and comfortable. Eventually the new United Center will get its personality."

THE GOLDEN YEARS

THE 1930S

The early part of the thirties was characterized by an assortment of different coaches doing stints behind the Chicago bench. Among these individuals were Godfrey Matheson, Emil Iverson, and Tommy Gorman.

GODFREY MATHESON

Godfrey Matheson, who began coaching the team in 1932, had absolutely no major league coaching experience. Upon being hired, he supposedly told his men that only six would get to play and the rest would serve as bench warmers. After Bill Tobin, who was still the Hawks' business manager, found out about his game strategy, he was fired, never to be seen again.

EMIL IVERSON

In 1932-33, Iverson was one of three coaches (Matheson and Tommy Gorman were the others) to stand behind the Chicago bench. Before his brief stint as head coach, Iverson, who coached hockey at State University, ran a camp at Vermilion Lake, Minnesota, where the team's players would train periodically during the summer.

TOMMY GORMAN

It was Tommy Gorman who would take the team all the way to the prized Cup in 1934. Gorman was also involved in the only game lost by forfeit in team history on March 14, 1933 against Boston. After referee Bill Stewart, who would later coach the Blackhawks to their second Stanley Cup, ejected him from the game, the players refused to return to the ice and the Bruins won 1-0.

Born on June 9, 1886, Gorman is an interesting man. As a youth, he served as a page boy in the House of Commons in 1895. Gorman was a tremendously funny man. Looking back on his days as a page boy, he once commented to a reporter: "The other guys used to stuff me in wastepaper baskets and lock me in closets." (May 16, 1961 *Toronto Globe and Mail*).

Quite a lacrosse player, he went on to become the winner of the 1908 Olympic Games First Prize at London, England, as a member of the Canadian Lacrosse Team. Recalling his early days as a lacrosse player, Gorman once told the following story in a 1957 issue of *Weekend Magazine*:

> *"My professional debut took place at New Westminster with Regina Capitals, Minto Cup challengers. There were 15,000 fans watching the powerful team we'd produced for Regina, with such stars as "Sport" Murton, Art Warwick, "Bones" Allen, Johnnie Howard, "Newsy" Lalonde, Jack Shea, and "Bun" Clarke.*
>
> *In the second period Tom Gifford hit me so hard he broke my jaw, cracked my nose, and knocked out four teeth. I woke up in [the] hospital with Sport*

CHICAGO BLACK HAWKS
NATIONAL HOCKEY LEAGUE
1933–1934

The Blackhawks' First Stanley Cup winning team in 1934, with manager Tommy Gorman (back row center) wearing a team jacket. He is a founding father of the National Hockey League. Back row left to right: W. Calfish (ass't. trainer), Abel, Couture, Trudel, Conacher, Thompson, Gordon (manager), Goldsworthy, Coulter, Jenkins, McFadyen, Leswick. Front row left to right: Starke, Cook, Romnes, Gottselig, March, Sheppard, Gardiner, E. Froelich (trainer). (Photo from the Hockey Hall of Fame/Ernie Fitzsimmons Collection.)

Murdoch and Jack Shea beside my bed. There was a terrible moaning from the next room. 'What happened?' I said. 'What's that moaning?' 'Sssssshhh,' said Sport, 'that's the guy who hit you.'"

Like his father, Gorman served as a sports reporter for the *Ottawa Citizen*. He gave up his duties there in 1921, however, to pursue sports management and promotion. He became one of the NHL's founders when he and another man by the name of Ted Dey purchased the Ottawa Hockey Association, whose owners were going to let it lapse. A friend loaned him half of the $5,000 asking price. "Hockey boomed following the war," he said in a

1957 issue of *Weekend Magazine*. "In January, 1925, I sold out to Frank Ahearn for $35,000 plus his shares in the Connaught Park Jockey Club."

During his lifetime, Gorman managed seven hockey clubs to Stanley Cup Championships: [Ottawa Senators: 1920, 1921, 1923, Chicago Blackhawks (manager and coach): 1934, Montreal Maroons (manager and coach): 1935, Montreal Canadiens: 1944, 1946].

After the NHL, Gorman was associated with the Ottawa Nationals of the Border Baseball League, who won the League Championship in 1948. He also served as president of the Ottawa Senators of the Quebec Senior Hockey League when they took home the Allan Cup in 1949. He passed away from cancer in Ottawa on May 15, 1961.

THE MEN

The Blackhawks won their first Stanley Cup with a truly amazing collection of athletic talent. Prior to the 1934 season, they had only reached the finals once, in the 1930-31 season, where they were defeated in the deciding game by the Montreal Canadiens. Men like Clarence "Taffy" Abel, Lionel Conacher, Tom Cook, Art Coulter, Charles Gardiner, Johnny Gottselig, Harold "Mush" March, Elwin "Doc" Romnes, and Paul Thompson made sure a defeat in the Stanley Cup finals didn't happen in 1934. Many considered Gardiner, Gottselig, and March to be the finest Blackhawks of the thirties.

Taffy Abel (photo from the Hockey Hall of Fame/Ernie Fitzsimmons Collection.)

CLARENCE "TAFFY" ABEL

Defenseman Clarence "Taffy" Abel, born on May 28, 1900, stood at 6'1" and weighed in at 225. He was the first U.S.-born hockey player to skate in the NHL. Abel didn't play his first hockey game until the age of eighteen, while living in his native town of Sault Ste. Marie, Michigan. In 1924, Abel carried the American flag as he took the Olympic oath for hockey players in Chamonix, France. Before breaking into the NHL as one of the original New York Rangers in 1926-27, Taffy also played for the Minneapolis Millers in 1925-26. His NHL career spanned eight seasons and 359 games (including the play-offs). Later, Taffy went on to coach and manage hockey. After retiring, he ran a tourist resort called Taffy's Lodge in Sault Ste. Marie until his death on August 1, 1964.

LIONEL CONACHER

Lionel Conacher, also a defenseman, spent only one season (1933-34) with Chicago during his distinguished twelve-season NHL career. Besides being an excellent defenseman, Conacher contributed in the scoring department as well, accumulating 23 points in 48 games that year. Besides playing for the Hawks, Conacher also played for the Pittsburgh Pirates, the New York Americans, and the Montreal Maroons. He came from a large hockey family, and was chosen as Canada's Athlete of the Half Century (1901-1950).

Arthur Coulter. (Photo from the Hockey Hall of Fame/Ernie Fitzsimmons Collection.)

ARTHUR EDMUND COULTER

Perhaps one of the most fearsome defensemen to circle the ice during the thirties was Arthur Edmund Coulter. Born in Winnipeg on May 31, 1909, Coulter broke into ice hockey with the Pilgrim Athletic Club in that city. He turned professional with the Philadelphia Quakers in 1929, and came to Chicago in 1931-32.

Often described as possessing incredible strength, endurance, and devotion to the team principle, Coulter was a driving defensive force in Chicago's 1934 Stanley Cup victory, where he shared defensive responsibilities with Clarence "Taffy" Abel. After being traded to the New York Rangers in 1935-36 for Earl Seibert, Coulter succeeded Bill Cook as team captain, and became a natural leader there.

During his entire career he was chosen to the second All-Star team three seasons in a row ('37-'38, '38-'39, and '39-'40). He scored 30 goals and racked up 82 assists. His emphasis was on playing defense and being the team's leader. After his last season in New York (1941-42), he joined the Canadian Armed Forces during World War II, which ended his professional career.

CHARLES "CHUCK" GARDINER

Goaltender Charles Gardiner, born in Edinburgh, Scotland on New Year's Eve, 1904, turned pro with the Winnipeg Maroons of the Western League in 1926. Howie Morenz claimed he was the hardest man he ever had to beat.

Gardiner became a Blackhawk during the 1927-28 season and remained in Chicago until his untimely death on June 13, 1934. Recording 42 career shutouts in 316 games, Charlie was a remarkable man and a tremendous athlete.

After coming to Winnipeg from Scotland at the age of seven, and learning to skate on corner lots, Charlie decided to become a net-minder because of his poor skating ability. By the age of 14, he began playing on an intermediate team in Portage La Prairie, Manitoba. He played minor hockey with Assinboines and the Winnipeg Tigers, and eventually the Selkirk seniors in 1925. Gardiner turned pro in 1926 with the Winnipeg Maroons and was sold to the Blackhawks in 1927.

Chuck Gardiner (photo from the Hockey Hall of Fame/Ernie Fitzsimmons Collection.)

Gardiner was a sprawling net-minder, who would often rush out of the net to stop the opposition. Even when the Blackhawks were losing, Gardiner had an unbreakable spirit and would always fight till the end. Because he would often come out of the cage to cut down the angle of opposing forwards, he was nicknamed the "Roving Scotsman," and was among the very first "roving" goaltenders who used this technique.

In *The Chicago Blackhawk Story*, by George Vass, Francis "King" Clancy said of Gardiner: "Charlie had everything, sure hands, good eyes, quick reflexes, no weak spots, and a fine team spirit. In his last season of 48 games, 10 of them were shutouts, and in 14 others he allowed only one goal."

King also commented on Gardiner's sense of humor: "I remember the night someone threw a derby hat on the ice. Charlie skated over, picked up the lid, slipped it on his head as though it was a helmet, and wore it while playing."

As a boy, Bill Mosienko, Chicago Blackhawk star of the forties and fifties got to meet Gardiner: "I got to meet him when he presented us with our medals at the Playground Championships. I'll never forget that, it was quite a thrill."

Gardiner's goals against average for seven seasons was a very respectable 2.02, and he received the Vezina Trophy in 1932 and 1934 for being the League's best goalie. He also made the All-Star team four times during his career, first team in 1931, 1932, and 1934, and second team in 1933.

Johnny Gottselig, former Hawk star of the 30s and 40s, said the following about Gardiner in a write-up he did many years ago: "[Charlie was] a keen thinker [who] was considered valuable for his generalship and his guiding advice to the players in front of him." Gottselig also commented on how daring Chuck was, "never hesitating to dive in among sharp blades for the puck or to skate out far from the net to break up a play in the making."

Losing and being scored on bothered Gardiner most of all. It has been said that he would get deeply upset when teammates scored on him during practice sessions.

When not playing hockey, Gardiner was known to be one of Canada's best trap shooters, as well as an excellent baseball and rugby player. He also owned his own sporting goods store in Winnipeg. In addition to his hobbies (singing, photography, flying, motorboating, and golf) Gardiner ran hockey clinics in Winnipeg, and always made himself available to charities for fund-raising events. Gardiner, who had a wife and a son, Bobby, had a reputation for being a clean liver. He never drank or smoked, and always had time to speak with his fans after the games were over.

The greatest sacrifice Gardiner ever gave quite possibly may have been his life for the 1934 Stanley Cup. Although very ill since the previous season, he never missed a game, always pulling through for his team despite frequent visits to the hospital. In a state of exhaustion, he collapsed during the third game of the best of five series against Detroit, allowing the Red Wings to win the game 5-2. It was the only game of the series that Chicago lost. Years ago, Johnny Gottselig commented that management sent Chuck to Milwaukee for two days of rest and relaxation. Gottselig explained that the often nervous Gardiner was a worrier, and losing often sapped his energy.

However, despite being extremely ill, he did the impossible and played the entire Stanley Cup final game on April 10, 1934. The game was scoreless for three periods, and it wasn't until the sec-

ond period of sudden death overtime that Harold "Mush" March finally scored the winning goal.

After winning the cup, Gardiner collected on a bet made with defenseman Roger "Broadway" Jenkins. Charlie, carrying a bouquet of roses presented to him by Lionel Conacher, was given a wheelbarrow ride around a Chicago Loop block.

Charlie died in Winnipeg's St. Boniface Hospital on June 13, 1934 after collapsing at his home. Some sources claim he had a chronic tonsil infection. Others say he had kidney and stomach trouble. However, it is accepted that a brain tumor caused by a head injury earlier in his career was the true culprit.

In George Vass's book *The Chicago Blackhawk Story*, Coach Gorman's comment on Gardiner after the victory appeared as follows: "He's the greatest goalie that ever donned the pads. He won the title for the Blackhawks. Without him, we wouldn't have made it." Major McLaughlin had named Gardiner team captain on November 6, 1933. He is the only goalie whose name appears on the Stanley Cup as being the captain of a Stanley Cup championship team.

During the 316 NHL regular season games in which he donned those pads, Gardiner allowed only 664 goals for a 2.02 GAA; 42 of those games were shutouts. Out of the 21 play-off games he participated in, Gardiner allowed only 35 goals for an incredible 1.37 GAA; five of those games were shutouts. All things considered, Charlie is most definitely one of the best goaltenders who ever graced the ice at Chicago Stadium!

Marvin McCarthy, who wrote for the *Chicago Herald-American* many years ago, and who looked fondly upon Chuck, wrote a short piece after Gardiner passed away. It is included here.

"Another valiant warrior lies at eternal ease in the shadow of professional ice hockey's symbol of courage, the Georges Vezina Trophy, for keepers of the goal, Chuck Gardiner is dead. Curly-headed Chuck, holy terror of the ice, young Blind Fury personified, who times galore has startled and thrilled us with headlong rushes into the very thing that I'm afraid, played a part in his death—the hurtling puck.

No onslaught that stout Chuck ever faced was so sudden or stunning as Death's swift charge that laid him low. Early Wednesday afternoon on June 13 Chicago hockey fans learned that Gardiner was ill at his home in Winnipeg. A few hours later the last red light had flashed for Chuck.

The best goalie in all hockey, who could stop rubber bullets, was powerless before his charge, and Death had scored a goal."

Charlie became a charter inductee of the Hockey Hall of Fame in 1945.

JOHNNY GOTTSELIG

Another Hawk great of the thirties was Johnny Gottselig. Born June 24, 1905 in Odessa, Russia, he played left-wing for Chicago from 1928 until 1945. During his career he racked up 372 points in 589 games. His best season was 1938-39 when he scored 16 goals and recorded 23 assists for a total of 39 points, placing him among the League's top scorers. After retiring from professional play,

Harold "Mush" March (photo from the Hockey Hall of Fame/Ernie Fitzsimmons Collection.)

he went on to coach the Hawks for three seasons and later served as their publicity director. He also did play-by-play radio broadcasts of Blackhawk games. Later, he became an executive with Stone Construction, a manufacturer of concrete pipes. Gottselig, who was extremely dexterous with the stick, made the All-Star (second team) in 1939.

Longtime off-ice official Jack Fitzsimmons remembers Gottselig as: "an entertaining hockey player. He had a special talent of killing penalties and probably was most unique. You don't see that anymore with killing penalties, [the way] he controlled that little black thing you push around."

HAROLD "MUSH" MARCH

The man that made it all happen for the Hawks in 1934 was Harold "Mush" March. Born on October 18, 1908, in Silton, Saskatchewan, March left his father's farm to play amateur hockey in Regina with the Falcons where he helped them win the Junior Championship of Canada during the 1927-28 season. It was also in Regina that he got his

Johnny Gottselig (photo from the Hockey Hall of Fame/Ernie Fitzsimmons Collection.)

nickname "Mush." Because of his small size (5'5", 154 lbs.) he was called "Mush Mouth" after a character in the "Moon Mullins" comic strip.

After being discovered at the age of 20 by Dick Irvin, March was signed to a contract and he played right-wing for them from 1928 until 1945. It was his goal in sudden death overtime that secured their first Stanley Cup ever.

"I can tell you a story about Mush when he started," said John Robertson, a longtime Hawks employee. "His father was dealing with Bill Tobin. Bill Tobin used a Michigan bank roll with all the big bills on the outside filled up with dollar bills on the inside (with a laugh). He signed Mush. It was one of those things where he went up to Regina to sign him. Mush was a great player. He had a terrific shot and he had a thing of putting his stick over his shoulder and spinning around after shooting, catching the [opposing] players beneath the chin. He had a knack of doing that real well. He was a great scorer, and a small man."

Recalling a funny story that involved March, Robertson said: "It's very different because now everything is plush, and in those days everything was plain old wooden floors. They didn't have the protective equipment they have today. I mean, you used to have to sew felt on long underwear. You'd go in the dressing room and [it would] smell like billy goats because if they were successful in winning they wouldn't even let you wash their underwear. I can remember when [Mush] March had a streak going he refused to wash his underwear and stuff. By the end of the season, it was getting pretty bad."

Although he was a forward, he was an effective two-way player, known for his defensive back-checking. Longtime off-ice official Jack Fitzsimmons explained: "It was a different program than it is now. He was a two-way performer, his offensive skills were always productive and at the same time he was a defensive hockey player. He had many, many skills. You can't compare the game from the 30s and 40s to the game today, it was different. But he was a credit to the sport and in fact, a credit to the sport world, whether it was hockey, football, or baseball. He was [also] a former golf pro. But the bottom line is he is a class act. He was then and he still is."

After retiring from professional play, March served as an NHL linesman for 11 years and was part owner of the General Bearings Company in Chicago. Still a big hockey fan, he now resides in Arizona where he plays golf frequently and has been a pro member of the United States Golf Association since 1961.

PAUL THOMPSON

Another incredible athlete of the 30s was a man who led the Blackhawks in individual scoring six times during the eight years he played in the Windy City. That man was Paul Thompson, born in Calgary, Alberta, in 1906. Brother of four-time Vezina trophy winner and former Chicago Blackhawk head scout Tiny Thompson, Paul came to Chicago in 1931 after spending five years as one of the original New York Rangers. While there, he aided them in winning their first Stanley Cup. He repeated this feat twice more with the Blackhawks, taking part in both of their first two Cup wins.

During his 13-year NHL career, Thompson scored 153 goals and racked up 179 assists for a total of 332 points. He was the scoring champion of the American Division in 1937-38 and made All-Star twice: first team in 1937-38 and second team in 1935-36.

"Paul Thompson was an excellent player," said Cully Dahlstrom. "He was great around the net and [at] shooting the puck. He was a good coach [coached the Blackhawks from the late 30s to mid-40s]. He wanted everybody to work hard and work as a team, which we tried to do. The first year [Dahlstrom's first year—1938] he was the [assistant] coach when we won the Stanley Cup. Bill Stewart [was the coach], but Paul Thompson was in there too."

When Thompson started out in 1926 as one of the original Rangers, he received a salary of $3,500, and moonlighted in Camel advertisements, which gave him $50 a week plus all of the Camels that he could smoke.

In a February 10, 1972 article appearing in the *Calgary Gazette*, he once commented: "I joined the Rangers from junior hockey when a lot of the oldtimers were going out. A lot of them gave me good advice saying: 'Look kid, I'm all through and never saved a dime...look after yourself, put a few bucks away, go into business, don't go out like I am.'"

Thompson quickly moved up the ladder, and was promoted to head coach in Chicago. After The Major fired coach Bill Stewart during the 1938-39 season, Thompson took the job, finishing out his last season as player/coach.

In later years, Thompson offered his feelings on his promotion in an article by Gyle Konotopetz, which appeared in the *Calgary Herald*: "I was offered a raise from $8,500 to $12,500 to coach," he said. "I was a damn fool and took it for the money. Quit in my prime. Now, guys like [Lanny] McDonald are through at 32. We had an easy schedule so you could play longer."

Surprisingly, much against The Major's tradition of canning coaches in a hurry, Thompson lasted six seasons behind the Chicago bench. In 1944, he even steered the team to the Stanley Cup final series where they were swept by the Montreal Canadiens. He was also successful coaching several amateur teams, bringing the Vancouver Canucks to the Pacific Coast League title in 1945. That same year they also won the United States Amateur title, defeating the Boston Olympics. Later still, he coached the New Westminster, B.C., Cubs to the Western Canada Senior B Title.

In the end, things seemed to work out well for Paul Thompson. After retiring from hockey he moved to Kamloops, British Columbia, and operated a cattle ranch. Later, he moved to Calgary and purchased the Westgate Hotel, which he operated until 1981, and then retired.

In the same *Calgary Gazette* article, Thompson remembered his most memorable game with the Blackhawks, explaining: "It was in Chicago Stadium [Feb. 3, 1938] the year I had 22 goals. This big truck driver was always yelling, 'take that bum Thompson off.' Well, I scored four goals that night. After the fourth one, I got a hell of a hand, then I heard that voice: 'I still think you stink, Thompson.'"

The former flashy left-wing thinks of the game differently today than he did back then: "It's not the same game. We used to carry the puck, make lateral passes and our goals were clean cut. Now they pile up in the corner and somebody shoots from the blue line. It hits somebody in the ass and goes in."

In the same *Calgary Gazette* article, Murray Murdoch, one of Thompson's former Ranger teammates once remarked: "Now Paul was the handsome devil on the team with that curly hair. When we went out, the boys would say he had the sex appeal and one of the other boys...well, his feet didn't smell too good—had sox appeal..."

THE FIRST TRIUMPH

"I was having my afternoon steak before a game. I poured a hell of a lot of ketchup on it. I'd just started to eat when my wife Beulah made some casual remark. For no good reason, I picked up my steak and threw it at her. She ducked and the steak hit the wall. The ketchup splattered and the steak hung there on the wall. Slowly it began to peel, and I stared at it. Between the time that steak hit the wall and then hit the floor, I decided I'd been a touchy goalkeeper long enough. By the time it landed, I'd retired."

That quote, taken from John DeVaney and Burt Goldblatt's book *The Stanley Cup,* depicts the feelings of former Detroit Red Wing goalie Wilf Cude after his retirement. Part of his touchiness, without a doubt, came from a shaking Chicago gave Detroit in 1934 that brought the Stanley Cup to the Windy City for the first time in history. Starting off the season with a 23-day training camp at the University of Illinois, which boasted daily schedules consisting of running, road drills, and over two hours on the ice, the Hawks eventually found themselves in the play-offs.

Once there, they defeated the Montreal Maroons and then faced off with Detroit, who were first place in the American Division. Prior to that, they hadn't won a game in the Motor City for over four years. In a best of five series, they beat the Red Wings three games to one.

The first game, held in Detroit on April 3rd, ended with a 2 to 1 Chicago victory. Lionel Conacher scored the first goal for the Blackhawks at 17:50 of the first period, giving them the lead. Then, as the game wore on through a scoreless second period, Detroit finally answered with a goal from Herbie Lewis late in the third. Finally, during the second overtime period Paul Thompson scored, giving the Hawks their first win in the series.

The second game, also held in Detroit, again ended with a Chicago victory. Couture got the puck moving early in the first period with one of the two goals he scored in that game. Other Chicago goals came from Romnes and Gottselig, resulting in a 4 to 1 Hawk victory.

During the third game held in Chicago, things turned sour as goaltender Gardiner wilted due to his illness. The Red Wings managed to defeat the Blackhawks 5 to 2, especially dominating the third period with three unanswered goals.

However, things would soon change on April 10th in Chicago in the fourth and final game. Opening at a fast pace, the Blackhawks dominated the first period with the line of March, Thompson, and Romnes, at the same time playing careful hockey to keep the Red Wings from getting out of control. Detroit's Gus Marker and Chicago's Rosie Couture both served two minutes in the penalty box for tripping before the period ended, and Doc Romnes came close to putting a shot past Wilf Cude, but it hit the post. It was said that after Marker was sent to the penalty box for charging Johnny Gottselig into the boards, the Hawks really began playing more offensively.

Early in the first period, Detroit's Herbie Lewis nearly scored on Gardiner with a high shot, and had a second chance on the rebound but the puck was swept away in the nick of time by Hawk defenseman Roger Jenkins. After that, the Red Wings went at full steam in an attempt to score, only gaining an advantage for a short while. However, their efforts were futile as the game's first period ended with no score.

During the second period, March completely escaped the Detroit defense on a mad rush for Cude, but his shot just barely missed the net.

The third period was played defensively, with most of the action occurring at mid-ice. The tension began to build as the game remained scoreless. Hap Emms gave Gardiner his toughest moment of the entire game with a high, hard shot which caused the ill goalie to fall, and after that he took a time out to catch his breath.

After the third period ended with no score, the teams progressed through two periods of overtime play. Several near fights developed, as the tension built, but no penalties were called. Then, at 10:05 of the second overtime period, Harold "Mush" March finally burst the bubble with a goal that secured the Chicago Blackhawks their first Stanley Cup ever.

Years later, in George Vass's book *The Chicago Blackhawk Story*, March recalled the memories surrounding that historic goal: "I was standing behind the face-off circle. The puck came right to me, about forty feet out from Wilf Cude. All I had to do was to take a couple of steps and fire. I put everything I had into that one. I think Cude was startled to see me diving in after it, but I just had to have it. It was probably the biggest goal I ever scored."

Today he feels much the same way, commenting in a reminiscent tone: "It was the greatest thing that ever happened to me," he said. "It was like everything happened just for me."

Thanks to a winning goal during the play-offs by March, who had been experiencing trouble scoring consistently throughout the season, the Hawks were able to move ahead on their road to this first victory. After he scored his famous game-winning Stanley Cup goal, March was escorted by teammate Louis Trudel away from center ice and around the rink for a victory lap, waving and grinning all the way. NHL President Frank Calder then presented the Cup to the Champions.

In that final game, Detroit's Cude stopped 53 shots while Gardiner had to stop only 40. It was a strange twist of fate that Gardiner and Cude played goal on the opposing teams. As boys, they were friends back in Winnipeg; walking back and forth to school together. Roger Jenkins had to pay up on a bet he had made with Gardiner, and because they had won the Stanley Cup, he wheeled him around a Chicago Loop block in a wheelbarrow.

After securing their first Stanley Cup, the Hawks continued skating onward. Coach Tommy Gorman, who led the Montreal Maroons to a Stanley Cup the very next season, was replaced by Clem Loughlin, a former Hawk defenseman who would coach the team until the 1937-38 season. Loughlin's replacement was baseball umpire Bill Stewart. Surprisingly, it was Stewart who would lead them to their next Stanley Cup that very season.

BILL STEWART

Perhaps the most colorful and dynamic coach the Blackhawks had during the entire decade, Bill Stewart was truly a remarkable man. Grandfather of present-day referee Paul Stewart, Bill Stewart had quite an affinity with the world of sports. Stewart's grandson, also named Bill, explained:

"My grandfather didn't play in high school. He didn't start playing till after World War I. He got a job from a George Brown, who was the owner of the Boston Arena. This was prior to the Boston Garden. He was one of the assistant general managers, picked up skating, and started playing. I have clips from old newspapers of him playing for various and sundry teams. They would put all those scores in the paper. We have a picture of him in old goalie pads in the cellar of the old Boston Arena, circa 1921-22. He later went on [to coach women's hockey at Radcliffe]. Radcliffe needed a hockey coach, and they played at the arena. I think George Brown was instrumental in my grandfather getting the job.

Milton Academy, in Milton, Massachusetts, as well as MIT, also needed a hockey coach, and Stewart ended up getting those jobs as well, juggling his schedule between the teams' different schedules, which were fairly short. Besides coaching hockey, Stewart also served as a baseball umpire in the National League. "He knew his stuff," continued his grandson Bill. "Obviously he came from the National Baseball League, but he was a referee in the National Hockey League [as well]. During the winter he refereed college hockey. The National Hockey League only played on specific nights, obviously set by the train schedule. On the nights he wasn't working [there], he'd work in the American League, or in the CanAm League prior to the American League, and [he] worked college hockey on other nights. So, he was always movin'."

Stewart was raised in a strict family. Bill recalled: "In his family, my great grandfather and great grandmother were very religious people. The fact that he was an athlete growin' up, was abhorrent to them. He used to win medals in track. He'd bring them home, and his dad was a silversmith. His father took all of his medals one day and melted them down and made door stops out of them."

Stewart was as tough as they came. Paul Stewart commented: "My grandfather was refereeing in the National Hockey League and ironically, in 1934, he refereed the only game that was ever forfeited. Tommy Gorman, who had coached the Hawks, punched him in the face in Boston [and]

my grandfather jumped over the boards and chased him out of the rink. They said he was a tough guy and wasn't the type of guy to be intimidated. He was the first guy to throw Jackie Robinson out of a game, he was the first guy to ever throw The Rocket [Maurice Richard] out of a game. So it was his make up. He was right when he was right and was a man of his convictions."

The most famous tale of Stewart's toughness is the scuffle that took place between him and Toronto's Conn Smythe prior to a 1938 Stanley Cup play-off game. However, one of his encounters may have gotten him the job as a National League Umpire. "He got hired, got a National League baseball contract because of the fact that he made [an unpopular] call down in York, Pennsylvania on a Sunday," recalled grandson Bill. "The fans came out of the stands and attacked him on the runway, about 15 of them. He held his own. He got bruised a little bit and they shot tear gas off right next to his ear. But two weeks later he got a National League contract and he was umpiring."

There were other encounters as well. "In 1936, he was umpiring on second base at Sportsman's Park in St. Louis," Bill continued. "He made a call and a guy came out of the stands. I think the guy woke up about five days later. He swung a roundhouse right at him."

A dapper man, Stewart was a celebrity in his home town of Boston. After the Hawks won the Stanley Cup in 1938, the mayor held a reception there in his honor. "I knew him as just the guy who after his career had a big house," said grandson Paul. "We used to go over and he had all sorts of pictures on the walls and hockey sticks in the corner and baseball bats and all sorts of W.W. I stuff—a little kids' dream—and a play room. He worked for Topps chewing gum and he was a baseball scout. He used to take us to the park and the Bruins [games] and that, and everybody knew him. I have a pocket watch with a Stanley Cup emblem on it and it said: 'World Champions—1938 Stanley Cup Champions—Chicago Blackhawks, Bill Stewart, manager.'"

It was Stewart's demeanor that got him the job with Chicago. "They knew my grandfather, they knew his reputation, because he had come from refereeing," said Bill Stewart. "One of the reasons he got hired was because somebody threatened him one night when The Major was there, and he told this one off and told that one off, and you can have my job if you want it, but that's the way it is. McLaughlin liked his stirring attitude and steadfastness, which eventually got him [fired]."

Stewart was a good coach. He was very knowledgeable of the game, and kept close track of what was occurring in the League, keeping the scores of every game written inside of his rulebooks, which he read on the train to pass the time. However, the fact that he was an American was a hindering force on his career. Bill explained: "He had an idea about the game, it's just that he was an American in a totally Canadian game. I don't think anyone took him seriously. They kind of did [after he won the Cup]. But, I've read books afterwards by various people who kind of belittle him because of The Major's reputation, being eccentric. And because of my grandfather's reputation [of] being a tough battler. [Due to the] flukiness of it, you know, the Alfie Moore part of it, they kind of belittled that team. And also that they had the worst record...The Hawks went in with a bad record, but they won the Cup, and nobody can ever take that away from them."

Besides coaching the Blackhawks to their second Stanley Cup, and being involved in several different sports in varying capacities, in 1957, Stewart became the general manager and coach of the U.S. national team. He put the same team together in 1960 and took home the gold medal.

Although some of the same talent from the previous Cup victory was still present, such as Gottselig, March, and Thompson, the Blackhawks had acquired some newcomers as well around the time of their second victory. This new blood came in the form of men like Michael Karakas, Carl Potter Voss, and defenseman Earl Siebert.

MIKE KARAKAS

Karakas, born in Aurora, Minnesota, on December 12, 1911, played for the Blackhawks from 1935-40. Karakas learned how to play the game in Eveleth, Minnesota, in a flooded lot near the Spruce Mine. Before coming to Chicago, he spent three years playing on the Eveleth High School team, and then went on to play for Eveleth Junior College, and the Rangers (an amateur team) who won the state championship in 1931. Next, he played for the Chicago Shamrocks of the American Hockey Association as a back-up goalie in 1931, and a regular in 1932, when he was named as that league's most valuable goalie.

During his stay in the Windy City, his goals-against average was 2.91, and he allowed only 15 goals during the Stanley Cup play-offs in 1937-38. "I played with Mike Karakas when we were with St. Paul," said former Blackhawk forward Cully Dahlstrom. "He was always a good goalie. We thought we had the best goalie in the league."

After 1939-40, Karakas spent three seasons with the Providence Reds of the AHL. He later went on to play for the Montreal Canadiens. Karakas returned to Chicago in 1943-44 and took the Hawks to the Stanley Cup finals against the Habs, but they lost. In 1944-45, he led the NHL in shutouts, along with Frank McCool of Toronto, and was named to the second All-Star team. After 1945-46, Karakas returned to Providence of the AHL and finished his career.

ALFIE MOORE

Perhaps one of the most famous Blackhawks of the late thirties was Alfie Moore. Although he only played in one very important game, his handywork will never be forgotten in Chicago.

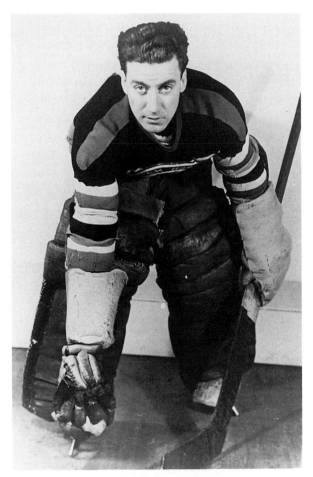

Alfie Moore got his "big break" into the NHL when Blackhawk goalie Mike Karakas broke his toe. (Photo from the Hockey Hall of Fame/Ernie Fitzsimmons Collection.)

It all began when Karakas broke his toe and was unable to play in the opening play-off game against Toronto. With their spare goalie Paul Goodman not available, the Hawks were at a loss for a net-minder.

New York Rangers' goalie Davey Kerr offered to replace Karakas, but the Maple Leafs wouldn't allow it and insisted that they use Toronto minor league goalie Alfie Moore. Feeling that they had received a sour deal, a fist fight broke out between then Toronto manager Conn Smythe and Bill Stewart.

"The two dressing rooms were side by side back in those days and my grandfather and Conn Smythe got into a fistfight in the hallway," recalled Stewart's grandson, Paul. *"I guess on the morning of the game...Smythe sent word to my grandfather that there was no way [he could use Kerr] and why didn't he suit up like Lester Patrick had done years previously. My grandfather took it a personal insult and he went whipping out of the room after him and they got into it. I guess Smythe in his own way was a tough guy and my grandfather was a tough guy and they went at it a little bit and the players had to pull them apart. You have to understand there weren't too many Americans in the league back in those days and there has always been that provincial attitude. Smythe, of course, was probably the most provincial of them all, and the interesting aspect [of it] is that he [Stewart] won the Cup and the Cup wasn't in Chicago when he won it because they thought it was going to Toronto."*

After looking for Moore at his house, they finally found him at one of the several taverns he had frequented that day. Johnny Gottselig was sent to find Alfie. In John DeVaney and Burt Goldblatt's book *The Stanley Cup*, Gottselig commented: "I

walked in and Alfie looked at me and said, 'By God, am I glad to see you. I'd love to get a couple of tickets for tonight's game.' And I said, 'Boy, Alfie, you got the best seat in the house.'"

Coach Stewart's grandson Bill recalled the story of Moore, explaining:

"The deal on Alfie, and I'm sure some of the older guys can back him up, [is that] he was in town and they found him sittin' in a bar havin' a pretty good time for himself. They brought him in the room and my grandfather said right away, 'No. No way. I'll play goal.' Of course, the guys wouldn't have any part of that. So they put him in the shower, and fed him some coffee to try and sober him up, I guess, and put him out on the ice. The first shot taken on him was scored. Then, he shut 'em out the rest of the way."

According to DeVaney and Goldblatt's book, after filling up with coffee, Moore, who was angry with Conn Smythe for sending him to the minors, claimed: "That Connie Smythe is going to rue the day he ever sent me down to Pittsburgh. I should have been playing up here instead of Broda [Toronto's goaltender], I'll show that Connie Smythe." And show him he did. Moore allowed only one goal in that game. After that, Toronto insisted that the Hawks bring Goodman up from Chicago and that was all of the action Alfie Moore would see. During the four years that Moore would spend in the NHL, he also played for the Detroit Red Wings and the New York Americans, playing in only 21 games. Surprisingly, 14 of them were losses, and the only play-off game he won out of the three in which he played was for the Blackhawks.

Years later, in 1961, Moore was present in the dressing room after the Hawks won their third Stanley Cup. When asked by a *Chicago Tribune* reporter if he was really intoxicated before the 1938 victory, he joked with him in an April 17, 1961 article (scratching his head in deep thought): "I've always been sorta hazy about that. I had quite a few beers that day and I just can't remember."

The Chicago Blackhawks' second Stanley Cup Championship in a decade. (Photo from the Hockey Hall of Fame/Ernie Fitzsimmons Collection.)

THE SECOND TRIUMPH

In 1937-38, despite not having the best possible season (14-25-9), the Hawks made it to the play-offs. In George Vass's book *The Chicago Blackhawk Story*, Alex Levinsky, who played defense for Chicago from 1934 to 1939, commented: "We were so bad that I thought we'd be eliminated in our first play-off series by the Canadiens. So I packed all my clothes in my car and sent my wife home to Toronto. But we kept winning and I was still living out of the car a month later."

It was also quite a season for Johnny Gottselig, as he went on to score one goal in each game of the opening round of the play-offs, helping them defeat the Montreal Canadiens. Later, in the opening game of the series against Toronto, he scored two goals, aiding them in a 3 to 1 victory and the chance to move on further in the play-offs.

The road to the Blackhawks' second Stanley Cup victory began in 1937-38 when they faced off with and defeated the Montreal Canadiens in the third place play-offs. Next they met the New York

Art Levinsky played defense from 1934–39. (Photo from the Hockey Hall of Fame/ Ernie Fitzsimmons Collection.)

Paul Goodman, goalie, almost missed the second game of the play-off series in 1938 because he was at the movies. (Photo from the Hockey Hall of Fame/Ernie Fitzsimmons Collection.)

Americans in the semifinals. Supposedly, in New York the Blackhawks were the victims of foul play when fans were caught holding the goal-judge's hands so he couldn't signify a goal made by Alex Levinsky. However, in the end the Blackhawks were the victors, beating the Americans two games to one in the best of three series.

Next came the big challenge, Toronto's Maple Leafs, who were first place in the Canadian Division. The Hawks had been able to beat the Leafs only once in six games during the regular season. The first game of that series, played in Toronto on April 5, resulted in a 3-1 Chicago victory. After the first period, both teams were tied at one with goals by Toronto's Gordie Drillon and the Hawks' Johnny Gottselig. After that, the rest of the game belonged to the Blackhawks as Paul Thompson scored in the second, and Gottselig once again in the third.

The second game, also in Toronto, was a different story as Chicago was routed 5-1 on April 7. Still without Karakas, whose broken toe stood in the way of his performance, and Alfie Moore as well, whom Toronto had refused to lend out again, the Blackhawks put their spare goaltender Paul Goodman, now available, in the nets. Supposedly, Goodman was nowhere to be found as game time grew near, and was found in a movie theater minutes before the game was to start. It is said that he believed Alfie Moore would be the one in goal that night. Besides a goal by Earl Seibert midway in the

first period, Toronto dominated the entire game. In the third period, the scoring combination of Toronto's George Parsons and Gordie Drillon managed to put three goals past Goodman in several minutes, at 11:08, 10:29, and 9:44.

The third game, back in Chicago, turned the tables back in the other direction as the Hawks skated away with a 2-1 win. After a Toronto goal in the first period by Syl Apps, Chicago dominated the rest of the game with a goal by Carl Voss in the second and Elwyn "Doc" Romnes in the third.

Then came the historic fourth game, held in Chicago on April 12. With 17,204 fans packed into the Stadium, the Hawks faced off once again with the Leafs. After one period of play filled with three fights, rough and tumble play, and flailing sticks, both teams found themselves tied at one. Carl "Cully" Dahlstrom scored first, followed by a goal by Toronto's Gordie Drillon. Fighting an equally powerful battle through three-fourths of the second period, Chicago finally answered the tie with a 10-foot shot by Carl Voss. Then, a little over a minute later, Jack Shill scored an unforgettable goal. One hundred and ten feet away from the Toronto cage, the defenseman lifted the puck into the air. Maple Leaf goaltender Turk Broda dropped to the ice to stop the easy shot, but got a surprise when the puck bounced over his stick and into the net, giving Chicago a 3-1 lead.

Toronto continually made desperate attempts to score during the third period, opening up in the process. Taking advantage of this, Harold "Mush" March, famous for having the last word in Stanley Cup finals, put a shot from right-wing past Broda with less than four minutes of play remaining. Chicago had won their second Stanley Cup by a score of 4-1. It was quite an accomplishment for the Blackhawks. During the regular season they had only beaten the Maple Leafs once in six games, and ended the season with a 14-25-9 record. The underdogs had done the impossible!

In an April 13, 1938, article columnist George Strickler of the *Chicago Tribune* commented: "It was pretty much of a joke. They had finished sixth in the National League race. No one took them seriously, although other play-off contestants were pleased to see them qualify."

Cully Dahlstrom, who played center for the team at the time, explains what enabled the team to keep winning in the play-offs, despite such a poor regular season.

> *"It [was] determination by the individual played. We seemed to have a group together there that didn't want to lose. And as such we played hard, and probably above our natural ability. That's why we won. When we [went] up [to] Toronto, they were kings of the hockey world at that time. We lost the first game quite badly, but then we got together and took control, so to speak, and we beat'em. It's determination, and the guys that don't want to get beat, they usually win!"*

NHL President Frank Calder had ordered the Stanley Cup sent to Toronto, because he had been told there was no way the Blackhawks would emerge as the victors. Alfie Moore was rewarded with $300, and an engraved gold watch for his services. Once again, Roger Jenkins lost the same bet he had made in 1934 with Gardiner, and he wheeled Karakas down State St. in a wheelbarrow in front of thousands of on-lookers. Little did they know that this pinnacle in the world of NHL hockey would not be reached again in Chicago for another 23 years.

National League baseball umpire Bill Stewart had become one of the year's most famous sports figures as he had brought the Blackhawks a Stanley Cup in his first season as an NHL coach. He was the first American-born manager to accomplish this feat in the NHL. After the victory, Stewart said: "My contract with the Hawks runs another year and we'll be out to repeat."

However, The Major canned his American born favorite after the Hawks again won only 14 games the next season, and completely missed the play-offs. Stewart's grandson, referee Paul Stewart, explains what was behind his grandfather being released.

> *"He told The Major to get the hell out of the dressing room," he explained. "The Major had come down and was berating a player in between periods. There had been the same type of interference from The Major, quite often, as with other owners such as Steinbrenner and Billy Martin. They have tried to usurp the authority of the coach and my grandfather wasn't the type to take orders from people who didn't know anything about it. He wanted my grandfather to coach the team from the first row of the balcony and shout down the orders by megaphone. Now with the headsets and so on, maybe The Major was a little ahead of his time. He came into the dressing room and said something to one of the players and my grandfather pitched him and they fired him for that."*

CARL "CULLY" DAHLSTROM

Carl "Cully" Dahlstrom, who was a rookie the year the Hawks took home their second prize, was born in Minneapolis, Minnesota on July 3, 1913. He began playing hockey at the age of nine, when he and his friends would knock cans around vacant lots with sticks. A center for the Blackhawks from 1937-38 until 1945-46, it was he who scored the first goal in the final game against Toronto, which the Hawks won 4-1.

After graduating at the top of his high school class in Minneapolis, Dahlstrom played junior hockey, and eventually found his way to the Minneapolis Millers of the American Hockey Association. It was there that he was given the nickname "Cully," after Cully Wilson, who had also played for the Millers.

After awhile, Cully was sold, along with several other players, to St. Paul by team owner Lyle Wright, who wanted to create a rivalry between the Twin Cities. It wasn't long before Dahlstrom was invited to try out for the Boston Bruins. However, things didn't work out at the time.

In a May 24, 1985 *Hockey News* article with columnist Randy Schultz, Dahlstrom offered a few comments about the tryout, and the days of hockey long ago.

"I just didn't have the natural talent like some kids do today to jump directly to the NHL...I can remember getting a tryout one year with the Boston Bruins and going to their training camp. After the first couple of days I realized that I wasn't ready to jump to the NHL yet. Those guys just skated circles around me. It was as though I was going in slow motion the way those players played. That's why it really didn't bother me when I went back to the minors. But when I got my tryout with the Blackhawks, that was a different story. Then I knew I was ready for the NHL."

After his unsuccessful tryout with the Bruins, Cully was discovered while playing for St. Paul by Bill Tobin.

"I kind of lost interest in possibly going to the National [Hockey] League," he said today, looking back. *"But then I got a call from Bill Tobin. He wanted me to come down to the training camp [at the University of Illinois, Chicago]...After a half-a-week of practice sessions, Bill Tobin contacted me and wanted me to come down to the office. At that time, he offered me a contract and I said I couldn't accept [it]. So I negotiated a little higher, which was still peanuts. Then I signed the contract and went to training camp. I tried out and was successful, at least I made the team and started in the National [Hockey] League for the first game."*

Dahlstrom not only did well in training camp that year, but after the season was over, he was awarded the Calder Trophy (League's best rookie). "This is honest," he explains today, "I thought there was a poor crop of rookies that year. I had no idea that I would be nominated for that position and accredited Rookie of the Year. But things happen, and [they] happened well for me. I had read a little bit about it, but I didn't think I would be a winner in that category."

Thinking back to the many hours he spent on the ice, Cully explains what kind of a player he was. "As an athlete, I also played in other sports," he explains. "I played softball [third base] and we went to the finals in the National Softball Tournament. [In hockey], I played an all-around center position," he explains. "I was good on defense. As a matter of fact, I did many, many terms of playing short-handed for the club. So, I was good defensively and reasonably good offensively, but not as good as some of 'em."

Including the play-offs, Dahlstrom scored 94 goals and 220 points in 371 games over the course of his eight-season NHL career. After hockey, Cully worked for Utah Radio Products Company in Chicago, and later as a real estate appraiser in California.

ELWYN "DOC" ROMNES

The 1937-38 Stanley Cup play-offs were also quite memorable for one of Cully's teammates by the name of Elwyn "Doc" Romnes. Born on January 1, 1909, in White Bear Lake, Minnesota, Doc was a center for Chicago from 1930-31 to 1938-39.

Elwyn "Doc" Romnes (photo from the Hockey Hall of Fame/Ernie Fitzsimmons Collection).

He also played for the New York Americans and the Toronto Maple Leafs for short periods during his ten season NHL career. Lionel Conacher once claimed that Doc was one of the best centers he ever skated with.

The reason the 1937-38 postseason was memorable for Romnes (46 career penalty minutes), is because at that time the 1935-36 Lady Byng Trophy winner (most gentlemanly player) had his nose broken in five places. As it turned out, the culprit was one of his former Maple Leaf teammates, Red Horner (1,430 career penalty minutes). Doc was the first Chicago Blackhawk to win the Lady Byng Trophy.

"Red Horner broke Romnes' nose with a body check, [an] elbow body check, it was a pretty good pop," said Bill Stewart, grandson of coach Bill Stewart "Of course, Romnes wasn't a big guy. So the next night, Doc's got the face guard on, so he's playin'. The puck goes down. The Doc takes his stick and swings it at Horner's head. According to my father, [he] just tweaked his nose, just clipped him a little bit. What we're talkin' about then goes on now. You take the big guy out of the game and the other guys back down. Horner was a bad dude. [Romnes] was a pretty mild-mannered guy, but he was pissed!"

After playing, Doc coached hockey at Michigan Tech and brought the Kansas City Pla-Mors to the United States Hockey League Championship and Play-Off Title in 1945-46. He later coached at the University of Minnesota from 1947 until 1952.

APPLE PIE

If anything odd could be said about the Hawks who circled the ice during the thirties, it would be that many of them, like Dahlstrom and Romnes, were born in the United States and not in Canada. Carl Dahlstrom, Roger Jenkins, Virgil Johnson, Mike Karakas, Alex Levinsky, Louis Trudel, Carl Voss, Elwyn "Doc" Romnes, Ernest Klingbeil, Paul Schaeffer, Al Suomi, Bun LaPrairie, and Milt Brink were all Americans. The situation was one that caused a certain degree of tension between many of the players.

Like former Boston Bruin Frank Brimsek, many of these American-born players, such as Karakas, and men who would later play for Chicago, such as Sam LoPresti and Johnny Mariucci, were coached by the legendary Cliff Thompson. Thompson coached hockey at Eveleth High school in Minnesota from 1920 until 1958, with a 534-26-9 record! Thompson took four of his teams to victory at the Minnesota state championship. He also coached at Eveleth Junior College, where men like LoPresti played for him. Eleven of the players he coached as youngsters went on to play in the NHL, and a few went on to the Olympics. Thompson was quite a coach. During the Great Depression, he went out of his way to make sure that many young hockey players had quality skates and decent equipment.

The reason that so many of these American-born players found their way to the NHL, and to the Blackhawks in particular, was because of The Major's obsession with having a completely American hockey team. Once, he even attempted to match only his American-born players against opponents in several games during the 1937 season, outraging the world of hockey by doing so. Art Ross of the Boston Bruins exclaimed that it was a disgrace to the game hockey.

In a May 24, 1985 article by Randy Schulz, appearing in *The Hockey News*, Cully Dahlstrom offered his opinion surrounding the whole affair. "I think that since his team was in an American City he wanted American-born players playing there," he explained. "But he soon found out that there weren't enough Americans to go around to build one team with. I don't think it took him very long to discover that."

Eccentric as he was, The Major had secured the Blackhawks two Stanley Cups in one decade. But, as the thirties died down and the forties grew near, the team would slowly lose its punch despite possessing some of the best talent in the league.

Sure,
heart-warming sentiments
have their place.
But not in a room
full of perfectly good
ice.

Congratulations to the 'Hawks
on 69 spine-chilling years.

Montgomery Ward
Things Are Changing

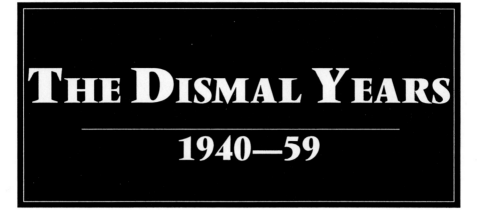

THE DISMAL YEARS
1940—59

Despite the forties and fifties introducing some incredible Chicago Blackhawk talent, the team would slowly slip in points after winning its last Stanley Cup. The Blackhawks, and the entire League, had survived the Great Depression, but now a new problem presented itself: World War II. Early in the decade of the 1940s, both Canada and the United States would find themselves involved in that bloody conflict. Even though some Chicago Blackhawks joined the military, among them Max and Doug Bentley, Chicago managed to pull through along with the rest of the NHL.

The team's worst slump of all would occur between 1947 and 1958 when it remained in last place nearly every season and only reached the play-offs once, in 1952-53. Luckily, the future had good things in store for them as the mid-fifties would mark the beginning of some truly successful years.

Blackhawks 1940-41 team, top row: LoPresti, Hergesheimer, Thoms, Seibert, Chad, Goodman, Frorlich (trainer). Center row— March, M. Bentley, Bill Carse, Gottselig, Bob Carse, Allen, Kelly. Bottom row: Dahlstrom, MacKay, Cooper, Thompson (manager), Mariucci, Wiebe, Portland. (Hockey Hall of Fame/Ernie Fitzsimmons Collection.)

George Allen–one of the "crowd pleasers" of the 1940s.
(Photo from the Hockey Hall of Fame/Ernie Fitzsimmons Collection.)

Hall of Famer Bill Gadsby, who played during this time period commented, "It was tough the first four or five years. We didn't have that good of a club, but we were in the NHL and that was number one and we were making good money, so that was number two."

George Allen, who played for the Blackhawks from 1939-40 to 1943-44 and also in 1945-46 gave his feelings on playing in the forties, an era that was slowly giving way to bigger stars and bigger paychecks:

"We were a real crowd pleaser. Oh yeah, we had crowds of seventeen, eighteen, almost twenty thousand. I remember the New York Rangers had a 21-game winning streak. We beat them in Chicago and I scored the winning goal. I was sold over there."

However, the profits from the huge crowds mostly went into the owner's pockets, explained Allen:

"We played when there was no money. I didn't do too bad, but some of the greats like the Bentley boys, why, they turned pro pretty cheap. I was working in the mines in Sudbury and I got pretty good wages. Of course, back in those days we thought $5,000 was a lot of money."

During the mid-fifties defenseman Pierre Pilote, who would be a major force for the team in the sixties, came to town. Recalling what it was like to play at that time, Pierre explained the training the team went through, and how it differed from that of today:

"There was no program set up for us. I guess the idea was that you went to training camp to get into shape. Guys went into camp ten pounds heavy and would drop eight and after they were playing ten years, they were twenty pounds heavier than when they started. The philosophy started changing a few years after that, but I'm talking about in the fifties [at] training camps where the guys would run for a couple weeks and do...some push-ups, something like that, but nothing too physical. You had to work in the summer back then because the salaries weren't that high. It's not like now where these guys can go to the gym everyday and stay in shape. We had to go to work. I remember I would start maybe two or three weeks before camp I would go to the park and do a little running and a few push-ups and that was it, go to training camp. It's quite different now, they're pushing weights and diets and three coaches and videos and all that. The game has changed, not for the worse, but it's a different game."

After the team secured its second Stanley Cup, former Blackhawk forward Paul Thompson took over as coach during the 1938 season. Thompson was the first NHL coach to employ the tactic of pulling the goaltender for an extra player. He used this maneuver during the last game of the 1940-41 season against Toronto. He was also chosen to coach the All-Stars the next season.

Chicago bench—Coach Johnny Gottselig (with hat on) having a discussion with the legendary referee Bill Stewart, Bill Gadsby in background. (Photo circa 1946, from Hockey Hall of Fame/Imperial Oil Turofsky Collection.)

Cliff "Fido" Purpur, who played for Thompson, commented on his former coach.

> *"I loved him. He wasn't a crab or nothin', and I think he liked his players. He played against me when I played for St. Louis and he said I was the toughest man he ever played against!"*

Johnny Gottselig, another All-Star coach, took the reins from Thompson for the 1944-45 season. Other coaches of this time period were Charlie Conacher, Ebbie Goodfellow, Sid Abel, Frank Eddolls, former forward Dick Irvin, Tommy Ivan, and Rudy Pilous, who would also coach up into the early sixties.

A funny thing about Charlie Conacher is an incident that he was involved in during the 1933 season, at the Hotel Lincoln in New York. His roommate Baldy Cotton, who was scared to death of heights, had gotten into an argument with him. To cool Baldy off, Charley held him by his ankles outside of a window, 20 stories up!

THE MEN

Among the best athletes of the forties were men like Sam LoPresti, Billy Mosienko, Doug and Max Bentley, Johnny Mariucci, Joe Cooper, Earl Seibert, Roy Conacher, Robert Hamill, Gaye Stewart, and Bill Gadsby.

SAM LOPRESTI

Sam LoPresti was born on January 30, 1917, in Elcor, Minnesota, and was raised in Eveleth, Minnesota. It was there that he developed into a top-rate goalie under coach Cliff Thompson, just like so many of the best hockey players from that area. LoPresti minded the nets for Thompson at both Eveleth High School and Eveleth Junior College. He also played goal at St. Cloud Teacher's College. Sam broke into the big leagues in the fall of 1939, after coach Cliff Thompson pointed him out to a scout for the St. Paul Saints of the American Hockey Association.

In 1940-41, LoPresti became a Blackhawk when Paul Goodman, then one of the Hawks' net-minders, hung up the skates. Although he only

BILL MOSIENKO

Bill Mosienko, undoubtedly one of the finest Blackhawk athletes of all time, was born in Winnipeg, Manitoba, on November 2, 1921. He played right-wing for the Blackhawks from 1941 until 1955, scoring 258 goals and recording 282 assists for a career total 540 points in 711 games. Mosienko is best known for a spectacular feat that, to this day, still remains an NHL record. On March 23, 1952 against New York Rangers goalie Lorne Anderson, Billy scored three goals in 21 seconds, at 6:09, 6:20, and 6:30 of the third period. He scored with both teams at full strength, helping Chicago beat the Rangers 7-6. The previous record for this feat was 1:04, held by Carl Liscombe while he was playing for the Detroit Red Wings in 1938. Teammate Gus Bodnar got in the record book by assisting on each goal. Bodnar also appears in the record book for holding the record for fastest goal by a rookie in his first NHL game while he was with Toronto in 1943-44 (15 seconds).

Sam LoPresti–goalie, made 80 saves against the Bruins in one game. (Photo from the Hockey Hall of Fame/Ernie Fitzsimmons Collection.)

spent two seasons in the NHL, LoPresti is well remembered for an incredible game in which he played. On March 4, 1941, in a 3-2 loss against the Boston Bruins, LoPresti made 80 saves! Boston goaltender Frankie Brimsek made only 18. To this day, his feat still remains an NHL record for most shots, one team, one game.

After the 1941-42 season, LoPresti entered the U.S. Navy. While aboard a merchant ship, his vessel was hit by a torpedo in February of 1943. Sam spent 42 days in a lifeboat at sea before being rescued. After returning home, he played senior amateur hockey in Northeastern Minnesota for a while and was inducted into the U.S. Hockey Hall of Fame in June of 1973. On December 11, 1984, LoPresti died at his home in Eveleth from a heart attack. He was 67.

Bill Mosienko still holds the NHL record of scoring 3 goals in 21 seconds against NY Rangers. (Photo courtesy of the Blackhawks.)

The March 24, 1952 *New York Times* proclaimed that "the crowd of 3,254 cheered Mosienko with a volume that seemed to come from twice that number when the record-breaking accomplishment was announced," and that "Anderson might have stopped Mosienko on the Hawk star's first shot, an open thrust from the center alley. But the second and third shots were neatly executed, and could have fooled any goalie in the league."

Reflecting upon his record in later years, Mosienko commented:

"It was quite an accomplishment, I hope it [the record] stays. After I scored the third goal, Jim Peters skated up to me and told me to keep the puck because I had set a new record. I was very happy and proud. It was like being on cloud nine."

Although Mosienko's best season point-wise was 1943-44, when he racked up 70, personally, he felt differently: "My best season would have to be 1945 when I won the Lady Byng Trophy," he said. "We were very successful that year." Always for fair play, Bill went that entire season without any penalties. He also received All-Star honors (second team) in the 1944-45 and 1945-46 seasons.

After retiring from the NHL, Bill went on to play for the Winnipeg Warriors. In *Hockey -The Illustrated History*, by Charles Wilkins, Dick Irvin once commented, "While killing a penalty, a Winnipeg player scored two goals in 14 seconds. Alf Pike, the coach, was going to change lines and Mosienko, who was on the bench, said, 'Leave him on. He's got a chance to break my record.' Shero [former NHL coach present at the game] claims the guy hit the post."

In Winnipeg, Bill was also the owner of a bowling alley, Billy Mosienko Lanes, for many years. "It's always been there to fall back on," said Bill, who was inducted into the Hockey Hall of Fame in 1965. "It was built in 1947 and opened for business in 1948."

Hall of Famer Bill Gadsby commented on his former teammate:

"Billy and I were good friends...nice man. I was on the ice the night he scored his three goals in 21 seconds in New York.

That was quite a feat for him, boy. It was tremendous. That record will never be broken, never. It was just fantastic, it was damn near the same play off of the face-off each one. He could really skate. He could skate with them today, really, he was that good. He could really fly and he scored those three goals. I mean, it was unbelievable just to watch it!"

Cliff "Fido" Purpur, who also played with Mosienko during the forties, offered his recollection of Bill:

"He and I were roommates. We had our own apartment at the Guyon Hotel. He was a wonderful guy. He didn't come from a rich family, ya know, they were a poor family. They called us the Gold Dust Twins [because] we were about the same height. [We were] both short, little old guys, ya know."

Mosienko was also part of one of Chicago's most electrifying scoring combinations of all time, the "Pony Line," (so-named because of their colt-like moves) on which he played with the Bentley brothers, Doug and Max. Mosienko said:

"We were a really good line. We had some real speed and our own 'automatic' plays. Unfortunately, they had to break us up. We were also a pretty good entertainment unit. Once we set an attendance record of 20,008. After that they had to limit attendance to 16,666 because of fire regulations."

When asked about the kind of training the Pony Line underwent, Mosienko commented: "I used to do a lot on my own to stay in shape. I did a lot of running besides my ice time. I can remember [with a laugh] my wife driving the car with me running behind."

Despite being an awesome scoring combination, the Pony Line was especially prone to injury due to the small size of its players. All three men were about 5'8", 145 pounds. During the 1946 season Mosienko and both of the Bentley's were sidelined with knee injuries, each tearing ligaments during a month's time. When asked about their vulnerability, Johnny Gottselig, then the team manager, gave his feelings in a March 4, 1946 issue of *Newsweek*: "We certainly are getting the works around the League. Every injury to our line is the same, and why? Because guys who couldn't hit the Bentley's and Mosienko with a handful of beans are hooking, tripping, and tackling them."

Speaking of famous hat tricks, the term *hat trick* came from a Toronto haberdasher named Sammy Taft. It's appropriate to mention Mr. Taft because he had a wealth of information regarding the days of hockey past, especially the Blackhawks. Mr. Taft owned and operated a hat store in Toronto for many years until his death in 1994. Back in the forties, a myriad of NHL players would stop in his store before the game at Maple Leaf Gardens and children would line up for blocks to get autographs. Mr. Taft offered a glimpse into the historic days of hockey past...how the hat trick began with a Chicago Blackhawk by the name of Alex Kaleta, a forward with the team in 1941-42, and from 1945-46 until 1947-48.

One day, back in the forties, the Blackhawks were in Taft's store before a game: "All of a sudden," explained Taft, "who walks in but Max and Doug Bentley, Mosienko, Mariucci, Mike Karakas, Big Joe Cooper, ya know, and before long the whole Chicago team. Well, they're all buying hats. Everything is going lovely, ya see. From outta nowhere, I look at this guy and I don't know 'em."

That man was Alex "Killer" Kaleta. Born in Canmore, Alberta on November 29, 1919, Kaleta was a flashy skater and a gentle natured man, quite the opposite of his nickname. After being introduced by Mike Karakas, Kaleta asked Taft to save a hat for him and he'd pay for it the next time the team was in Toronto. He had just walked on the team and hadn't been paid yet.

Teammate Mariucci offered to pay for the hat, but then, for some reason, unknown even to himself, Taft came up with a proposition:

"He looked like a nice, fresh kid, ya see. I said, 'I'll tell ya what to do Alex.

"The Most Famous Hat Trick" created, in essence, by Toronto Haberdasher Sammy Taft (left) and Rookie Alex Kaleta (not pictured). Taft offered to buy Kaleta a hat if he scored three goals against The Maple Leafs that night. Taft is pictured here with Bill Mosienko, who scored perhaps the most famous hat trick in League history. (Photo courtesy of the Blackhawks.)

"The Pony Line" —Bill Mosienko, Max Bentley, and Doug Bentley, so-named because of their colt-like moves on the ice. (Photo courtesy of the Blackhawks.)

You go out there tonight, score three goals, and I got a surprise for ya.' He looks at me and smiles. 'You get three goals and you'll have that hat tonight.'

"He goes out there and bing, bing, bing, he gets the hat trick. Eddie Fitkin [publicity man, former writer with the Toronto Star and Globe and Mail] picks up the scoop and the next thing I know, on the late hockey news at eleven o'clock, they blast it from coast to coast: 'Rookie Alex Kaleta scores a hat trick,' with the whole story of Sammy Taft and how it all happened."

DOUG BENTLEY

The Bentleys were the other big attractions in Chicago. Doug, the eldest of the Bentley brothers was born in Delisle, Saskatchewan, on September 3, 1916. Playing left-wing from 1939-44 and 1945-52, he received the Art Ross Trophy for highest total points in the 1942-43 season and made All-Star (first team) in 1943-44 and second team 1948-49. Besides leading the NHL in goals in 1943-44, he led

the Blackhawks in points three times. After leaving Chicago and racking up a Blackhawk career total 53 points, he went on to serve as player-coach of the Saskatoon Quakers of the Western League.

However, Frank Boucher managed to coax Doug away from Saskatoon so he could play with his brother Max for one last NHL season in New York. When the brothers were reunited once again it was quite an event. In Stan Fischler's book *Those Were the Days*, Bentley commented:

"I was doing a spot playing with the Quakers. On top of that I had been having a bad time with my nerves. I didn't think the NHL would help that condition. That's why I was against the move. But Boucher kept after me and, finally, he offered me the biggest money I ever got in my life; even in my best days with the Blackhawks. The money did it. That and the fact that I knew I could help Max; I could assist him on the ice and help settle him off the ice."

In their first game together, the brothers combined to rack up eight points, bringing the Rangers to a 8-3 victory over the Boston Bruins, who were then in fourth place. Doug scored one goal and three assists and Max scored two goals and two assists. In Stan Fischler's book *Those Were the Days*, Doug once commented on that historic game:

> *"Once the people started to holler for us, I knew that was it. I knew we'd really go. I knew because right off the bat I could tell that Max hadn't forgotten any of his tricks or mine either."*

Longtime Hawks employee John Robertson remembers a humorous story about the Bentley brothers.

> *"There was a small little lad, a midget, that used to sell flowers along West Madison Street. In those days the players all stayed at the Guyon and Paradise Hotels at Washington and Crawford. This little lad used to come down with the Bentleys. They thought that he was a little boy. He'd pal around with Doug. Doug would bring him down [to the locker room]. He would get down there and get the starting line-ups, the scratches and that. In those days the gamblers had card tables set up the stairs on the mezzanine in all four corners of the building. They'd bet on the starting line-ups and that. Little Jessie would get up there to tip their players off. Our trainer in those days used to pick him up (laughing) and put him on the training table."*

Douglas Wagner Bentley was inducted into the Hockey Hall of Fame in 1964, eight years before his death in 1972.

MAX BENTLEY

Doug's younger brother Max, also from Delisle, was born on March 1, 1920. Nicknamed the "Dipsy Doodle Dandy from Delisle," he played center for the Blackhawks from 1940-43 and from 1945-48. During his stay in the Windy City he scored 102 goals and 137 assists for a Blackhawk career total of 239 points. Leading the league in points in the 1945-46 and 1946-47 seasons, he secured the Art Ross Trophy twice. Besides receiving All-Star honors (first team) 1945-46, (second team) 1946-47, he was also awarded with the Lady Byng Trophy in 1943, and the Hart Trophy in 1946. Topping off his list of accomplishments, he was inducted into the Hockey Hall of Fame in 1966.

Max got his break into the major leagues when his brother Doug, who had made quite an impression in Chicago, told the management that if they thought he was good, they should see his brother. Many considered Max to be the better play-maker and stick-handler of the two. Whatever the case, he was known for his agility on the ice and his electric wrist shot, which according to his brother Doug, came from the strong wrists he got from milking cows on the farm.

Max's best game of all time was on January 28, 1943, when he scored seven points (4 goals, 3 assists) against the New York Rangers' goalie Bill Beveridge. That evening, the Blackhawks went on to devastate the Rangers with a 10-1 victory.

In a recent interview, Max's wife Betty offered some of her opinions and memories concerning his career in the NHL. When asked about some of Max's fondest memories of his days spent with the Blackhawks, she replied: "Oh gosh, just playing, just being with the Blackhawks. It was a real thrill for him just to turn pro and to be with his brother and Mosienko. He used to talk about that all the time. He'd always said how great they were together."

Betty Bentley was also quite a fan:

> *"We never missed a game at home [Chicago], but we weren't allowed to go on the road trips. I would just love to hear that crowd one more time and that big organ. It was truly something to have lived in that era and to go to the Stadium and hear that beautiful organ. Oh, the atmosphere at the rink! You just couldn't help but get excited, you just had to get into the game. There was so much magic, and they still got that magic [the Blackhawks]."*

Commenting on the days surrounding Doug and Max's retirement, Betty Bentley replied:

> *"We had a wheat farm [in Saskatchewan]. Doug coached in Saska-*

In an attempt to get back into the play-offs the Hawks traded star center Max Bentley (back left), and winger Cy Thomas (back right) to Toronto for Bob Goldham (back left), Ernie Dickens (back right), Bud Poile (bottom left), Gus Bodnar (front middle), and Gaye Stewart (front right) in one of the biggest trades in NHL history. (Photo from the Hockey Hall of Fame/Ernie Fitzsimmons Collection.)

The Bentleys also had another brother, Reg, who played on the same line with them for a short while. Said Betty:"Reg was only there [in Chicago] for a very short time. He [with a laugh] liked the pool room too much."Betty said that Reggie regularly played pool with many Chicagoland gangsters.

Max's career with Chicago ended after he was traded with Cyril Thomas on November 4, 1947, to Toronto in one of the biggest trades of all time. In return for Max, the Blackhawks received Gus Bodnar, Gaye Stewart, Bob Goldham, Bud Poile, and Ernie Dickens. The trade was carried out by Bill Tobin, who took over the team on August 15, 1946, when he purchased "controlling interest" for $340,000. Later, with his brother, Max spent a season with the Rangers before retiring.

Johnny Gottselig, then serving as team manager commented on the trade in the November 4, 1947 issue of the *New York Times*:"It had to be done," he explained, "because we needed fresh blood and no other club wanted any of our players except Max Bentley."

In that same article, Clarence Campbell, then the League President, ranked the trade with the Maple Leafs' purchase of King Clancy from Ottawa for $35,000 and Art Smith years before. "It is the biggest deal in the NHL in a long, long time and only goes to emphasize the worth of such a player as Bentley and puts him on a very high plane," he explained. "Chicago needs manpower," he continued, "and they certainly will benefit by getting such

toon for quite a while and Max continued to play hockey in Toronto after Doug retired. When Max came home he coached our oldest son and then coached in Alberta, besides the farming. They coached in the winter and farmed in the summer. Connie Smythe always wanted Max to stay in Toronto, but he was the type that wanted to be with all of his family in that little town of Delisle."

NHL caliber players from the Leafs. The trade indicates that Toronto is willing to sacrifice the players for a man like Bentley who can give the Leafs the nucleus for a top-notch third line."

Remembering his teammates of days past, former defenseman George Allen commented: "Oh, they were good guys. Hell, I played against them [the Bentley brothers] before I got into the big leagues. I even played against their older brothers. Yeah, I clobbered 'em [with a laugh]."

CLIFF "FIDO" PURPUR

Although he wasn't one of Chicago's star players during the forties, the Blackhawks acquired Cliff "Fido" Purpur in 1941-42. According to Purpur, he was originally picked to play on the line with the Bentley brothers. However, he became seriously ill in the summer of 1940 when the Blackhawks signed him on.

"I was laid up in bed for two months straight before coming to Chicago," he said. "I almost went. The doctors didn't even know [what I had]. That's where I lost a lot of my speed and everything. That was a sad deal. I waited all my life to get to Chicago. [However], my dreams came true [just because I made it]. I played a lot of games without a wink of sleep. [Once, I] played in Toronto on Saturday night without a wink of sleep, and played in Chicago on Sunday night. They [Chicago] figured I'd be greater than I was."

Thinking back, Fido recalled his most memorable game with the Blackhawks during the early forties.

"[It was] the night I got the hat trick against the Rangers," he said. "Old Paul Thompson, he said 'Go Fido!' They dropped the puck and I went down and scored. He kind of figured that he was the instigator of it. I got three goals, and they bought me a hat. You see, we got a hat when we scored three goals. I went down and got the hat, went over to Lake Shore Drive, went around the corner and my hat blew off! She blew down the street and got all greased up. By the time I caught up with it, it was shot."

Purpur played for Chicago until 1944-45. Besides hockey, he was a good baseball player as well. He played softball in the World Championship at Soldier Field twice for Grand Forks, North Dakota. "It was every state in the Union, ya know," he said. "We came in damned near third one time. We had a hell of a team, boy. There were some great teams in that tournament!"

After retiring, Purpur coached hockey at the University of North Dakota for seven years, and then built up hockey in North Dakota, taking the high school team to their first state championship, and the Grand Forks city team to the national tournament in Toledo, Ohio.

The Hawks also had other great athletes on their roster during the forties. Among them were defensemen Joe Cooper, who led the team in penalties four times during his seven-year career ('39-40, '40-41, '41-42, and '44-45), Johnny Mariucci, and Earl Seibert. Roy Conacher, Robert "Red" Hamill, and Gaye Stewart were some of the better forwards.

JOHN MARIUCCI

Born on May 8, 1916, John P. Mariucci was perhaps both the best and meanest Hawk defenseman of the forties. Standing at 5'10", and weighing 200 pounds, he played for the Blackhawks from 1940-42, and from 1945-48.

Before his professional hockey career, he played football at the University of Minnesota. He also played hockey at Minnesota, starring on their undefeated team in 1939-40. During his five seasons with the Blackhawks, he accumulated 308 minutes in penalties, leading the team twice consecutively, first in 1945-46 with 58 minutes, and once again the next season with 110 minutes. That latter season (1946-47), he was second in the League in penalty minutes.

Mariucci played for St. Louis of the American League, St. Paul and Minneapolis of the United States League, and the Eastern Amateur League's United States Coast Guard team before hanging up his skates in 1951.

After retiring from professional play, he coached hockey at the University of Minnesota from 1953-1965, and also coached for the U.S. Olympic team. In addition to his coaching, he was also involved with the Minnesota North Stars organization for some time. Mariucci is an inductee of both the U.S. Hockey Hall of Fame and the Hockey Hall of Fame in Toronto (as a builder).

Earl Seibert received All-Star honors 10 years consecutively. (Photo from the Hockey Hall of Fame/Ernie Fitzsimmons Collection.)

John Mariucci—tough-as-nails player who racked up the penalty minutes. (Photo from the Hockey Hall of Fame/Ernie Fitzsimmons Collection.)

EARL SEIBERT

Another great of the forties was Earl Seibert. Playing defense for Chicago from 1935 until 1945, Seibert was given All-Star honors ten consecutive seasons. He began this feat while playing for the Rangers in the 1934-35 season and then continued to do so every season through 1943-44.

ROY CONACHER

Roy Conacher, whose Blackhawk career lasted from 1947 until 1952, scored 102 goals, and recorded 125 assists for a total of 227 points. He led the Blackhawks in points for three straight seasons in 1948, 1949 and 1950. Roy's brother Lionel also played for the Hawks in 1933-34 during their first Stanley Cup season, and was named Canada's Athlete of the Half Century (1901-1950).

Roy Conacher—leftwing, led the Blackhawks in points for three straight seasons. (Photo from the Hockey Hall of Fame/Ernie Fitzsimmons Collection.)

BILL GADSBY

Born on August 8, 1927, in Calgary, Alberta, Bill Gadsby played defense for the Blackhawks from 1946-47 to 1954-55, and spent a total of 20 seasons in the NHL. He got his start in hockey at an early age:

"I lived in the city of Calgary [as a boy] and started playin' on the outdoor rinks. I never knew an indoor rink. They only had one indoor rink in Calgary. Then I went to Edmonton and we played in the junior league there. That was a four-team junior league. I turned pro when I was 18. I went with Chicago and [played for] the Kansas City Pla-Mors. That was the number-one farm team for the Chicago Blackhawks. I came up [to Chicago] ten games later, in '46, I was lucky."

Blackhawk scouts had their eyes on Bill all the way from bantam to junior. When the six-foot tall Gadsby broke in with the Blackhawks, he was described as having a hard, accurate shot with passing abilities on a par with, if not better than, most men playing in the League. He was known for his "play for keeps" style of play, and his ability to block hard. Because he made a good number of his moves right out in open ice, he seldom was penalized. Reflecting more closely upon his earlier days, Gadsby said:

"I played junior in Edmonton, Alberta, with the Edmonton Canadiens, and they were sponsored by the Chicago Blackhawks. In those days each NHL club had two junior clubs across Canada they sponsored. Chicago had Edmonton and Moose Jaw...Players like Bert Olmstead and Metro Prystai and Abel Francis all came out of Moose Jaw and went to the Chicago Blackhawks. I came out of Edmonton. They had scouts watchin' us all of the time. That's how I got tied up with Chicago."

Thinking back, Gadsby commented on one of his most memorable games:

Defenseman Bill Gadsby spent 20 seasons in the NHL and is a member of the Hockey Hall of Fame. (Photo from the Hockey Hall of Fame/Ernie Fitzsimmons Collection.)

"In one game, I scored the winning goal with one second to go. It was a fight-filled game with only three players on each side left on the ice. We were playing against Detroit. I was on the ice with Doug and Max Bentley and I scored at 19:59 of the third period and we won 3-2. That was my first year. I was only 18 years old and I think that was a great thrill."

Bill, who coached the Red Wings after he finished playing, currently runs 12 hockey schools in the Detroit area. "I have six boys' camps and six adult camps," said Gadsby. "My instructors are all former pro hockey players. Johnny Wilson, Alex Delvecchio, Don Murdoch, Dennis Hextall, they all live in this area [Detroit] so I'm kind of fortunate to have them. I'm on the ice all the time with them."

Incredibly, Gadsby just hung up his skates from playing alumni games in 1995. "I got arthritis in my feet and in my hands and I kind of suffer the next day, so I packed it up and now I'm a spectator, but I love it." For a man who spent 20 years in the NHL and retired from the League in 1966, 29 years ago, this is quite an accomplishment.

Things were also a lot different during Bill's playing days. When asked about the kind of conditioning he underwent to stay in top shape, both in camp and out, he replied:

"Actually, I didn't stay in shape in the summer that good. I ran for months before, and played a lot of racquetball and handball maybe six weeks before I went to training camp to get a fairly good amount of conditioning."

Gadsby, recalling time spent at the long time sites of the Blackhawks' camps, North Bay and Pembrooke, Ontario, said:

"We went to a whole month of training camp, where today they're in for 7, 8, 10 days and they start playing exhibition games. We knew we had a month to get in shape, so we really didn't have to get in tremendous shape during the summer."

Gadsby was an avid baseball player during the off season in his younger days, and he ranked among the best catchers in Western Canada. In 1952, Gadsby got polio, but battled his way back from the illness, and was the runner-up for the Norris Trophy in 1956, 1958, and 1959.

Today, besides running his hockey schools, Bill is involved with the Detroit Red Wings' alumni organization. Over the years, these alumni games have raised money for several worthy causes.

"Our Red Wing Alumni play about 20 games a year for charity. They've raised close to 3 million bucks over the last 25 to 30 years. We've never played Chicago, but we play Toronto and Montreal quite a bit, and they play a lot of over-30 leagues in this area, ya know.

"They get a bunch of guys together from another team and they'll play for the burn center or the Cancer Society, or any charity they want...and the Red Wing Alumni are glad to do it.

"It keeps the guys together. The Red Wing Alumni are very active. We meet once a month in Joe Louis Arena. We've got our own room. I think Chicago is getting very active now, too."

Commenting on the changing game, Gadsby said:

"I think they're bigger and they skate better [today's players]. I think they're faster today...the art of stick handling and the better plays aren't as prevalent as they used to be. It's less of a finesse game. You don't see the body checkin' in the neutral zone like you used to, you see too much high stickin.' Somebody's gonna get hurt badly, I think, if they don't do something about the high stickin'. You don't see the finesse too much anymore, like with Max Bentley and those great stick handlers years ago."

Gadsby, who served as the Blackhawks' team captain while in Chicago, played in 1,315 games (including the play-offs) over the course of his career. He scored 134 goals and 460 assists for a total of 594 points, at the same time racking up 1,631 penalty minutes. A seven-time All-Star, he was inducted into the Hockey Hall of Fame in 1970.

THE NOT-SO-NIFTY-FIFTIES

Things continued to look grim for Chicago in the 50s. However, it would be a time of dramatic change as well. As the team continued to slip farther and farther down hill, winning only 12 of their 70 games during the 1953-54 season, it was evident that something would have to be done if the Blackhawks were ever to get out of the basement. Stadium crowds were reportedly so sparse that the Blackhawks played some of their home games in Indianapolis and St. Louis. Eventually, the NHL even called a "help the Hawks" meeting to help Chicago get back on its feet.

Early in the decade, on September 11, 1952, Bill Tobin surrendered his controlling interest of the team to the men that owned Chicago Stadium; James D. Norris, James D. Norris, Jr., and Arthur M. Wirtz. However, the elder Norris passed away two months later, leaving his former partners in charge of the sickly Hawks, badly in need of repair.

Blackhawks 1950-51 team, top left to right: Guidolin, Babando, Brown, Bashoway, Lumley, Bodnar, Morrison, Bentley, Mosienko. Bottom left to right: Gurenovich (trainer), Stewart, Gadsby, Dickens, Olmstead, Goodfellow (manager) (inset photo), Dewsbury, Conacher, Stasiuk, McCaig, Lundy. (Photo from the Hockey Hall of Fame/Ernie Fitzsimmons Collection.)

Recalling the condition of the club during the mid-fifties, and how things eventually improved, defenseman Pierre Pilote said:

"When I first came up they were in their rebuilding years. About two or three years prior to that I think they were the lowest attendance-wise. I can recall where the crowds were small, three, four, five thousand probably, and remembering maybe playing on a Sunday, and we'd play against Toronto or Montreal and we would draw probably ten [or] eleven thousand. We seemed to play pretty well, even though we might lose 2-1, or 3-2, or tie. Even though we didn't have an equal club then, we seemed to bring the best out of us and make a good game out of it. As we got more players, we started winning more games and we became a factor in, I guess, in the sport world in Chicago. I guess when Bobby came into his own, Bobby Hull, and Mikita, and Glenn Hall and all these guys, and then I guess winning the Cup [in 1961], that kind of took us over the hump. Then we were there to stay as a top draw, packin' the house.

I guess when Tommy Ivan came there, they were at about the lowest. [Then] they started rebuilding. They didn't have much of a farm system. I think that's when they first bought Buffalo, and with that came St. Catharines, because Buffalo owned [them], it was a minor league club. They owned an awful lot of players. Then a few trades with Detroit, I guess.

But it [the empty seats at the Stadium] was interesting to see. I think they were broadcasting television games, CBS I think. They used to make sure that the crowds would sit along the boards so that it seemed like we had a full house. That's where the cameras would pan. It took four or five years. We were not number one in town. The Bears and the White Sox and the Cubs were number one. We finally did it, but it took quite awhile."

TOMMY IVAN

Determined to rebuild the team no matter what, Norris used his influence with the Detroit Red Wings, which was owned by his family, to acquire a new general manager by the name of Tommy Ivan. Now vice president of the team, Ivan is the man to whom the Hawks owe thanks for their rebirth during the late fifties. As stated in the *Chicago Blackhawks 1991/92 Official Yearbook*, Ivan's "rebuilding of the Hawk farm system, drafting of players, and strengthening of team spirit led to a Stanley Cup Championship in 1961, and a club that reached the finals in 1962, '65, '71, [and] '73." Ivan learned many of his hockey skills under the wing of Jack Adams while with Detroit, and he led the Red Wings to three Stanley Cup victories and six first-place finishes during a seven-season stretch as their coach.

"The biggest obstacle," commented Ivan, when asked about his role in rebuilding the team, "was just getting a contender... When I came over to Chicago and eventually got a contender, it was a big thing, at least to me it was." It certainly was a big thing. Because of Tommy Ivan the whole city of Chicago got to see the Chicago Blackhawks get back on their feet once again.

An example of Ivan's no-nonsense approach to the game can be seen by looking at a game during the 1958 season. While serving as G.M., he fined every man on the team $100 for "indifferent play" when they were beat by the Canadiens 9-1, with five of the Montreal goals coming in the third period.

Ivan was quoted in the October 25, 1958 *New York Times* the day after the game:

"It [the game] was a lousy effort from a bunch of players who call themselves major leaguers. Any time a team can score nine goals against you in one game, it's obvious that the players aren't putting out. That third period, when Montreal scored five goals against us, was a disgrace. I know Montreal always is tough on home ice but we were never in the game at any time. We have tried everything without getting any results. Maybe this will do some good—hitting them in their pocketbooks."

Ivan was reportedly the first G.M. in the history of the League to fine an entire team. Born on January 11, 1911, in Toronto, Ontario, Tommy Ivan was first involved with the game as a player. However, while playing junior hockey, he was injured and turned to coaching and officiating in Brantford, Ontario. During World War II, he served in the capacity of gunnery instructor in the Canadian Military.

After coaching in the United States Hockey League and the American Hockey League, Tommy Ivan became a coach, and later general manager, of the Detroit Red Wings. After becoming G.M., he led the team to six straight League championships and three Stanley Cups in three years!

"The biggest thrill I got, as far as coaching is concerned, was when I was coaching Detroit," said Ivan, remembering a favorite moment of his streak with Detroit. "I think it was '52, you'd have to go through the record books. At that time there were only six teams. In the first round of the four-of-seven series, we won four straight. In the finals, a four of seven series, we won four straight. It was pretty incredible."

Longtime off-ice official Jack Fitzsimmons described Ivan as:

"A great gentleman and an outstanding part of [Chicago's] hockey machinery for many years. Tommy Ivan is one of the most highly respected and intelligent hockey individuals the game has ever seen," he said. "He knew what he wanted, he was a competitor, he knew how to appraise talent and get the most out of them. An indication of that was his performance in Detroit, where he had that club up at the top for several years. I could never quite understand how come [he came to Chicago] at the time...But [now] I know why he came into Chicago, it's because of Jim Norris. But the point is that at that particular point, Detroit was a well-oiled machine with nothing but success and Chicago was down at the bottom and they had top control of the last position of the National Hockey League at the time. So when Tommy Ivan came in, he reorganized the whole orga-

nization and of course within a few years he brought the Stanley Cup to town. With a great effort from people like Glenn Hall and Bill Hay, Murray Balfour and stuff."

Through numerous deals, Ivan also acquired many key players, including the likes of Ed Litzenberger, Eric Nesterenko, and Pierre Pilote. These men would make important contributions to the team for years to come. After spending enormous amounts of the owner's money, Ivan finally established a farm system made up of 11 teams and over 300 players.

Today, Tommy Ivan is very active with hockey. He is involved with both the U.S. Hockey Hall of Fame in Eveleth, Minnesota, and the Hockey Hall of Fame and Museum in Toronto, Ontario. He also attends most Chicago Blackhawk home games.

Ed Litzenberger

Although he spent his last season with Chicago playing on the Stanley Cup team of 1960-61, Ed Litzenberger spent the majority of his career with the Blackhawks playing in the mid to late fifties. Ed, who played right-wing for Chicago from 1954-55 to 1960-61, came to the Windy City as part of the *Help the Hawks Plan* at the age of 22 from the Montreal Canadiens organization. It was Montreal that discovered him when he was playing for the University of Denver. While with the Habs, he played in only five NHL games over two seasons, being overshadowed by superstar right-wingers Rocket Richard and Boom-Boom Geoffrion.

However, once the Neudorf, Saskatchewan, native found his way to Chicago, he began to shine, taking home the Calder Trophy for Rookie of the Year during his first season with the Hawks. He was the first Blackhawk to win the award since Cully Dahlstrom in 1938.

Recalling his departure from Montreal and arrival in Chicago, Litzenberger said:

"They were going to move the franchise from Chicago because they weren't drawing any people at all. They had what they called the 'Help the Hawks Plan.' I was selected from the Montreal Canadiens, and a very dear friend of mine, Harry Watson, from the Toronto

Ed Litzenberger–right-wing/center. (Photo from the Hockey Hall of Fame/Ernie Fitzsimmons Collection.)

"I scored the winning goal the night before to put us up one point against the Detroit Red Wings, and I was traded the next day. I did hold a record in the league for awhile.

"I played 29 games with the Montreal Canadiens and 44 with Chicago for a total of 73 games in a 70 game schedule. Then they changed the schedule, I don't know what they play now, 80 or 90 or 100."

Maple Leafs and Metro Prystai from Detroit. That's how we wound up in Chicago, and it turned out that Harry Watson, who played about nine or ten years in the league, ended up playing on the same line. He was a big strong guy who was extremely respected. Nobody messed with him and he gave me all the confidence in the world. A nice guy to have on your left side, huh?

"I was lucky enough to win the Calder Cup as rookie of the year. If it hadn't been for Harry and Red Sullivan and some people, I would figure I was just a lucky guy. I worked so hard. When you have a name like Litzenberger and you play right-wing...and you're trying to break in with the Montreal Canadiens and they have people like Maurice "The Rocket" Richard and "Boom-Boom" Geoffrion and my name is Litzenberger. So I changed it to Eddie Litzenberjae. Of course that's not true. It was tough to break in.

After a tragic auto accident on a Chicago expressway in which his wife was killed in January of 1960, Ed recovered and took part in Chicago's third Cup victory. During '56-57, '57-58, and '58-59, Litzenberger scored over 30 goals each season.

After his days with the Blackhawks were over, he continued to make big contributions to hockey in Toronto and Detroit. With the Maple Leafs, he took part in their '61-62, '62-63, and '63-64 Cup victories. He even led the Leafs' farm team to victory towards the end of his career. "I got lucky," he once said in an article appearing in *The Hockey News*. "Even when I got sent down to Rochester...we won the Calder Cup two years in a row."

When asked about playing for so many winning teams, in the same *Hockey News* article he explained: "I was lucky to be on teams like that. When you consider that guys like Bill Gadsby [20 seasons in the NHL] never won one [Stanley Cup] in all their years."

Litzenberger went to Regina College and Central Collegiate. After hockey, he went to New York and became a stock broker. Today, he is still involved with the market in a different aspect. He went into business with his brother George at one point, and they operated their own industrial casting company, as well as a construction company which is now in dissolution.

Alex Kaleta–left-wing, scored three goals in exchange for a hat from Sammy Taft's haberdashery; indirectly coined the term "hat trick."
(Photo from the Hockey Hall of Fame/Ernie Fitzsimmons Collection.)

Pete Conacher, one of the members of the famous Conacher hockey family.
(Photo from the Hockey Hall of Fame Archives.)

Frank Brimsek–goalie during the "dismal" 50s, nicknamed "Mr. Zero." (Photo from the Hockey Hall of Fame/Ernie Fitzsimmons Collection.)

Harold (Mush) March, Max Bentley, and Doug Bentley — some of Chicago's finest players of the 40s. (Photo courtesy of the Blackhawks.)

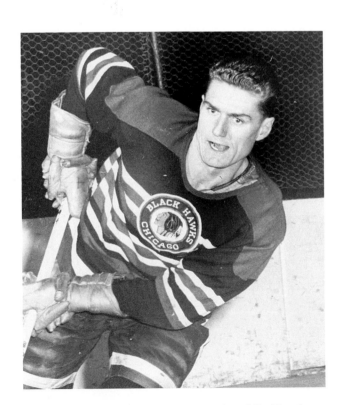

Allan Stanley—defenseman for the Hawks during the mid-50s. (Photo from the Hockey Hall of Fame/Ernie Fitzsimmons Collection.)

Art Wiebe played 11 seasons for the Blackhawks. (Photo from the Hockey Hall of Fame/Ernie Fitzsimmons Collection.)

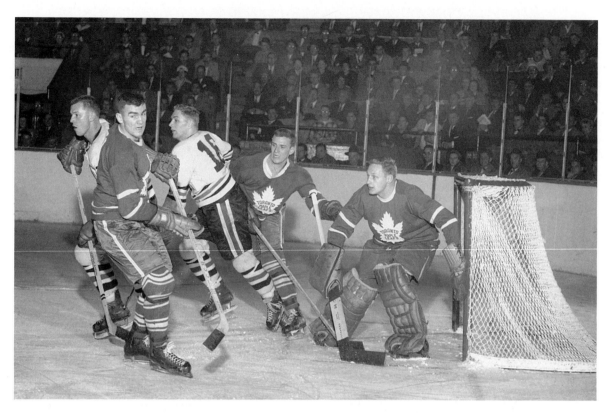

By the end of the 1950s, the Blackhawks were finding their way out of a 20-year slump. Players like a young Bobby Hull (#16) above and goalie Glenn Hall below were coming into their primes. Skating in the photo above from left to right are: Ron Murphy (Blackhawks), Brian Cullen (Maple Leafs), Bobby Hull then #16, Maple Leafs Noel Price, and goalie Ed Chadwick. Photo below shows the Hawks' Pierre Pilote checking Toronto's Paul Masnick, as Glenn Hall looks on. (Photos from the Hockey Hall of Fame/Imperial Oil Turofsky Collection.)

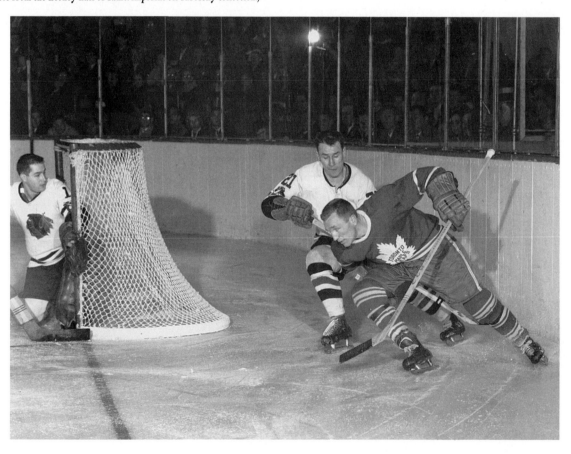

Tommy Ivan was the architect who rebuilt the Blackhawks at the end of the 50s. (Photo courtesy of the Blackhawks.)

Bobby Hull (circa 1957-58 season) one of the Blackhawks "immortals." (Photo from the Hockey Hall of Fame/Ernie Fitzsimmons Collection.)

THE IMMORTALS

Of all the athletes that graced the ice at Chicago Stadium during the team's history, none match the caliber of the four "greats" Bobby Hull, Stan Mikita, Glenn Hall, and Tony Esposito. Their career accomplishments make them not only outstanding in the NHL, but among the greatest athletes of all professional sports as well. Therefore, this entire chapter is set aside for the four Chicago Blackhawks whose retired numbers hang from the rafters at United Center. Hull #9, Mikita #21, Hall #1, and Esposito #35.

BOBBY HULL #9

Born on January 3, 1939, in Pointe Anne, Ontario, Robert Marvin Hull, also known as "The Golden Jet," is the biggest star ever to play for the Hawks, and without a doubt ranks among the best who ever played in the League. Bobby Hull played left-wing for the Blackhawks from 1957-58 until 1971-72. While with Chicago he scored 604 goals (666 including the play-offs) in 1,036 games, placing him near the top of the list for the League's all-time goal-scoring leaders.

Boasting a hefty collection of awards, Hull received the Art Ross Trophy (top scorer in the League) in 1960, '62, and '66, the Lester Patrick Trophy

Bobby Hull—"The Golden Jet" one of the Blackhawks and hockey's all time "greats." (Photo courtesy of the Blackhawks.)

in 1969 (outstanding service to hockey in the U.S.), the Hart Trophy (most valuable player) in 1965 and '66, and the Lady Byng Trophy (most gentlemanly player) in 1966. Hull certainly deserves credit for the latter trophy, due to all of the heat he took from the shadows on opposing teams. The Golden Jet also received All-Star honors 12 times (first team: 1960, '62, '64, '65, '66, '67, '68, '69, '70, '72) (second team: 1963, '71).

Thought of by many as the greatest left-wing of all time, Hull is remembered for many different things. Perhaps the most unforgettable is his devastating slap shot, which depending on the source, traveled anywhere from 115-120 m.p.h., making it a dangerous weapon that scared the pants off of opposing goaltenders. His shots were known to send goalies backwards into the net, numb their legs through their pads, and tear their gloves from their hands. Describing a Hull shot as seen from between the pipes, a retired goalie once commented that the puck resembled a pea when it left his stick, and often disappeared as it picked up speed on the way to the net. Many times, if Hull shot from 20 feet or closer the goalie would be unable to move before the puck reached him.

Recently, former teammate Glenn Hall reflected on the many practices in which he faced Hull years ago: "Well, I didn't really enjoy it much. The one thing Bobby enjoyed was shooting the puck. He didn't care who he was shooting at or where he was shooting, he just enjoyed shooting it. I don't know if there's anybody today that shoots a puck better than Bobby did."

Bobby, together with teammate Stan Mikita, developed the curved hockey stick, which allows better control of the puck than straight sticks. This, along with the muscular physique possessed by Hull, explains the lightning-fast shot for which he was so well known. Described by many as the "perfect mesomorph," sports reporters of days past used to dwell on the thick musculature of Bobby's back and his biceps which at 15½ inches were fully ½ inch thicker than those of former heavy weight champion boxer Muhammad Ali. At 5'10", 197 pounds during his playing days, the Golden Jet's superior strength came not from weights, but from hard labor on his cattle ranch, which he relished.

Besides possessing superior physical strength, and coming from a competitive family of 11, Bobby's talent can be traced back to his early childhood, as

Bobby Hull in action against the Montreal Canadiens Jacques Laperriere #2 and Dave Balon #20. (Photo provided by the Hockey Hall of Fame Archives.)

with so many professional hockey players. In an article by James Atwater, Hull once recalled:

"When I was older, oh, starting maybe when I was six or seven, I can remember getting up at six-thirty in the morning and stoking up the fire in the kitchen stove. I'd put on the water for the oatmeal and call mum so she could get up and put the salt in the cereal and start getting ready. And then I'd go off to the open air rink we had in the neighborhood. I'd be all by myself out there on the ice, practicing my shot up against the boards. It made quite a racket. I must have [woken] up the entire neighborhood."

His hard work most surely paid off. After starting to skate at the age of four and playing organized hockey at age ten, NHL scouts had their eyes on him by the time he was 12. Like other Hawk greats, Bobby played junior hockey with the St. Catharines Tee Pees under future Hawk coach Rudy Pilous, at the age of 18. In the same James Atwater article, Bobby once commented:

"I think of my father and how he gave up what might have been a great career in pro hockey to raise a family. I thank him. I remember the games I played in the Juniors at St. Catharines and how he and Mum would come to the games, and Mum would sit at one end of the rink and my father would sit at the other. When the games were over he would say 'You only had two goals, you should have had five!' Mum would say, 'Nice game, son.'"

After finishing a productive 33-goal season with the Tee Pees, Bobby was called up by Chicago to play in a 1957 pre-season game against the Rangers. Hull then commented that he "got lucky" and scored two goals on Gump Worsley, who was between the pipes for New York.

"Bobby was a guy with lots of potential," said Pierre Pilote, Hull's former teammate. "[He had] skating ability and shooting ability, and all of a sud-

den he came into his own after two, three years in the League. I got to see him comin' up when he was 18 with brown loafers with a penny in them, you know, a penny at the top. The first time I saw him was in training camp in St. Catharines. He practiced with us and then he played a game against New York, I think it was, and he got [two] goals. Tommy Ivan said 'Why, you're comin' home with us. You're not gonna play junior hockey anymore.'"

During his career Bobby took his fair share of abuse from shadows on opposing teams, and often chose to play with injuries that would place any ordinary player on the bench. After fracturing his jaw in a December 19, 1969, game against Detroit, he remained in the line-up, and continued to play with his jaw wired shut, wearing a football helmet for protection. Despite having to take all of his meals through a straw, becoming weaker all of the time, he stuck to his guns and continued to play. It would be that season, after the wire was removed from his jaw, that he would score his record total of 58 goals.

Earlier still, as stated in Gary Ronberg's article "Open Season on Bobby Hull," in the January 20, 1969 issue of *Sports Illustrated,* during the 1963 Stanley Cup Play-Offs, Hull "played with a nose so severely smashed that the fracture extended into his skull. With the Hawks one game from elimination, Hull ignored the orders of his doctors, checked out of a Chicago hospital and flew by himself to Detroit. That night, with both eyes blackened, his nose encased in tape, and blood draining into his throat, he played against the Red Wings."

Jerry Toppazzini, who played for both the Bruins and the Red Wings, commented on what it was like to play against Hull: "There is no question that Bobby Hull was the best left-winger. He could play in any era, and he had everything-size, strength, skill, stamina, and soul. After I ran into him a couple of times I predicted that Hull was for real. He weighed 190 solid pounds, running into him was like running into a cement wall. If you ran into him dead center he would go right over you like a Sherman Tank. He was so strong, a powerful skater, and a great finesse player who could really shoot the puck," (from *Hockey Digest*).

Amazingly, during his career Bobby was clocked at speeds up to 29.2 m.p.h. Because of this, Billy Reay used to work him extra hard during practice, once commenting in an article by James

Atwater: "He skates so effortlessly that he can go for two minutes at top speed while the others can go perhaps one minute and fifteen seconds." During his playing career, Gordie Howe once commented that everybody felt slower when Bobby took to the ice.

In a February 2, 1983 *Chicago Tribune* article, Hull's longtime friend and former teammate Stan Mikita once recalled days of long ago when the two attended high school together: "The first time I met Bobby was when I was about 15 years old in St. Catharines, Ontario. I'd heard of him because he was supposed to be the next big hockey star with the St. Catharines Tee Pees," Mikita explained. "We played football together in high school. He was a half-back, and I was sort of a flanker back. Even in football, the way we played the game was completely different. I'd try to run around the guy where Bobby would try to run him over."

Although nobody thought the record could be broken, the Golden Jet surpassed Rocket Richard's and Bernie Geoffrion's record of 50 goals in a season when he scored 54 in the 1965-66 season, and later 58 in the 1968-69 season which to this day remains a Chicago Blackhawk record.

The former record of 54, however, didn't come without a great deal of sacrifice and tension. After missing five games of the season with a knee injury, the Golden Jet had a total of 50 goals with 13 games remaining in the 1965-66 season. The tension was building everywhere as Bobby went scoreless game after game. The team was suffering badly, due to changing their usual style of play to set Bobby up for extra scoring opportunities. Then, on March 12, 1966, in Chicago everything came together as Hull scored his 51st goal in front of a Stadium crowd of over 17,500. After going more than 11 periods with no goals, Chico Maki got things rolling for Chicago when he scored early in the third period. Then, Bill Hay passed to Lou Angotti who quickly fed Hull who made a 50-foot slap shot from center ice at 5:34 of the final period, tying the game at 2-2. The shot was screened by Eric Nesterenko, whom Cesare Maniago, the opposing goalie, claims lifted his stick to allow Hull's goal. Although he scored three more goals that season, none were so difficult as that number 51.

After contract disputes with the Hawks, Bobby went on to play with the Winnipeg Jets of the WHA from 1972-1978 after signing a $2.75 million contract at the age of 33. Before allowing him to play, the NHL used every legal method possible to prevent him from playing.

Around the time that he signed with the WHA, Hull gave his impression of the whole situation in the June 28, 1972 issue of the *Chicago Tribune:*

"This whole thing has made me wonder what the hell they [the Blackhawks] were thinking. They must have thought I was bluffing or they must have thought they'd gamble that the Winnipeg offer would fall apart. They must not have known me very well. I can't figure out what they were doing about signing me, or rather, what they weren't doing. If anything, I made their side of it easier when I said publicly at the start of all this that I wanted to stay in Chicago and I didn't expect them to come close to matching the Winnipeg offer. They didn't need me as much as the new league did and I knew that. But they never took any serious steps to offer me a contract, not even sit down and talk and start negotiating. I guess there was pride involved on both sides. They felt I should come to them and I felt they should come to me."

Recently, in Gordie and Colleen Howe's book *After the Applause*, with Charles Wilkins, Hull elaborated on his jump to the WHA, which is thought to have cost the Blackhawks close to a billion dollars over ten years because of drops in attendance: "All I ever wanted was a contract from the Hawks! And they didn't offer me one until well into June. They hand delivered it—$250,000 a year for five years. And I said to the guy who brought it, 'You can take this back to Mr. Wirtz—it's too late.' A few days earlier, the WHA had been in touch to say they'd raised half a million. The next day they phoned to say they were at $750,000. At that point I said, 'I'm gone...'"

In the WHA, Hull came down with an ulcer due to the strenuous schedule, sometimes having to play eight or nine games in a straight stretch under conditions that were poor in comparison to those found in the NHL. In the Howe's book *After the Applause*, Hull explained: "In New Jersey it was hilarious, we'd put on our equipment in the Holiday Inn, then bus over to the arena in our street shoes and go into a little dressing room in shifts to put our skates on. The room was so tiny we couldn't all go in at once. And the rink was tilted! By the end of the period, with the snow built up on the ice, you really had to be able to shoot the puck just to ice it." Besides the games, there were also a myriad of interviews and public appearances that he had to attend.

Today Bobby raises cattle, and has been involved in farming and running Hereford breeding operations across Canada since 1959.

Even though Bobby is in the cattle business, Glenn Hall recently commented: "He loved to shoot the puck. I'm sure, right now, if he had a choice of anything to do, he would go out and shoot...and not care if the shot hit the net or the boards...just [to] get something on it. That's what made him such an effective scorer." Bobby Hull, the incredible Golden Jet, will always stand out as one of the greatest athletes in all of hockey.

Stan Mikita #21

The other half of Chicago's dynamic scoring duo of days past was Stan Mikita. Born in Sokolce, Czechoslovakia, on May 20, 1940, Mikita came to Canada as a youngster to live with his aunt and uncle who had adopted him. Adjusting to life in another country wasn't easy for Stan. "I didn't know the language," he said. "When you don't understand something, you always think that people are talking about you. I thought they might have been making fun of me, which at times they might have been."

However, it beat remaining in Communist-occupied Czechoslovakia. "I liked the idea of being able to do whatever you wanted without somebody looking over your shoulder, because of the way it was with the Communist rule," he said.

Like most young boys in Canada, Mikita began to learn the importance of the stick and puck. "The way it all started was that some kids were playing road hockey in front of the house. That's how I got into the game. I'd just look at them from inside the house through the curtains, then from the porch for a couple of days, and finally from the sidewalk. Eventually they said: 'Why don't you come and join us?' and that took probably a good week."

Stan Mikita—the ultimate playmaker. (Photo courtesy of the Blackhawks.)

As all great things have small beginnings, so did Mikita's career. Reflecting upon years past, Stan commented, "The Canadian Legion had just started sponsoring the little league program in St. Catharines, [Ontario]. They had six teams that were named after the original six NHL teams. I played for the NY Rangers."

It wasn't long before the ultimate play-maker found his way to the St. Catharines Tee Pees, a junior A team sponsored by the Blackhawks. Once there, he played with other future Hawk stars like Bobby Hull. "I was drafted by the coach of the St. Catharines' team whose name was Rudy Pilous. They would draft a kid from bantam to a junior club. Once you were drafted you automatically belonged to whatever big team sponsored that farm team, which in my case was the Chicago Blackhawks. So theoretically, I was 13 years old and I belonged to Chicago."

It wouldn't be long before Mikita broke into the big leagues. Said Stan: "I was 17 or 18 and I came up for three games in 1958 because of an injury to one of their centers." Once there, Stan made his mark as one of the NHL's most aggressive players, leading the League's centers in penalties on a number of occasions.

Mikita's former coach, Rudy Pilous, recently recalled the day Mikita got called up to the big club in Chicago. Said Pilous:

"Mikita was playing junior hockey for me and I phoned from Chicago to the man that was lookin' after the team and said, 'If we're ahead at the second period, don't play Mikita anymore. Undress him and take him to Welland [Ontario] and put'em on the train. I need him here, we're short players.' So they put him on the train and the guy said: 'It's pretty short notice to get a sleeper [car], but I'll have a sleeper for ya in a few minutes.' But, the conductor forgot about the goddamn kid and when he got to Chicago, I went there to meet him. He was havin' a cup of coffee and a cigarette, and I raised hell with him about the cigarette. He said 'Why you cheap bugger, you wouldn't get a sleeper for me.' I said, wait a minute now, there's something wrong here.

Anyways, we played him that night. We were playin' the Canadiens, and about two minutes before the end of the second period I told him, 'You look after yourself there,' and I sent him out to face-off against Beliveau. Beliveau was more mesmerized: 'Who in the hell's this kid!' They dropped the puck and he grabbed it and damn near scored. So that was his first effort in the National League."

During his career with Chicago, Mikita received All-Star honors eight times (first team: 1962-64, 1966-68, second team: 1965, 1970) and earned a large assortment of awards for his achieve-

ments. He became the first athlete in NHL history to win the Art Ross, Hart, and Lady Byng trophies in one season (1967). Amazingly, Mikita repeated this feat the next year, again claiming all three trophies. He had also taken home the Art Ross trophy in 1964 and 1965, before performing his triple crown miracle. Among his other accomplishments were the Lester Patrick Trophy in 1976 and Team Canada in 1972. When Mikita played an exhibition game for Team Canada that year against Czechoslovakia, the fans and the media treated him like a god.

The Lady Byng trophy was quite a surprise to many, since Stan was such an aggressive player. However, he changed his habits dramatically in 1966, and in doing so used his time for scoring points instead of sitting in the penalty box. During his career, Stan once joked that with a wife, two kids, and a mortgage, he could not afford all those fines for racking up misconduct penalties.

In an article by Bob Verdi, which appeared in the September 23, 1983 issue of the *Chicago Tribune*, Stan once reminisced about those early days when he first came to Chicago:

"When I came to Chicago in '59, Bobby [Hull] had been there a couple of years already," he explained. "We lived in Berwyn for a spell before we got married. Along with Tod Sloan, Ron Murphy, then Jack Evans. We all chipped in $50 to buy a '49 Pontiac. [It had] holes in the floorboard which we'd patch up with cardboard.

"I was the kid, so I was assigned to drive the thing every place. It didn't have power steering, and that's how I built up my arms. One day the bloody thing wouldn't run anymore, so we just left it on a street corner someplace. We got a lot of miles out of it, and a lot of laughs. I just sort of followed Bobby around at the start, learning the ropes. He never told me how to make this play or that play, but he could see that I was excitable, and he reminded me to calm down. I learned about the pluses and minuses of being in the public eye, like Bobby was."

Stan Mikita waiting to take to the ice for another brilliant shift. (Photo from the Hockey Hall of Fame/Frank Prazek Collection.)

Years ago, Mikita's longtime teammate Glenn Hall once gave his impression of Mikita explaining that he was so talented that he could change his mind in mid-stride while skating or shooting, which drove goalies crazy, thinking they had him figured.

More recently, in Gordie and Colleen Howe's book *After the Applause*, with Charles Wilkins, Hall of Fame defenseman Bill Gadsby offered his impression of Mikita at the time he broke into the League and was playing a super-aggressive game. He described him as:

"a miserable little pain in the butt...He'd cross-check you, he'd spear you in the belly. You'd be going around the back of the net, and he'd spear you in the calf—down you'd go. I used to watch the better players, pick out their bad habits, and do my best to exploit those habits. Stan had a very bad habit of passing to the left side and then looking to see if it was a good pass. If you came from his blind side, while his head was turned, you could really crank him a good one. I nailed him dozens of times, but I've got to give him credit, he always got back up. I remember hitting him hard during the play-offs one year and telling him, 'Boy, one of these times you're not going to get

up.' And he said, 'Ah, get lost, you old man, that was no body-check at all.' I'd hit him some nights and he'd have to crawl to the bench. But he'd always be back for the next shift. He had a lot of guts."

A good portion of Stan's career was spent under the wing of coach Billy Reay. "He pretty much left you to yourself," said Mikita. "He'd say: 'Here's what we have to work on,' and we'd go out and try to do the job. He was kind of a quiet coach in comparison to other coaches who are a little louder and what have you. In his own way, he got the point across."

Reay thought a lot of Mikita back in his coaching days, once commenting in George Vass's book *The Chicago Blackhawk Story*: "I have to say that I have never seen a better center. Maybe some could do one thing better than Stan, like skating faster or shooting harder. But none of them could do all the things that a center has to do as well as Stan does. And very few of them came close to being as smart as he is... he's about the brightest hockey player I've ever seen...He's a hard-nosed hockey player. One of his biggest assets is that he has got a lot of pride."

Today, when asked about his fondest memory of playing for the Hawks, Stan replies: "I still have a lot of fond memories of some of the games, and the camaraderie and friendships that were made. I think we were [a close-knit group] and many of us still remain friends to this day."

During his 22 year career with the Blackhawks, Mikita played in 1,394 NHL games, scoring 541 goals and 926 assists for a total of 1,467 career points. When the Hawks lost some of their key players to the WHA, such as Bobby Hull, Ralph Backstrom, and Pat Stapleton, Mikita chose to stick with Chicago and played a big part in keeping the team's head above water. Seventeen games into the 1979-80 season, he retired from the NHL.

Today, Mikita is involved in both business and hockey endeavors in the Chicago area: "I was in the golf business for about seven years," he said. "Then I went into business with Glen Skov, who used to play with us. We are manufacturers representatives in the plastics industry, representing injection molders, blow molders, extruders, and packaging."

Stan's present involvement with ice hockey is a truly rewarding experience. "I run a hockey school for deaf kids," explains Mikita, "It sure is [rewarding]. We usually run it the second week of June in Northbrook and Glenview. The kids come from all across the country. It's the only one that I know of that's done in the United States. We hold it here because we have the facilities."

The Stan Mikita Hockey School for the Hearing Impaired, as it is called, is operated at the Northbrook Sports Complex in Northbrook, Illinois. The school, which has been going strong for 20 years, came into existence due to the efforts of a Chicago businessman, Irv Tiahnybik. Irv, who is the former owner of Leon's Sausage Company in Chicago, had experienced problems with his hearing-impaired son. His son Lex had experienced communication problems as well as unfair treatment from other players on his independent youth team, the Chicago Minor Hawks.

From these difficulties sprang the Mikita School and what is known as the American Hearing Impaired Hockey Association (AHIHA). The AHIHA is a large, non-profit organization, formed in 1973, that operates year round. It helps players acquire language and speech therapy, diagnostic evaluations, counseling, hearing aids, auditory training, as well as funds for one child to receive a cochlear implant. Financial assistance is also given to families in certain cases.

Because of the efforts of instructors and volunteers who come from all over the U.S. to help

out, hearing-impaired individuals, especially younger ones, are able to break out of their shells, boost their confidence levels, and just play hockey.

Some of the instructors at Stan's school have included Chris Chelios of the Hawks, Tony Granato, and Jim Kyte, the 6'5", 210-pound defenseman for the Calgary Flames who retired as the only hearing-impaired player in the NHL. Kyte also started a similar school in Ottawa, Ontario.

In an article with Brad Herzog, which appeared in *Sports Illustrated*, Kyte offered his feelings concerning the Mikita school: "Being a professional athlete, you're a role model, whether you want to be or not. And because I'm hearing-impaired, I'm a role model for hearing-impaired children. I come here not because I'm obligated, but because I want to."

In 1992, those who participated in Mikita's hockey school ranged in age from 5 to 28. The AHIHA varsity team plays a game against Stan and some of his former teammates from the Hawks. Among them are such men as Keith Magnuson, Cliff Koroll, Bob Murray, Ivan Boldirev, Dale Tallon, Reggie Kerr, and others.

Also involved with the Chicago Blackhawk Alumni Association, Mikita touched upon what kind of activities the Alumni are involved in: "We give a scholarship to a young high school hockey player. That works out pretty well. We have our golf tournament as a fund-raiser. We have meetings every so often. Also, we try to keep up on what some of our members need. If they need some help we try to help them."

On a March 9, 1993 broadcast of Sports Channel America, which covered the Alumni's awarding of hockey scholarships, former Blackhawk defenseman Keith Magnuson, now the Alumni president, stated: "It's very important for a young man to realize that athletics is wonderful, it teaches you a lot about life. But you also [have to realize] that at the same time while you're improving your body, [it's important] to improve your mind and to further your education as far as possible."

In 1983, Stan was inducted into the Hockey Hall of Fame along with Bobby Hull. "It took me completely by surprise," he explained to Neil Milbert in the June 8, 1983 *Chicago Tribune*. "I thought you had to wait five years, and I've only been retired three years. Our old teammate, Billy Hay, is on the selection committee. He called me early this morning and told me I was going to be voted in. But Billy kids a lot. I didn't know if I should take him seriously until I asked: 'Who else got in?' and he said 'Bobby and Ken Dryden.' Then, I knew he wasn't kidding."

GLENN HALL #1

If any one goaltender in NHL history could be thought of as truly incredible, it would have to be "Mr. Goalie," Glenn Hall. Born in Humboldt, Saskatchewan, on October 3, 1931, Hall played forward as a boy on his public school's team. However, the goalie quit one day, and nobody would take his place. As captain of the team, Hall got between the pipes. That's how he began playing goal.

Hall is best known in the world of hockey for his NHL record for consecutive games played by a goaltender, which to this day still remains unmatched. His consecutive streak of 502 games lasted from the beginning of the 1955-56 season and continued until the thirteenth game of the 1962-63 season when he injured his back in a game against the Boston Bruins on November seventh. Incredibly, the streak consisted of 30,120 successive minutes in front of the net!

All things considered, Hall was an iron-man in every sense of the word. In addition to the 502 consecutive games he played in the NHL, Hall did not miss a game during the period (lasting nearly eight years—four in junior hockey and almost four in the minors) before he turned pro.

Glenn broke into pro hockey when he was offered a contract from the Detroit Red Wings. Playing for their minor league team in Windsor, Ontario, he honed his skills to a fine edge, stopping all kinds of shots from opposing teams that continuously penetrated Windsor's defense. In his second season there, he was named MVP.

Like his fellow superstars Hull and Mikita, Hall, who was acquired from the Red Wings, also boasts quite an impressive collection of awards. He was awarded the Calder Trophy in 1956, the Conn

Glenn Hall—"Mr. Goalie," best known for consecutive games played by a goaltender, his streak of 502 games is still unmatched. (Photo courtesy of the Blackhawks.)

Smythe in 1968, as well as the Vezina in 1963, 1967 (with Denis DeJordy), and 1969 (with Jacques Plante). Hall's averages for his three Vezina seasons, in that order, were 2.55, 2.38, and 2.17, all very respectable. Besides these honors, Hall received All-Star honors 11 times, (first team: 1957, '58, '60, '63, '64, '66, '69, second team: 1956, '61, '62, and '67). Topping everything off, he was inducted into the Hockey Hall of Fame in 1975, and the Canadian Sports Hall of Fame in 1993.

Those awards didn't all come overnight, but throughout a career that spanned 18 seasons of NHL hockey. Today, looking back with modesty, Hall discusses his view of making it through the grind of so many seasons: "It wasn't that bad, really. I mean, you're back and forth. You're gone for a few days, but as far as that goes, it wasn't extremely difficult. I suppose that it got long physically as well as mentally, but you were home with the family quite a bit. The biggest thing in those days was that you were away at Christmas time a lot, and that's what bothered me." Hall sees the practice of not scheduling games on Christmas Day as an advancement.

Glenn also elaborated modestly on the number of seasons he spent in the NHL:

"The 18 years is a little deceptive. They still put it in [the record books] but one year I came up and I think I played two games one year, six games another year, just when I was with the Detroit organization and [Terry] Sawchuk was hurt. For some reason, they still call that a year. And then, at the other end of it, expansion really prolonged the careers of lots of athletes, the old guys, hockey players, particularly the goal keepers. They all seemed to want an old goal keeper in there. With so much expansion, I personally got four more years and some of 'em even got more than that."

Years ago, in *Sports Illustrated*, William Barry Furlong described Hall's unique style of net-minding: "Hall meets the shot with his feet wide, but his knees close together to form an inverted "Y". Instead of throwing his whole body to the ice in crises, he'll go down momentarily to his knees, then

bounce back to his feet, able to go in any direction." It was this style of play that allowed "the ghoulie" to record 84 shutouts in 906 games, leading the League in this department six times during his 18-year NHL career that lasted from 1952-53 to 1970-71. Of these 18 years, Hall donned the pads in Chicago for ten, recording 51 shutouts in 618 games.

The son of a railroad engineer, Hall was skilled in many ways, from his fast legs and hands to his ability to play the angles. In Stan Fischler's book, *Those Were the Days*, Johnny Gottselig, former Blackhawk star of the thirties and forties, once commented on the similarities between Charles Gardiner and Hall: "There was lots of similarity between Hall and Gardiner," he said. "Gardiner was a better stick man but Charlie didn't have to concentrate as much as Hall did in the modern game. When the screened shot and the hurried pass and slapshooting came along, a goalie like Hall didn't know where 60 percent of the shots were coming from. That's murder. Gardiner wasn't close to Hall as a glove man."

An unusual thing about Glenn is that he would often get violently nauseated before games. However, once past this, Hall felt better, and said that he had no real problems once the game was under way. In a recent article with Brad Rauer of *Chicago Hockey Weekly*, Glenn offered further insight into this phenomenon: "I just built myself up to an unbelievable peak. It was a combination of fright and desire. I was a little afraid of being hurt badly, but I was scared to death of playing poorly."

Once, while in town to receive a "Milestone Award" for long, meritorious service along with Stan Mikita and eight other retired Hawks, Hall had lunch with Mikita. "This noon, Glenn Hall and I had lunch together at Lawry's, and I warned Chef Hans, 'If he gets sick and runs for the bathroom, don't think it's your food. It'll just be because Glenn is reliving his hockey career,'" explained Mikita to Neil Milbert in the February 2, 1983 issue of the *Chicago Tribune*. "All goalies are strange," he continued, "but I never saw anybody like Glenn. He'd throw up before games. But you never saw a player with more courage."

Like Mikita said, Hall displayed a great deal of courage, as well as determination and dedication. Once, while playing for Detroit in a 1957 play-off game against Boston, he was hit in the mouth by a

Glenn Hall making a save against Toronto's Tod Sloan during the 1957-58 season. (Photo provided by The Hockey Hall of Fame/Imperial Oil Turofsky Collection.)

shot from Vic Stasiuk. After taking approximately 25 stitches in his mouth, he returned to the ice and finished the game.

"It wouldn't happen today with the two goalkeeper system," explains Hall, remembering some of the painful experiences of days when goalies didn't wear masks. "I remember getting hit bad twice in the play-offs. Once with Detroit and once in 1967 in the spring, the last year before expansion. Obviously, today the goalkeeper is lying on the ice and crying when they got a little hang nail or something. I got up, not because I was tough or anything, but because Charlie Rayner and Turk Broda and Frankie Brimsek and all of those guys prior to me, that's what they did. The goalkeeper considered himself bein' tuff. That was foremost in my mind; 'Don't let down the tradition.' Boy, you go in the closet and cry. Don't cry on center ice. I think that ya didn't get up for yourself, ya got up for the old goalkeepers."

Although his injuries could have been prevented by wearing a mask, Mr. Goalie only wore one in practice, once explaining that in games, you were paid to take risks.

The fact that Hall experienced nervousness before games to the point that it made him miserable wasn't because he felt responsible for every goal scored against him. Hall once revealed a bit of his philosophy in a *Sports Illustrated* article by William Barry Furlong, explaining: "Only 10 percent of goals are the fault of the goalkeeper. The rest are the result of mistakes made up the ice that let a guy through to take a shot. The goalkeeper either makes the last mistake or makes the great save that wipes out the other mistakes."

Before retiring from the NHL, Hall spent his last four seasons in goal with the St. Louis Blues. Because he got to live in the country while playing there, and the team's style complemented his own, St. Louis was where Glenn enjoyed playing the most. Hall recorded a 2.48 average in his first season with St. Louis, and a 2.17 average the next season (with Jacques Plante).

Today, Glenn resides near Edmonton, Alberta, where he is a part-time scout and goaltending coach for the Calgary Flames. "I travel a little bit and get down to quite a few games," said Hall, who retired after the 1970-71 season with a NHL career average of 2.51. "I enjoy it very much. I enjoy the kids. I've been with them long enough to see the young fellows come up, [and] can see why one is capable of making it and why the next one is not capable of making it, so it becomes very interesting."

While working with the Calgary goalies, Hall doesn't necessarily teach his old style of net-minding. "I really let the guy figure it out. But I believe skating is the most important ingredient, [and] boy, oh boy, the mind runs very close to second. I think intensity. With no intensity you're not gonna play well. I like a competitor...I'll talk on position; how high up you are, how and why the puck went in."

In The *Hockey News' Awards Special 1993,* Calgary Flame's coach Dave King commented on Hall's abilities as a goaltending coach. Although he sometimes uses video replays to show players where they make mistakes, most of the time he uses his head: "It's amazing," said King. "He can tell you every minute move that led to a goal."

In that same source, Hall listed some of his favorite goalies of today. "The guys I like most are the battlers, the guys like Grant Fuhr, Tom Barrasso, Ron Hextall, and Mike Vernon."

Tony Esposito—"a sure-fire thing" that the Blackhawks had during the 70s. (Photo courtesy of the Blackhawks.)

To top off his distinguished career, at the age of 61, Hall was awarded The Hockey News/Itech King Clancy Memorial Award in 1993 for his continuing service to the sport of hockey.

TONY ESPOSITO #35

One sure-fire thing that Chicago had going for them during the seventies, and even into the eighties, was Tony "O" Esposito. Born on April 23, 1944, in Sault Ste. Marie, Ontario, Tony learned to skate from his brother Phil on the streets and neighborhood rinks of the Soo.

As a youth Esposito considered giving up hockey because playing Junior hockey would mean leaving home and quitting school. However, his father and a friend became part owners of a new Junior team right in the Soo, and persuaded him to play, resulting in a future hockey scholarship to Michigan Tech.

After graduating with a degree in business and All-American hockey honors from Michigan Tech in 1967, Tony turned pro with Vancouver of the Western League. He also spent some time with Houston of the CHL in 1968-69 before going to the Montreal Canadiens that same year.

Tony came to Chicago in 1969-70 after being acquired from the Montreal Canadiens organization on June 15, 1969 for $25,000. He remained with the Hawks until 1983-84. Over the course of his entire 16-season NHL career, he recorded 76 shut-outs in 886 games, and has a career average of 2.92. In 1969-70 Tony set what is considered the modern season record with 15 shutouts.

Esposito boasts quite a collection of trophies. He was awarded with the Calder (outstanding rookie) in 1970, the Vezina (best goaltender) in 1970, '72 (with Gary Smith), and '74 (with Bernie Parent), and the NHL Challenge Cup in 1979. He also played for both Team Canada and Team USA. During his career, he received first-team All-Star honors in 1970, '72, and '80, as well as second-team honors in 1973 and '74.

A story from John Devaney and Burt Goldblatt's book *The Stanley Cup* tells that a rumor once surfaced regarding Tony being traded to the Boston Bruins. When Tommy Ivan, who was serving as General Manager at the time, was confronted with it, he exclaimed: "I haven't taken leave of my senses. If I ever mentioned trading another Esposito to Boston, they'd run me out of town!"

Years ago, in George Vass' book *The Chicago Blackhawk Story*, when asked about Phil and Tony playing in the NHL, their father stated:

"They were very good hockey play-ers as boys, very good, indeed. I never dreamed they'd be that good. I really never thought they'd make it in the NHL. I thought Phil was pretty good with his stick and Tony a smooth skater, even bet-ter than Phil. But I didn't see anything in them as boys that stood out. They've gone far beyond anything I dreamed they could do..."

Esposito forcing Montreal's Cournoyer to shoot high in 1972-73 season. (Photo provided by the Hockey Hall of Fame/Frank Prazak Collection.)

People often criticized Tony for his unorthodox, sprawling style of net-minding, stating that since he was a "horizontal" goalie, that he was in no position to make second plays.

In an article by Frank Orr, which appeared in the March 20, 1972 *Maple Leaf Gardens Program*, former coach Billy Reay explained his philosophy surrounding the heat that Esposito would receive:

> *"Esposito is very alert. A few goalies are a split-second behind the play but Tony's that split-second ahead of things. He may be awkward but he's rarely out of position. It's a bit funny that people have knocked him for his lack of great style. He keeps the puck out of the net doesn't he?"*

During Tony's career, Reay had mentioned that many similarities existed between Esposito and Glenn Hall in terms of their moves and the way they both displayed intensity by yelling on the ice. He also pointed out that one of Tony's biggest assets was his keen alertness, and that having him on the ice was almost like having a third defenseman out there.

Esposito's former teammate Pit Martin commented on what it was like playing with Mr. Zero: "Tony was probably among the top goaltenders of all time. At least from my memory from the time I was a kid until now. He did [hold the team together] on the ice. He was very quiet off the ice. Never said a word, and you didn't dare talk to him at all in the dressing room before a game. Maybe after a game you could approach him, but he was bound and determined nothing was going to get past him. Amazing goaltender."

Grant Mulvey, who came to the Hawks during the mid-seventies, gave this description of Mr. Zero: "Tony Esposito was the best player through the seventies that Chicago had. He should have been the MVP every year. Without Tony, in the seventies [when the Hawks began slipping defensively]...we were getting out-shot 40 to 20 and we were in the ball games, and at some points we were winning them, being out-shot two to one. Tony was an amazing athlete, and he'll go down, in my eyes, as one that was the most instrumental in the seventies."

One of Mulvey's most memorable games involved Tony. "Probably the best single game that I saw an individual play," he commented, "was when we were in the play-offs against Boston. Boston out-shot us an astronomical number like 68 to 16, and we beat Boston 2 to 1. At that point, Tony was in the nets and he was just incredible."

A common sight when Tony was in goal was the way he would rock his body during the National Anthem because of pre-game nervousness. "I get very nervous before a game," he once explained in the April, 1970 issue of *Hockey Pictorial*. "I have trouble with my emotions and nerves. I keep my food okay because I eat about seven hours before game time. But I worry about making a mistake. If I make a bad play, the puck is in, and everybody sees it. That feeling is what makes me sick." Esposito held firm with the theory that no matter how the rest of the team was playing, he had the last word if any goals were scored.

Early in his career, Tony once revealed a bit of his philosophy on being a goalie in an article by Bill Libby, which appeared in the April 14, 1972 issue of *The Hockey News*. Said Esposito:

> *"You learn all the time. You can always improve. Some goaltenders seem to get better with age. If they survive. It's a tough racket. Some nights when the guys aren't going good, a goaler can pull his team through. Other nights when the guys see you're not having a good night, they can give you extra protection. It's a team thing and it sure helps to play on a good team with a good defense. It's worth a goal or two a game, the difference between being on a top team and a bottom team, which is why it's so hard to rate goaltenders. It is tough out there and I don't mind getting some rest now and then."*

Esposito was known for his dedication and focus on the game. Former teammate and coach Keith Magnuson once explained that Tony had a set routine when preparing for games, which began with his thinking about the games the night before and that never changed over the years.

Elaborating upon his philosophy of the game in *Pro Hockey Heroes of Today*, by Bill Libby, Tony once explained:

"Who the hell likes to have pucks shot at them at a hundred miles an hour from fifteen or twenty feet? I tell them in practice, take it easy, don't blast away. But they do, they crank up from ten or fifteen feet out. If that puck goes into that mask at one-hundred and-twenty miles an hour, it will ring your bell, all right. A concussion maybe. The mask keeps it from splitting your face open. But there's still places exposed on your head you can get cut. And having the mask banged against your face by a puck can break your bones. But in games, I'm only afraid of being scored on. I don't back up. I forget the fear of getting hurt. I push it out of my mind. It's giving up the goals, the getting beat that bothers me. It's a job and it pays good, so I do it. But I don't like it. No, I don't like it. I do it because I can make a good living at it."

During his long career, Tony recorded 423 wins. In 1983, a year before the end of his days in pro hockey, Esposito was still highly regarded by many. "Tony is a very good first-shot goalie," explained Wayne Thomas, then New York Rangers' goal coach, in an article by Tim Moriarty appearing in the February 7, 1983 issue of *Newsday*. "Okay, he's not your classic goalie. He plays the percentages. I know he's been criticized a lot down through the years because of his style, but he's still playing and a lot of his critics are not around anymore."

Unfortunately, Esposito's last days in the NHL were sour ones. In 1984, at the age of 41, he attempted to have Blackhawk president Bill Wirtz terminate his contract by the March 6th trading deadline because he wasn't spending very much time on the ice. Wirtz, who feared he would sign with Minnesota and help them in the play-offs, refused him. He refused to play in the last regular season game. In 1985, he wasn't invited to training camp, and his NHL career ended. In the September 7, 1984 issue of the *Toronto Globe and Mail*, Bob Pulford, who was serving as General Manager at the time, commented: "Tony has been a great goaltender, but there comes that time in everyone's career."

Since retiring from professional play, Esposito has coached goalies for Team USA in the Canada Cup tournament, been involved with the NHLPA (National Hockey League Players Association), and is currently the director of hockey operations for the Tampa Bay Lightning. He was elected to the Hockey Hall of Fame in 1988.

The city of Chicago was very fortunate to have tremendous athletes like Bobby Hull, Stan Mikita, Glenn Hall, and Tony Esposito playing for its NHL team in days gone by. Their achievements and contributions to both the team and to the sport of professional ice hockey will most certainly never be forgotten, and will live on in the hearts of fans for years to come.

Born Again

THE 1960s

esides the big stars like Hull, Hall, Mikita, and Esposito, the '60s and '70s introduced a great deal of Chicago Blackhawk talent, as well as the third Stanley Cup in team history in 1960-61. After some disappointing years during the 1940s and '50s, the Blackhawks became one of the League's most powerful teams during the sixties. After the 1960-61 Stanley Cup victory, they made it back to the finals in 1961-62 where they were beaten by the Maple Leafs, and once again in 1964-65 where they were beaten by Montreal.

During the sixties, Chicago had coaches like Rudy Pilous, who brought them to their third Cup, and Billy Reay who coached the team from 1963-64 until the 1976-77 season when he shared the job with former Hawk defenseman Bill White.

Rudy Pilous

Rudy Pilous, who coached the Blackhawks from 1957-58 until 1962-63, was once described by *Sports Illustrated* writer Arlie W. Schardt as "the master of the soft sell," resembling a "jolly song leader in a German beer hall." At the same time he was alert and shrewd with an unusual and acute instinct for commanding grown men. During his last few months of life, Pilous retained his wonder-

Coach Rudy Pilous with Pilote, Hull, Fleming, and Vasko. (Photo courtesy of the Blackhawks.)

ful sense of humor, explaining to me before our interview that he would only charge me $1,000 per question. As a boy, Pilous worked exercising race horses in Winnipeg with the famous jockey Johnny

Longden. He also coached minor league hockey in Houston, San Diego, and Louisville.

In 1943, Pilous founded the first Junior A club in St. Catharines, Ontario, the Falcons, and served as the team's coach and manager. He left a secure job in St. Catharines, with General Motors to coach the Blackhawks farm team in 1945, which at that time was located in Buffalo. He had never coached a professional team before in his life. In a *Sports Illustrated* article with Arlie W. Schardt, Pilous once commented:

> *"The security of knowing that I had a pension and all was very good, but my bloody head was so thick with boredom that I jumped at the chance to go to Buffalo. They had me scouting, promoting, publicizing—even buying equipment. I learned every phase of the game."*

In 1953, Pilous coached the St. Catharines Tee Pees to their first Memorial Championship. He later became the owner of that team as well, and the Tee Pees went on to win the Memorial Cup again in

1961. While in St. Catharines, Rudy coached some of the men who would later play for him in Chicago. Among these men were: Bobby Hull, Stan Mikita, Ab McDonald, Chico Maki, Pierre Pilote, Elmer Vasko, and Wayne Hillman. Nearly 75 players Pilous coached in the minor leagues made it to the NHL.

Finally, in 1957-58 it was time for Rudy to step up behind the big bench at Chicago Stadium. However, Pilous once explained that he had to consider taking the position, since the Hawks had been in the basement of the League for so long. "When they offered me the job it seemed as crazy as winning the Irish Sweepstakes," he exclaimed in Schardt's *Sports Illustrated* article. "Even at that, I had to think it over for awhile, though, because this was the graveyard."

Pilous' style of coaching created a spark, as the Hawks took home the Stanley Cup in 1961. In the same article by Arlie Schardt, Pilous explained how he related to his players:

> *"They're men. I don't know much about their personal lives. I never check*

Traditional stock photo of some of Pilous' young team members in the early 1960s. (Photo courtesy of the Blackhawks.)

up on them. They know what they have to do. I don't fraternize with them in a social way. I have to have their respect. I have to be humble and firm at the same time."

Pilous was excused from his duties as the Hawks' coach shortly after the 1961 Stanley Cup victory.

"Tommy Ivan and I did not have very good communication. He didn't care to have me in Chicago. Tommy Ivan there was saying that we should've wound up in first place, and we were one point behind first place. After we won it in '61, he didn't think I did too good a job in '62, so he let me go."

After coaching the Blackhawks, Pilous coached the Winnipeg Jets (then part of the WHA), to two championships. He then returned to St. Catharines to coach the Maple Leaf's AHL affiliate, the Saints, from 1982 to 1986. Sadly, Rudy passed away in 1995 from a heart attack at the age of 80. He was inducted into the Hockey Hall of Fame as a "builder" in 1985.

William T. Reay

After Pilous was excused from his duties, Billy Reay took over as head coach for the Blackhawks in 1963-64, and remained so until 1976-77, when he shared part of his last season with Bill White. He coached the Blackhawks longer than anyone in the team's history and brought them to two Stanley Cup final appearances.

Billy was born on August 21, 1918 in Winnipeg, Manitoba. As a player, he turned pro with the Detroit Red Wing's farm team in Quebec City in his early twenties. While there, he served as a player/coach, and at the same time led the club in scoring, helping them to win the Allan Cup (given to senior Amateur hockey champs years ago). Later, he played on two Stanley Cup teams, and one championship (first place) team, while spending eight seasons as a center with the Montreal Canadiens. Reay lists the Stanley Cup teams, and a four-goal game in the playoffs against the Bruins one year as his career highlights.

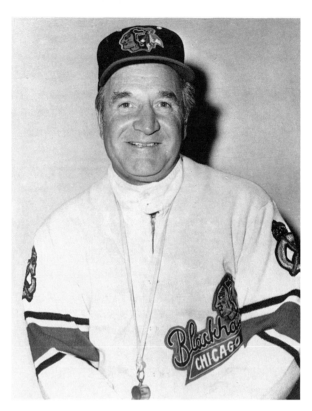

Billy Reay, coach from 1963 to 1977, held the position longer than any other, led the Blackhawks to two final Stanley Cup appearances. (Photo courtesy of the Blackhawks.)

While playing for the Habs, Reay earned a reputation as being a pesky checker and play-maker, playing on the same line with Boom-Boom Geoffrion and Paul Meger. When asked about playing with Geoffrion, Reay said:

"It was very, very, good. Boom-Boom had a terrific shot and I was a pretty good face-off man, so we took advantage of that. He [Geoffrion] was younger than I was, and we played very well together."

After coaching the junior Canadiens and retiring from NHL play, he spent time as player/coach for Victoria of the Western League. Eleven years later, after more coaching stops in Seattle, Rochester, Toronto, Sault Ste. Marie, and Buffalo, he came to coach the Blackhawks. During his reign behind the Chicago bench, he coached the team through 1,012 games. Of these, 516 were wins, 335 losses, and 161 ties.

Years ago, in a *Sports Illustrated* article by Mark Mulvoy, Reay was described as "a surly little tyrant who tried to bring Bobby Hull and Pat Stapleton to their knees, a media manipulator who invented the French-speaking Designated Talker for post-game interviews with English-speaking journalists, and the muddled trader who sent Phil Esposito to Boston." Whatever the case, he brought the Blackhawks to six, first-place division finishes.

In that same *Sports Illustrated* article, one Hawk who played for him noted, "People don't realize it, but Billy, more than anyone else, has kept this club together. He has rebuilt us overnight about five times. Without him, who knows where we'd all be?"

Recently, former Blackhawk forward Dennis Hull remembered playing for Reay:

"Billy Reay is the one who made it possible for me to play in the NHL. I was pretty raw talent when I got to Chicago. He worked with me long and hard; not only about hockey, but about life and everything else. He was just a great guy. He was honest and when he said it, he meant it. You could always take his word for it. He didn't back down from anything. I think that's what the guys respected most. If he said you weren't playing, you weren't playing, and if he said you were gonna do this, that's what you did. I think honesty is what everybody's looking for in a friend. He knew who to yell at and who to pat on the back; I think all coaches should be able to do that. I think a lot of times you see coaches today, they're trying to treat everybody the same way and to have them play the same way, and it just doesn't work that way."

Former Blackhawk defenseman Pat Stapleton remembers Billy Reay: "As a friend. I think that I was very fortunate to play for Billy," he said. "He was certainly a player's coach, he was a man's man. He demanded that you play well in the game. From then on you were on your own. There were no childish things from Billy at all. He wanted you to produce. If you produced and played well for him, it was adequate with him."

Former forward Jim Pappin was also a big Reay backer, explaining:

"He was the best. I played in Toronto for Punch Imlach and I hated every day. Then I got to Chicago, and Billy Reay was completely opposite. He dealt with you as a man, person to person. He didn't scream or holler in front of teammates at you. If something was wrong, he called you into his office or into his hotel room on the road. That was the big thing about him. He could communicate with a person. If you were struggling or anything on a road trip, he'd just leave a message in your hotel box to be in his room at such and such a time and you went up there and he just talked to ya about the problems and you came out of there feeling great. He was a man's man. He didn't holler or scream at you. He was a good hockey man, he knew the game and he was a good coach. A lot of the players took advantage of him, but they only hurt themselves, they didn't hurt him. He had curfews every night, but he never checked a curfew in the 15 years that he coached the Blackhawks. If there was an important game, he used to call a meeting at ten o'clock at night. Then, once you got in your hotel room, nobody wanted to go out anyway. You won't find anybody saying anything bad about him."

Today, looking back, Reay describes his coaching philosophy, and how it developed from his beginnings as a minor league coach.

"I think you serve a good apprenticeship in the minors, and you learn how to handle players and realize that they all have different personalities and they all can't be treated the same. I think that I understood players pretty well, having been a player myself. I understood what they went through. I had a lot of young players play for me and I always tried to encourage them and not do anything to hurt them. I think quite a few of the coaches [today try to coach all of the players the same way]. And I think some of the coaches that never had the opportunity to coach in the minors are sort of

handicapped. When you coach in the minors and you come to the big leagues, you have perfect control of the way you think. You know that you know what you're doing. But if you don't have that experience, it's very, very tough."

Thinking back, many high points came to mind when Reay thought about all of his years behind the Blackhawks bench. However, he picked out several as high points. "We never won the Stanley Cup, but we should have," he said. "One of the greatest victories was when Boston had their great team. Bobby [Hull] had left our club and we played them in the quarter finals, which was two games out of three. We beat that great team with Orr and Esposito and all those guys in the third game, six to two."

After retiring as Head Coach of the Blackhawks, Reay took six months off, and then went to work for Cameo Container Corporation in Chicago in sales and public relations. He is now semi-retired, and still lives in Chicago.

Billy Reay asking Santa for another Stanley Cup.
(Photo courtesy of the Blackhawks.)

A Different Era

Providing a feel for what it was like to play for the Blackhawks during the sixties, Glenn Hall offered some of his comments on the era.

Elaborating upon the training camps and conditioning Pilous and Reay put the team through many years ago, he said:

"Everything was on-ice conditioning in those days and now it's off-ice conditioning. We basically looked at training camp as a conditioning-type practice, it was to get in shape. There was no program set up in the summer to be in good condition like there is now. It was nothing then, it was up to the individual. Most of us felt it was beneficial if we did come in reasonably good condition."

Recently, Hall also described what it was like to be a key hockey figure in Chicago when he was playing:

"We were doing something we enjoyed. I don't think you have to be a star. I think it really helped you do well if you enjoyed it. I don't care what you're doing, if you're a blacksmith and you enjoy doing your job, you're going to do a good job.

We were a close-knit team. We more or less socialized with each other, like on off days and all the way along. The team concept was quite good... My best friends were my teammates and you enjoyed being with them. Also, the best friends of my wife were the wives of my teammates, so we just got along.

Possibly, it's not happening as much today as it did then, everything now being such high profile. Even in the old days, Bobby was very recognizable. But the rest of us, we could run and hide and have no problem. I think with today's athlete, it's a little bit tougher. He can't do the same things that we were able to do because he would be recognized.

We certainly didn't have to worry about going to see our banker or stock-

broker or something like that. All we had to worry about was if we had enough money to last to the fifteenth and again to the first, so they made it quite easy for us."

In a September 11, 1988 *Chicago Tribune* article with Mike Kiley, Bobby Hull also offered his feelings on what it was like to play in the 1960s and '70s.

"I think when the players leave the Stadium these days they split in eighteen different directions," he commented. "They don't get to see each other again and realize what they're here for until suddenly it's game time. We were always together. We were a family put together for the purpose of entertaining the people in the seats. Hockey was our life. We weren't absorbed in ourselves to the point that we wore fur coats and drove Lamborghini's, Porsche's, and all the rest. When we played it was for very few reasons. One was that it was a boyhood dream to play in the National Hockey League, and it had come true. Even better was to compete with the greats of the game, and to be able to do it on a par with them was about the greatest thing that had ever happened. Now it's become too commercial. Hockey allowed agents to get control of the players' minds and their business. That caused players to think of more than playing the game. When I pulled the crimson sweater over my head, my only thought was not to embarrass myself, my teammates, my family, and my organization. Everything I did was with pride."

Former Chicago Blackhawk forward Billy Hay also gave his impression of what it was like to play in Chicago during this era. First, he explained that the big deal the media made about friction between the regular players and stars like Bobby Hull, Glenn Hall, and Stan Mikita wasn't altogether true. "[That] didn't bother the team," he explained. "That was just the media. Of course they had their job to do, but in the dressing room and once the game started,

there were no stars…[Bobby], Stan Mikita, and Glenn [Hall] were as good as you'll see in the game and they all got along so well with the whole team. I think that was important. You'd bring up young players and new players and they'd all become part of the team and we'd enjoy having them around."

Commenting further on what it was like to play pro hockey for the Hawks during the '60s, Hay explained:

"We had so much fun…The exciting thing was we played hard, we worked hard, [and] we didn't have much money, so simple humor was sort of an outlet. We had some good people, like Al Arbour. He quotes those teams with a lot of character. I think that's very explicit. We had a lot of good guys. Once the puck dropped, we all knew what we were there for, but off the ice we really had a lot of fun. We didn't have lawyers and accountants that we were talking to all of the time. We made our own fun and we had to make our own decisions."

Recalling some of that fun, Billy Reay described one of the practical jokes the team pulled, of which he was the victim.

"One time we were in Oakland. We always had a meeting at eleven o'clock the day of the game. [At the meeting], there was a knock on the door, and an FBI guy [appeared]. He asked for me and started questioning me about the race track or something. The players had put him up to it, but I kind of guessed it. That was one really funny thing."

Playing the game itself was different in the past than it is today. Former Hawk forward Jim Pappin explains:

"We played a more respectful game. The hitting was still hard, and all that stuff. But nobody wore helmets, so nobody really hit anybody over the head with their sticks. There was no spearing and the hooking and holding and slashing. Today, everybody grabs on and

hooks to slow the opponent down. You couldn't do that in our day because you didn't wear a helmet. If you ever hooked somebody or grabbed somebody's stick, the guy would just punch ya in the nose. You didn't have that protection. Now they don't care. But that's the League's fault anyway. They could stop all of that hooking and holding. [There were more finesse plays back then] because the game was not as fast as it is today. There was a lot more skill back then as far as playmaking and being able to skate with the puck. Players today, they can do everything else a lot better than we could. The only thing they can't do [is] they can't skate, and puck handle because the game is different. Now they're taught to move it up quick, get it in the other team's end and forecheck hard. The equipment has [also] changed. The equipment is all lighter, so naturally that makes everybody faster. The skates have more support, so you're a much stronger skater today. Our skates were made of leather and you had to get them stitched up to keep them stiff. There are very few wooden sticks anymore. All the sticks are uniform so everybody can shoot the puck through the end of the rink now. Guys growin' up have sticks they can practice with. When we grew up as kids, we couldn't do that because we couldn't afford to, we'd break the sticks practicing shooting all day. The only reason I ended up being able to shoot the puck fairly decent is because I was always a rink rat, a stick boy for visiting hockey teams, so I always had a basement full of sticks. But most kids, their dads had to buy them sticks, so they couldn't afford to practice taking slap shots and breaking the thing in about ten minutes."

Pappin points out that things weren't all that bad while he played during the sixties and seventies, explaining: "I don't think I'd trade them places even though they do make a lot of money," he said. "When we played, it sure was a lot of fun. But the money, if you look at things in a different way, I could buy a house back then for $60,000 that they'd have to pay $400,000 for today. I bought a Mercedes in '74 for $12,000, it'd be $80,000 today. I mean, we still lived a pretty good life, as far as the money goes that way. I mean, when we were done playing we weren't set for life like these guys will be, that's about the only difference."

The Men

Besides greats like Hull, Hall, and Mikita, the Chicago Blackhawks had many other key players on the ice during the sixties. "We had great talent," comments Billy Reay. "At the time of the first expansion, why, I thought we had the best team in the League overall. We had…a lot of good hockey players. I was very blessed to have a team with so many good hockey players."

In goal was Denis DeJordy, backed by defensemen Pierre Pilote, Elmer "Moose" Vasko, Doug Jarrett, and Pat Stapleton. They also possessed forwards like Ken Wharram, Bill Hay, Lou Angotti, Reg Fleming, Doug Mohns, Ab McDonald, Murray Balfour, Eric Nesterenko, Phil Esposito, and Chico Maki. The team had other noteworthy athletes as well, such as the tough, competitive Reg Fleming, who was with them from 1960-64.

Denis DeJordy
Denis DeJordy, born on November 12, 1938, in St. Hyacinthe, Quebec, played goal in the NHL for 11 seasons, seven of those with Chicago. DeJordy stood at 5'9" and weighed 185 lbs. Often described as a quiet Frenchman whose teammates knew they could count on him to get the job done, he played his first organized hockey with his brother Roger in Jonquiere, Quebec. Oddly, it was he who played forward, and his brother who manned the pipes. Eventually they switched positions and began shining as quality players who were rivals during their pro careers. While playing in the minor leagues, Denis already had the looks of a future superstar. While with the Buffalo Bisons of the American League, the season he came up to Chicago, he was awarded both the Les Cunningham Trophy (MVP) and the Harry Holmes Memorial Trophy (goalie allowing the fewest goals in a season). That season, he had a 2.79 average, allowing 187 goals in 67 games.

DeJordy was awarded with the Vezina Trophy, which he shared with Glenn Hall in 1966-67, his first full NHL season since he began playing for the Hawks in 1962-63. That year he recorded a 2.46 average. One of his best moments perhaps was in the 1967-68 Stanley Cup playoffs when he helped the Hawks win four straight games, and recorded a 2.00 average in the series even though they eventually lost the semifinal.

In comparison to Glenn Hall, with whom he shared goaltending responsibilities for several seasons, DeJordy's style was a lot different. Rather than relying on his reflexes as did Hall, Denis was more of a stand-up, positional goaltender. Also, with the exception of Pat Stapleton and Doug Jarrett, many hold the opinion that Hall spent the majority of his career behind more developed and experienced defensemen such as Elmer Vasko, Pierre Pilote, Al MacNeil, and Larry Hillman.

During his career, Denis once commented on the difficulties of goaltending in the March, 1969 issue of *Hockey World* in an article by Keith L. Jackson:

"It is particularly tough when the puck and the players are in the crease. You can't take your eyes off it or you will be in deep trouble. Breakaways are also extremely tough. You try to hold back to the last second in committing yourself and if it's an experienced forward, he plays the same game and holds back. Once you make your move it [had] better be the right one or the man will score."

However, it was he who was known for making important saves, and specialized in stopping breakaways. During the 1967-68 season, Denis made an incredible save on Toronto's Frank Mahovlich, in which he came about 30 feet out of the net and dove onto his stomach to knock the puck away from Mahovlich who was racing alone towards the net. This action resulted in Chicago being able to keep the lead, and preserved a 1-0 shutout victory!

Unfortunately, because Hall was the Hawks' star goaltender, DeJordy spent a good deal of his time rusting behind the bench. Upon his request to play a 40-game schedule, Reay sent him to the Hawks' farm club in St. Louis, and got Dave Dryden

to serve as Hall's back-up goaler. As Tony Esposito was on his way in, DeJordy was on his way out the door to Los Angeles, Montreal, and Detroit before retiring after the 1973-74 season. He exited from the NHL with a 3.13 career average after eleven seasons.

Pierre Pilote

One of the Hawks' most outstanding defensemen from 1955-56 to 1967-68 was Pierre Pilote. Born in Kenogami, Quebec, on December 11, 1931, Pierre spent 13 seasons with Chicago. In an era where high-scoring defensemen were uncommon, Pilote scored 80 goals and recorded 418 assists for a NHL total of 498 points in 890 games. The winner of the Norris trophy three years in a row (1963, 1964, 1965), he also received All-Star honors eight years in a row, (second team: 1960-1962 and first team: 1963-1967). Topping off his list of accomplishments, Pierre was inducted into the Hockey Hall of Fame in 1975.

Legendary Blackhawk goalie Glenn Hall described Pilote as one of the best, most influential Hawk athletes of the '60s and '70s.

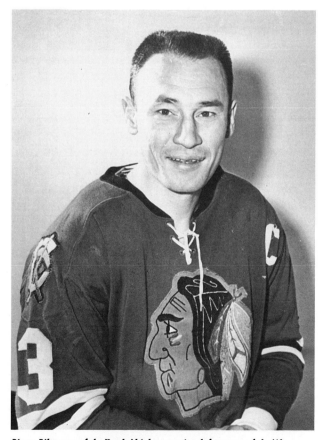

Pierre Pilote one of the Hawks' highest-scoring defensemen of the '60s. (Photo courtesy of the Blackhawks.)

"Pierre changed the game quite a bit. He was even pre-Bobby Orr. With the defense moving in to be part of the offense, he was certainly influential."

Pilote recently commented on his offensive game, explaining: "Well, it was natural because I first started to play as a centerman, when I was about 16, 17. I guess there were more centermen than defensemen, so the guy [his coach] asked me to play defense, so that's how I made the junior B-club. And then [when] I started playing defense, I had to learn the position, but I was always thinking offensively, if you know what I mean. I guess it evolved when the Blackhawks started getting guys like Hull and Mikita and stuff like that. We became more offensive-minded I guess. I was involved with that kind of trend."

After finishing junior hockey with the Tee Pee's of St. Catharines, Ontario, Pilote went on to play with Buffalo of the AHL for four-and-a-half years before being called up to Chicago. As one can see by looking at his stats, Pilote was considered a truly effective two-way player, contributing equally well both offensively and defensively.

Remembering his first game with the Hawks, Pilote commented:

"I remember it was in Toronto, and I didn't think I would start. In those days they brought you up and either they put you on there for a minute or two if you're winning high, or if you're losing. I had come up from Buffalo and I was all dressed up and ready to go. Dick Irvin, he was coachin' then, came into the room and announced who was gonna start. And he said 'Pilote and [Frank] Martin.' I couldn't believe it.

So anyway, Todd Sloan that year played [for] Toronto as a centerman and [got] some 40-odd goals that year. A really great year. I was standing at the blueline at the beginning of the game. Todd had a little trick that when the puck would drop, he would slip it past the other centerman and away we go. Of course I had never seen that. I didn't know all the tricks of the players in the NHL. At first you're kind of at their mercy. You

have to learn their tricks and moves. I froze right there, he took two or three steps, and boom! He was around me. The goaltender for us was Hank Bassen, and he went right in on Hank. Hank stopped it and the puck went in the corner and I picked it up and made a pass and kept on going. I'm sure if they would have scored, that would have been the end of me, but I kept on playing for about 20 minutes. So I always thank Hank a little bit because I'll never forget how I froze at the blueline."

Accumulating 1,205 minutes in penalties during his career with the Blackhawks, Pierre was quite a policeman. Stan Fischler said in the *Sport Magazine* article, "Pierre Pilote: Rough, Tough, and Talented," that in one of his memorable games, "he knocked out Ray Timgren with a single left hook and then swung around and dropped Elliot Chorley with one right. 'They went down like punctured balloons,' Pilote said. Pierre once commented: 'I've started many a feud. When I was younger, people really used to hate me. Every two games a guy was carried out on a stretcher case.'" Although he was a rough player, Pilote wasn't a mere goon like many believed him to be. His emphasis was on the game, and not getting into scraps.

When asked to recall a few of the more memorable scraps he had during his career, Pilote explained:

"Scraps? Well, I've had a few of them. I guess the [most memorable ones are the] ones I lost. I remember one time, there was a big brawl. I had never really fooled around with this guy, [Bert] Olmstead. He was a big tough guy. I had never seen him fight, or had any entanglements with him. We were in Toronto, and all of a sudden a big brawl broke out, and I happened to be with him. Well, I threw a couple of punches. He threw one. Boom! The next thing I know, he's got me by the neck and I'm on the bottom and he's holdin' me, I couldn't move. I thought he was going to break my neck. So, that's one that I remember not winning too well.

At first you have a few. Then you kind of establish your position and nobody [messes with you]. Well, there's always the odd challenge, ya know. I think I fought more in the American League than in the National Hockey League. There were a lot of tough guys down there trying ya out.

I had a fight with the Richard brothers one time. That was kind of exciting. Luckily, I had Harry Watson to help me on that one. We were playing in Montreal I think and I had a little tussle with the Pocket, Henri Richard, and then his brother came in. I was tussling with him too and then all of a sudden big Harry Watson came in, and took the big brother out of there. So that made things easy for me."

After Ed Litzenberger was traded to Detroit in 1961, Pilote was given the responsibility of team captain, and proved himself to be a natural leader and liaison between the athletes and the brass.

Pierre spent the 1968-69 season with Toronto, where he was traded for Jim Pappin who, at the time, was unhappy with the Leafs. In an interview after the trade, Tommy Ivan stated that the team was reluctant to let him go, but they would honor his wish to be traded.

Later, Pilote went on to coach in the Metropolitan Toronto Hockey League in which his son Pierre, Jr. played, and pursued various business ventures in such areas as the luggage industry, farming, carpentry, and has owned a doughnut shop, laundromat, and automobile dealership.

Elmer "Moose" Vasko

At 6'3", and weighing anywhere from 210-220 pounds during his 13-year NHL career, Elmer "Moose" Vasko was, at one time, the biggest man in the entire League. Playing defense for the Blackhawks from 1956-57 to 1965-66, Vasko and his counterpart Pierre Pilote made a terrific defensive pair during their playing days.

Born on December 11, 1935, Elmer played hockey with the Blackhawks' junior club in St. Catharines. Playing in 641 games over the course of his 10 seasons with Chicago, Vasko racked up a

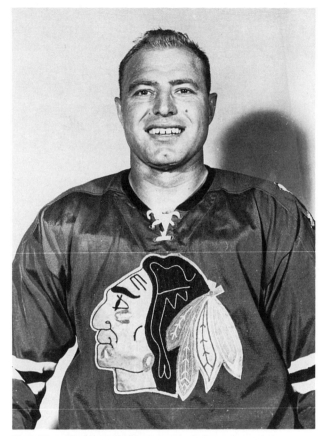

Elmer "Moose" Vasko was the biggest man in the league at one time. (Photo courtesy of the Blackhawks.)

surprisingly low number of penalties (606). Moose made All-Star (2nd team) in 1962-63 and 1963-64.

Former Blackhawk defenseman Pat Stapleton said:

"[Elmer Vasko] was a very capable athlete. He was, at that time, probably one of the biggest athletes that played in the NHL. [He] was very, very capable and worked extremely well on defense with Pierre Pilote. They complemented one another in their style of play. They both possessed great attributes. Both of them were pretty fair puck-handlers. Both of them could rush the puck and the more, I guess, that Pierre handled the puck offensively, Moose became more of a defensive hockey player. But, they both possessed great puck-handling skills, or good puck-handling skills."

When asked if Elmer was a very intimidating player because of his size, Stapleton said:

"At that time I don't think it was necessary. I think he did his part. He played his position very well…When people are individually big, [other] people expect them to be more of a physical force, and I don't think that was Elmer's nature. He played the game and was very capable of playing the game the way it was supposed to be played."

After spending a season in Salt Lake City of the Western League, Elmer spent two seasons with the Minnesota North Stars, and then retired after three weeks in training camp with the Buffalo Sabres. Today, Moose lives in the Chicago area.

Doug Jarrett

Doug Jarrett, who played defense for the Hawks from 1964-65 to 1974-75, was born in London, Ontario, on April 22, 1944. Known for his effective hip-checks, a trivial tidbit about the 6'1", 205 pound "Chairman of the Boards," as he was called, involved eating potatoes to improve his game. He began his career with an impressive rookie season, but later began to fizzle out in the middle of his career with the Hawks, experiencing trouble weakening late in games and performing in doubleheaders. He had to remedy this problem by adding starch to his diet, receiving some vitamin shots, and playing five pounds overweight.

"He's a more even type of defenseman," Billy Reay once said in a February 4, 1972, Bob Verdi article that appeared in *The Hockey News*. "While he may not overly excel at one thing, he is able to do everything. He isn't very flashy but he is very respected around the league."

Although he was quite a hitter, Jarrett didn't get into scraps as often as his scrappy defensive partner Keith Magnuson. In the same *The Hockey News* article, he gave his views on fighting, explaining:

"I don't think I could fight my way out of a paper bag. But a lot of fights start when somebody gives you a stick or something. I just try to check clean, and I don't think most players mind taking a good hit. It may hurt, but there's no reason to fight."

Jarrett later played for the New York Rangers before retiring in 1976-77. Over the course of his 13-year NHL career, he played in 775 games, racking up 220 points and 631 minutes in penalties.

Pat Stapleton

Born on the fourth of July, 1940, in Sarnia, Ontario, Pat "Whitey" Stapleton played defense for the Blackhawks from 1965-66 to 1972-73. During his NHL career, which began in 1961-62, Pat racked up 386 points (53 goals, 333 assists) in 700 games including the play-offs.

An instant favorite with Chicago Stadium fans, many believed that the 5'8" Stapleton was too small for an NHL defenseman. But "Whitey," as he was called, went on to have a spectacular career in the Windy City after Tommy Ivan got him from Boston. While he played, many fans thought of him as one of the League's most exciting and colorful players.

On the ice, Pat Stapleton was mainly a puck-carrying defenseman with good rushing and passing ability. He was very effective at setting up goals for the forwards, and keeping the puck in the

Pat Stapleton—one of the fans' favorite defensemen in the '60s. (Photo courtesy of the Blackhawks.)

attacking zone. He was an expert checker and puck-handler with quick reflexes and was known for his accurate shot from the point.

It took a little time for Pat to make the climb up to the NHL and become a regular. He played Junior A hockey for the St. Catharines' Tee Pees with Stan Mikita and other future teammates.

While playing Junior, Stapleton worked as a milkman in his birthplace of Sarnia, Ontario. "It was a good life," he once explained to *Toronto Sun* columnist Jim Coleman on March 20, 1972. "I finished my route by noon and, I could spend the rest of the day fooling around with my family. I got a kick out of driving a horse-drawn milk wagon. They took most of the fun out of a milkman's life when they replaced the horses with motor trucks."

Pat later played under former Blackhawk coach Billy Reay for one of the Hawks' farm teams in Sault Ste. Marie, Ontario, as well as four-and-a-half seasons with the Buffalo Bisons after he played junior hockey.

Eventually, he was drafted by the Boston Bruins where he spent one-and-a-half seasons, before being sent off to Kingston and then the Western Hockey League Portland Buckaroos.

In Portland, he was voted the WHL's most outstanding defenseman. He also gained valuable experience that would help him later in his career. "Hal Laycoe was coaching the Portland team and he took me under his wing and rebuilt my confidence," Stapleton once told Keith L. Jackson in the December 1968 issue of *Hockey Pictorial*. "For a while I was used at center and this experience has given me the insight to understand the thinking of the forwards. Hal suggested I take off a little weight and when I moved down ten pounds to 180, my present playing weight, I found that I was able to move with much greater speed and became more valuable to the team."

While with the Buckaroos, the Maple Leafs picked him up for about 24 hours in a trade with the Bruins on June 8, 1965. However, the next day, the Leafs failed to protect him in the NHL draft.

It was then that the Blackhawks picked him up. But, as fate would have it, they shipped him away to their Central League team in St. Louis. It was a "lucky break" that turned Whitey into a Blackhawk regular. After one of Chicago's regular defensemen, Moose Vasko, broke his toe, Pat was called up for duty and never left for the minors

again. He became an instant hit not only in Chicago, but in visiting cities as well.

"Life takes some peculiar twists," he told *Toronto Sun* columnist Jim Coleman on March 20, 1972. "If Moose Vasko hadn't broken a toe, I might still be driving my milk wagon in Sarnia."

Today, Pat feels the same way, explaining:

"I think, no question about it, timing has a lot to do with it; being in the right place at the right time. I guess you could say it was someone's injuries that allowed me the opportunity to move in and play on the defense. That training camp,...I had come back to Chicago. I had spent the first couple [of] months in St. Louis and then there was an injury and I got called up. I was fortunate enough to score a goal in the first game and it just seemed to multiply from there."

During his first season with the Blackhawks, Stapleton made second-team All-Star, and did so twice more; in 1970-71 and 1971-72.

Pat also displayed courage while playing. Once, in a 1967-68 game against the Maple Leafs, Bob Pulford injured him when the point of his stick shattered Pat's sinus cavity and cut him below the eye. The Hawks were struggling to make the play-offs at the time, and Pat was one of their key players.

Even though coach Reay was against it, Pat returned to the ice several games later wearing a football-like helmet. Although his eyes were all right when tested separately, they didn't focus right together, and he saw double. He played anyway, and his presence allowed Chicago to move ahead in their play-off pursuits, although they didn't win the Stanley Cup.

In February of 1969-70, he suffered a severe left knee injury when he smashed into a goal post. That season, he would only play in 49 games. In an article by Bill Libby appearing in *The Hockey News,* he commented:

"You can't believe how bad the pain was! It was just agonizing. Dr. Ted Fox, the Chicago Bears' team physician, who took care of me, said he couldn't believe how bad my injury

was. There are injuries and there are in-juries. There are knees and there are knees. My knee injury was bad. And the rehabilitation exercises were torture."

When he finally did come back, it took him a while to get back on track and play on the par that he had been on. His 6'2" defensive partner Bill White had to pick up the slack while Whitey struggled to regain his form.

Looking back over his career, Stapleton described himself as a player.

"I think assets that I did have were puck-handling skills and passing skills. Being able to move the puck out of our own end and having the ability to control the puck in our defensive zone. I would think that [those] would be some of the main assets [I had]. Being able to position guys so it was to my advantage, not to their advantage."

A career such as Stapleton's is certain to be filled with many unforgettable memories. Today, reminiscing about those years, Pat lists the games in which the Hawks clinched first place for the first time (1967), and in which Bobby Hull scored his 51st goal as memorable. He also elaborated on some other special games, one of which was a milestone in his playing career.

"There was [a] time when I was for-tunate enough to get six assists in one game [March 30, 1969 vs. Detroit] that stands out in the Chicago Stadium. The record at that time was 47 assists for a defenseman. I think it was the last game of the year, if I remember right, or the second to the last game and I got six as-sists to break the record and end up with 50 assists, which at that time was a record in the National [Hockey] League."

In July of 1973, Pat jumped to the WHA Chicago Cougars for a 5-year, $1 million contract and a $125,000 bonus. "This gives me the opportunity to expand my hockey career and to have control of a team," he told Reid Grosky of the *Chicago Tri-bune* on July 25, 1973. "The Kaisers [owners Jordon and Walter] are ready to spend some money and they've given me complete control of the opera-tions. We'll be going after the proven NHL players, and I have some in mind."

Later, with teammates Ralph Backstrom, Dave Dryden, and lawyer Jeff Rosen, he became part-owner of the team. Besides the 350-acre farm he owned while playing for the Hawks, he also owned ice rinks in Downer's Grove and Carol Stream, Illinois, and ran summer hockey schools and a prep league in the Chicago area.

Today, looking back on his switch to the WHA, Stapleton said:

"I think it was just simply a busi-ness decision. It came down to what was best for me and my family at that time. After having spent eight years with Chi-cago, it looked like the right thing to do.

"I'm really proud that I had the op-portunity to play with the Blackhawks. They were more than generous with me from the standpoint of giving me the op-portunity to participate at the level that I had dreamed about from [the time I was] a kid.

"It [playing for the Chicago Cougars] was a different experience altogether. We played in a different building. It was to-tally different from the number of people that went to the games [at the Stadium]. It was [different] from a standpoint of coaching and, being involved in the management side of it.

"In the second year we did [get in-volved in the ownership]. We kinda kept the team together. The owners that were there decided [not to participate] any longer because it didn't look like they were going to build the rink where the Cougars were supposed to play, which was eventually built at O'Hare [Rosemont]. The owners, at that time, felt as though it didn't look like it was com-ing on stream as fast as they had wanted it to. It was just at the beginning of the season and our main purpose was to keep the team stationary for the year and

then let the chips fall where they may, because it was difficult enough for everybody. People had kids in school, players had homes, so that was our main purpose to do that."

Stapleton is involved in several different pursuits since he retired from playing professionally. Among them are farming in Ontario, and a youth hockey program reaching children throughout Canada and the U.S.

"Basically, we've been involved in farming ever since I was in hockey. [I] started a little company that is more of an educational company as far as the sport of hockey [is concerned] and helping young people get the best out of the game and play the sport for the life skills it teaches you. I guess if there was a mission [it would be] that they could enjoy it as much as I've enjoyed it and my family's enjoyed the sport of hockey. It's such a great game. We fail to tell people that it is the most difficult sport to play and that the players that play it are the greatest athletes in the world.

"It [the program] was in Canada in the eighties, and now we've branched off into the United States. It works with the skills on the ice. It works with the parents off the ice and how they support their athletes, [helping them] have an understanding of what a great game it is and how to support the athletes that are a part of their family.

"It's an in-depth program. I've taken my 47 years in the game and documented it to the point where other people can follow the recipe and what it takes to be a complete hockey player."

Kenny Wharram

Born in Ferris, Ontario, on July 2, 1933, Kenny Malcolm Wharram arrived in Chicago in the early fifties. He played right-wing for the Hawks in 1951-52, 1953-54, 1955-56, and from 1958-59 to 1968-69. It wasn't until the early sixties that he really began to shine. When he was put on the famous "Scooter Line" with Stan Mikita and Ab McDonald

Kenny Wharram—member of the "Scooter Line" with Stan Mikita and Ab McDonald. (Photo courtesy of the Blackhawks.)

(and later Doug Mohns) in 1960, he became a very productive hockey player.

"The Scooter Line" was one of the most famous scoring combinations of the 1960s. What made it click so well was the combination of Mikita's superior playmaking and athletic abilities, Wharram's speed and agility, and Mohns' size, checking ability, and "heavy" slap shot. At their peak, in 1966-67, the line scored a combination of 91 goals (Mikita 35, Wharram 31, and Mohns 25) and 222 points! Their final season was 1968-69 when they scored 82 goals (Mikita and Wharram each scored 30, and Mohns scored 22).

Wharram's former teammate Ed Litzenberger said this about his teammate:

"Kenny could skate a 100 miles an hour, but he really didn't come into his

own until he hooked up with Stan and
Ab McDonald. Stan had the ability to
slow the game down. Kenny would come
from behind and would give him [Stan]
the puck, and he could put the puck in
the net. Ab would grind it out of corners
and it was a marriage of talent is what
it was. [Kenny] was a quiet guy. A good
guy."

Although he wasn't as good a stick handler as
Mikita, Wharram had a hard, accurate shot and was
a gifted skater. Many remember Wharram for his
"patented" shot from the right side, 30 feet out from
the goal. During his 14-season career he scored
268 goals and recorded 308 assists for 576 points
in 846 games (including the play-offs). Wharram
once commented on how he functioned as a player
in George Vass' book *The Chicago Blackhawk Story*.

"My speed helps me overcome what
some might consider to be lack of size.
By keeping on the move all the time, with
my head up, I don't give the defensemen
time to set me up for solid checks. Also,
when they do hit me, they usually get just
a little piece and not enough to ride me
out of the play entirely. I try to go all out
all the time when I am on the ice. You
only get out of a sport what you put into
it, and I owe it to my teammates and
myself to give my all."

Former Hawk center Pit Martin commented:
"I didn't play with Kenny Wharram very long but
he certainly was a contributor in a very quiet kind
of way." Just before the 1969-70 season, Wharram
was forced to retire because of a heart condition.

Billy Hay

William Charles (Red) Hay was born on December 8, 1935, in Saskatoon, Saskatchewan. Standing at 6'3" and weighing in at 197 pounds, Hay
played center for the Blackhawks from 1959 to
1967, scoring 113 goals and 273 assists in 506
games. His best season point-wise was 1961-62,
when he scored 11 goals and 52 assists in 60 games.
Describing his earliest memories of learning
to play the game, Hay commented:

"My earliest memory [was] when I
was five years old in Saskatoon,
[Saskatchewan]. We had a rink across
the back alley and my mother used to
send me out there. I would cry and come
back in and she would kick me back out."

However, Hay soon learned to like the world
of ice hockey that most Canadians grow up in.

"From there you learned how to be
competitive and how to enjoy the game.
That was all there was to do in the winter in Saskatchewan. That's how you
grew up to play the game; once the creeks
froze [until] the natural ice melted."

Bill Hay came from quite a family. His father,
Charlie, was a goalie for the Regina Pics in 1923
when they were defeated by the legendary Toronto
Granites. Bill's mother Florence (String) was an
outstanding track and field star, and his uncle Earl
Miller was a forward for the Blackhawks from
1927-28 to 1931-32. Hay explained:

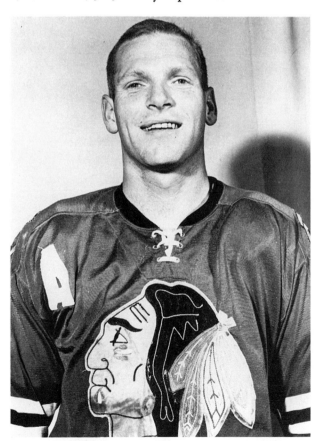

*Bill (Red) Hay was one of the first college graduates to play in the NHL.
(Photo courtesy of the Blackhawks.)*

"[My uncle] was a fellow who grew up playing in the Saskatoon area for senior hockey and minor pro [teams]. Then he played a couple of years with the Blackhawks. His sister, who was my mother, was a good athlete [university basketball, track and field]...and my father Charlie Hay was, I guess, not a bad goaltender for the University of Saskatchewan and senior hockey teams around western Canada."

Bill also had a brother who played basketball, hockey and football, as well as a sister who was quite athletic. "It was a lot of talk around the breakfast table," he explained with a laugh.

Bill played his first hockey for the Junior Pats near Regina. Before coming to the NHL, he played college hockey for the Colorado College Tigers in Colorado Springs where he received a degree in geology. He then went on to play for the Calgary Stampeders of the Western League, scoring 24 goals and 30 assists.

At the time that he broke into the League he was one of the first college graduates to make an appearance, and it had an effect on his initial acceptance into the NHL. "They looked at me as if I was a little different," said Bill when asked about the experience.

"It [college] wasn't the normal route to get to training camp and then be successful [enough] to make the team. It's all in the timing. It's no different than being a rookie. They looked at me a little differently when I went to school because I was supposed to turn pro and go the normal route."

When he reported to his first NHL training camp, Hay had to tell the players he had played for the Regina Pats the year before. He did this because, as he put it, it was "an organization they could relate to."

When asked if anyone ever gave him a hassle as to what his priorities were (a geology career or a hockey career), Hay explained: "I think down deep they were happy to see that somebody could come up through the college system. Being the first fel-low, you had to take some knocks along the way, but that didn't bother me. You became a pal and a teammate if you could help them and play the game and that's why I worked so hard at it."

Recalling memories of years gone by, Hay remembers the first Blackhawk game he suited up for.

"The first game I ever played I never got on the ice. The New York Rangers were in town. It was the first game the Hawks played, the first NHL game that I'd ever seen. New York was ahead of us a couple of goals and between periods Rudy Pilous, our coach, kept saying that the Zamboni was going faster than half you guys. I had to go out and, sitting on the bench, I asked the guy sitting next to me what number did Zamboni wear because he must be having a good game; I'd never seen an ice-making machine either."

After coming up to the big leagues, Bill won the 1960 Calder Trophy for Rookie of the Year during his first NHL season. He scored 55 points that year, placing him thirteenth in the League. Said Hay of his early accomplishment:

"You're [always] surprised at winning any individual award [but] that really wasn't on my mind at all. It was winning hockey games and fitting in with the team. There were so many good veterans around that had been there for awhile that I was learning from. Any sort of individual award never crossed my mind. It just happened and after that it didn't linger. You went into another season and the next season we won the Stanley Cup, which was as exciting as it could get."

Along with the late Murray Balfour, who was acquired from the Canadiens' organization in the same deal with Hay, Bill saw his first ice time playing on the Million-Dollar line with Bobby Hull, which would develop a real reputation.

"My first ice time was in Toronto," explained Hay, as he remembered back to when he was paired with Balfour and The Golden Jet. "It was Christmas time, really, when Rudy [Pilous], because of injuries, put Bobby together with Murray Balfour and myself. We just happened to play good and that's the lucky break that we needed."

When asked how long the "Million Dollar Line" (so-called because of the way Norris was spending money to rebuild the team) was together, Hay explained:

"Oh, three or four years. Then, as the game is today, it started to change. As soon as you went into a slump they'd change the line-ups. But I liked playing with all the young kids."

Bill Hay is involved in many different endeavors since retiring from professional play, and has served on the Hockey Hall of Fame selection committee since 1980. "I ran a drilling operation, oil well drilling, for Bow Valley Industries for 25 years, around the world. And that was all areas of the world that you could get to," he explained. "That would be a half billion in assets, so that was a sizable operation. Then, I retired in 1990 and spent one year as President of Hockey Canada, as a volunteer. Then, for the last [few] years, I've been President and CEO of the Calgary Flames."

Billy Hay has also been active in other pursuits over the years. "I was on the board of Hockey Canada since 1974," he continued. "So I've been close to the game, ya know. I helped build the Olympic Saddle Dome here [in Calgary], and ran the Saddle Dome foundation along with my job at Bow Valley, so I never really got out of it [hockey]. I've spent a lot of time around the game continually. I like the people, I like the game."

Murray Balfour

Born in Regina, Saskatchewan, on August 24, 1936, Murray Balfour began his career with the Montreal Canadiens in 1956. A member of the Million Dollar Line with Bobby Hull and Billy Hay, Murray Balfour played for the Blackhawks from 1959 to 1964. He was instrumental in the team's 1961 Stanley Cup victory. During the semifinals against the Habs, he scored a goal in the third overtime, and scored five goals and five assists in 11 play-off games. Sadly, he died in 1965 of lung cancer.

Remembering Balfour, former coach Rudy Pilous said:

"As a player he was what they call a digger, ya know. He always was on the checking-side. In other words, if their line messed up and the opposition got the puck, Murray was always back. Bobby wouldn't back-check too much, but Murray Balfour did the back-checking."

Former teammate Ed Litzenberger remembered Balfour:

"Murray came from my alma mater, he was after me. Murray never smoked or drank. He was a clean living guy. He would drive a thousand miles for a poker game but he never smoked or drank or chased girls. He was a tough kid, again my kind of guy. I was playing for Rochester and we played in Hershey. Murray had been sent down and I was talking to him after the game. He was coming up here to Toronto after he had his operation. I didn't even know he had been sick [and that] he had a tumor in his tummy about the size of my fist. He said his girlfriend, who was a stewardess, was going to join him. I said 'listen, when you get to Toronto call me and stay at my place. I got all the room in the world you can come and go as you please.' The next thing I know, my brother called me at 1:30 in the morning [and said] that Murray had passed on. He was a good guy. He died too young, it wasn't fair."

Pierre Pilote also remembered Balfour in a positive light, commented:

"He was a lovable, carefree kind of guy. A wind-blowing-in-his-hair type of guy. He loved to play cards. He was tough. He was a hard-nosed type of guy, tougher then Reggie Fleming in a way. He was not the biggest guy, about 185 or so, but well built. An only child I think. I

liked him a lot. I think he was well-liked by everybody. He was always smiling. He would mind his own business. He was a kidder, [and he] loved to play poker."

Lou Angotti

Born in Toronto, Ontario, on January 16, 1938, Lou Frederick Angotti played center for the Chicago Blackhawks from 1965-66 to 1966-67, and then from 1969-70 to 1972-73. A 1962 graduate of Michigan Tech University, he was sold to Chicago by the New York Rangers. Before getting a regular seat in the Windy City, Lou spent time circulating to Philadelphia and then Pittsburgh before returning back to Chicago. Later, he went on to play for St. Louis, after which his 11-season NHL career ended.

Hall of Fame referee Bill Chadwick once gave his impression of Lou in the February, 1970 issue of *Hockey World:* "He is always out of position and never seems to be where he is supposed to be," said Chadwick. "I would compare him with Eddie Shack. He can lift a team when it gets behind and his style of play is dangerous and injury prone."

Lou Angotti played center from 1965-67 and 1969-73, famous for setting up Bobby Hull for his 51st goal while sitting on the bench. (Photo courtesy of the Blackhawks.)

Interestingly, it was Lou Angotti who set up Bobby Hull for his famous 51st goal in 1966, while sitting on the bench!

Angotti said in the same *Hockey World* article:

"I kicked it over to Bobby from just in front of our bench and he went over the Ranger line and drilled it past Cesare Maniago who was in goal for New York in those days.

"We were changing lines and I just happened to be still on the ice when Hull came on. As soon as I got the puck to him I stepped onto our bench and was actually sitting when he scored."

Angotti, who was known for his explosive style of play and team dedication, centered a line with Eric Nesterenko and Hull while he played for the Hawks. In the same article, he commented:

"I think Nester and I are lucky. Frick and Frack could get points playing with Bobby...When you play with Bobby you have to be better. You are free wheeling so much that you have to score more because the other team is concentrating so hard on Bobby Hull that it often forgets about you."

Eric Nesterenko

Known both as the "Flin Flon Flash," and "Mr. Elbows," Eric Nesterenko was born in Flin Flon, Manitoba, on October 31, 1933. After breaking into the NHL with the Toronto Maple Leafs in the 1952-53 season where he spent his first four years, Eric almost didn't make it to the Chicago Blackhawks when he decided to quit hockey and pursue college football. Fortunately for the Blackhawks, Eric separated his shoulder during training camp and Tommy Ivan convinced him to give hockey a try in the Windy City, where Conn Smythe had sold him as part of an effort to help the Hawks "rebuild" themselves.

Over the course of his 16-year career as right-wing with the Blackhawks, Nesterenko scored 207 goals and recorded 288 assists for a career total of 495 points in 1,013 games. Altogether, he spent 21 seasons in the NHL (1951-52 to 1971-72). Includ-

Eric Nesterenko, known as the "Flin Flon Flash," was the thinking-man's hockey player. (Photo courtesy of the Blackhawks.)

ing the play-offs, he racked up a career total of 611 points (263 goals) in 1,343 games.

Although he was never a great goal-scorer, Nesterenko's particular strength was defense. Many believed him to have exceptional puck-handling ability, but at the same time he seemed to lack the thundering shot necessary to make him a great offensive threat. Nesterenko often played while either injured or sick. Often described as a thinking-man's hockey player, he was an excellent penalty killer, and one of the best defensive forwards of his era.

Former Hawk forward Bill Hay gave his impression of Nesterenko.

> *"He had such solid talent and was so smart about the game and special teams and special circumstances, [that] he was as good as there was. He liked the important games; the play-off games in which he performed well."*

Billy Reay said this of Nesterenko:

> *"Nesterenko was a very valuable member of the Blackhawks. Grant you, he didn't score 50 goals, but he did as a junior [with a laugh]. He got around 20 goals and had the opportunity to score about 50. He was a unique guy. He had his own style and he kind of floated around the ice. He liked to think that he was like Sonja Henie, ya know. He was a very interesting guy and a college graduate and played for the Hawks for a long time. He could kill out penalties well. He played on Bobby's line at one time. He could score goals when he had to. Very good skater, very strong skater. The thing that stuck out in my mind was the number of chances that he got to score goals and that he didn't capitalize on. If he would have capitalized on three quarters of his chances he would probably have scored 40 goals a year."*

"Eric Nesterenko was a hell of a skater and a very knowledgeable guy," said Rudy Pilous, who coached Nesterenko before Billy Reay. "He was always gonna be himself. He was a hard guy to coach, but he helped the team."

The following excerpt from Studs Terkel's book *Working*, reveals some of Eric's thoughts concerning his childhood beginnings in ice hockey:

> *"I lived in a small mining town in Canada, a godforsaken place called Flin Flon. In the middle of nowhere, 400 miles north of Winnipeg. It was a good life, beautiful winters. I remember the Northern Lights. Dark would come around 3 o'clock. Thirty below zero, but dry and clean. I lived across the street from the rink. That's how I got started, when I was four or five. We never had any gear. I used to wrap Life Magazines around my legs. We didn't have organized hockey like they have now. All our games were pickup, a never-ending game. Maybe there would be three kids to a team, then there would be 15, and the game would*

go on. Nobody would keep score. It was pure kind of play. The play you see here, outside the [Chicago] Stadium, outside at the edge of the ghetto. My father bought me a pair of skates, but that was it. He never took part. I played the game for my own sake, not for him. He wasn't even really around to watch. I was playing for the joy of it, with my own peers. Very few adults [were] around. We organized everything. I was a skinny, ratty kid with a terrible case of acne. I could move pretty well, but I really never looked like much. Nobody ever really noticed me. But I could play the game. In Canada it is part of the culture. If you can play the game, you are recognized. I was good almost from the beginning. The game became a passion with me. I was looking to be somebody and the game was my way. It was my way of life."

After the NHL, Eric spent some time playing for the Chicago Cougars of the WHA in 1973-74, coaching, and later, acting. He played the role of an aging hockey player in the CBC drama series "Cement Head," and later was both actor and consultant in the 1986 box office hit "Youngblood," starring Rob Lowe and Patrick Swayze. An avid skier, Nesterenko has spent time working on various ski patrols and serving as a ski instructor.

Phil Esposito

Another influential forward who played for Chicago during the 1960s was Phil Esposito, who later became a superstar with the Boston Bruins. Born on February 20, 1942, in Sault Ste. Marie, Ontario, Phil broke right into the minor leagues from the amateur leagues. After playing for the OHA St. Catharines Tee Pees in 1961-62, where he scored 32 goals, he went on to play for the St. Louis Braves. Once there, he scored 36 goals and 54 assists during his first season.

Although many thought he was a little awkward when he made his NHL debut in February of 1964, Esposito went on to center a line with Bobby Hull for several seasons. He was branded with the nickname "Garbage Collector," since many of the goals he scored were off rebounds of shots made by Bobby Hull that didn't go in.

In one of the most one-sided trades in NHL history, Phil was sent to Boston on May 15, 1967, along with Fred Stanfield and Ken Hodge. In return, the Hawks got Pit Martin, who was to be a speedier center for Bobby Hull's line. They also got Jack Norris and young defenseman Gilles Marotte. It was one of the biggest trades in franchise history, and one of the most foolish in the eyes of many. Esposito and Hodge went on to become very successful with the Bruins.

Over the course of his 18-season career, Phil Esposito scored 778 goals and recorded 949 assists in 1,412 games (including the play-offs). He took home the Art Ross Trophy (highest point total) in 1969, '71, '72, '73, and '74, the Lester Patrick Trophy (outstanding service to hockey in the U.S.) in 1978, the Lester B. Pearson Award (outstanding player) in 1971 and 1974, and the Hart Trophy (MVP) in 1969 and 1974.

Besides the hefty collection of trophies he took home over the years, Espo was also named to the first All-Star team in 1968-69, '69-70, '70-71, '71-72, '72-'73, and '73-74, as well as the second All-Star team in 1967-68 and 1974-75. Phil Esposito was truly a remarkable hockey player.

Chico Maki

Another notable Hawk forward of the 1960s and 1970s was Chico Maki. Born in Sault Ste. Marie, Ontario, Chico, whose real name is Ronald, was nicknamed after the eldest of the famous Marx Brothers. In an article by Randy Schultz, which appeared in the September 6, 1985 issue of *The Hockey News*, Chico once recalled various aspects of his career. Commenting on his nickname, he explained: "Before I was born my mother used to go to the movies with the Marx Brothers in them. I guess that Chico was the character that she enjoyed the most."

Like many Chicago Blackhawk athletes of the time, Maki played junior hockey with the St. Catharines Tee Pees, and then for the Hawks' minor league team, the Buffalo Bisons of the AHL. During his (rookie season in Buffalo, he scored 72 points (30 goals, 42 assists) and was awarded the AHL rookie of the year award. That same season, the Blackhawks even called him up to assist them in their successful drive for the 1960-61 Stanley Cup. After that, he spent one more season in Buffalo, and then became a Blackhawk for good.

Chico Maki was great for setting up scoring opportunities for Hull, Esposito, Angotti, and Nesterenko. (Photo courtesy of the Blackhawks.)

"We really played well together as a line. You couldn't get anybody much better than Bobby at left-wing and I knew that Phil had a real great scoring touch if really given the chance."

During his career, Chico was never a high-production goal scorer, but rather focused his abilities on setting up Hull, Esposito, Angotti, and Nesterenko for scoring opportunities. Chico's brother Wayne was also a forward for the Blackhawks from 1967-68 to 1968-69, and later played for St. Louis and Vancouver. He was involved in a high-sticking incident during a 1969 exhibition game in which Ted Green of the Boston Bruins suffered a fractured skull and was sidelined for a whole season. Sadly, Wayne passed away from a brain tumor in 1974.

As if the death of his brother wasn't enough, prior to the training camp in 1974-75, Chico's 11-year old son was involved in a serious farm accident when his foot got caught in a combine that Chico was operating. After the accident, Chico temporarily retired from hockey, but later returned for another season. Maki said in an article by Bob Verdi, appearing in the February 20, 1976 issue of *The Hockey News:*

"My boy was going through tough times, and when he said that he wanted me around, that's all I needed to hear. I couldn't have lived with myself if I had tried to continue playing when he was hurt."

After retiring from the NHL for good, Maki operated a farm near Simcoe, Ontario, and has been involved in the hotel-restaurant ownership business.

During his 15-season NHL/Chicago Blackhawk career, in which he alternated from right-wing to center, Maki played in 841 games, scoring 435 points (143 goals, 292 assists). He has been described in many ways. Bob Verdi, who was then writing for *The Hockey News,* once described Maki as a winner, true-grit performer, splendid penalty killer, and unselfish checker.

From 1964 to 1967 Maki played on a line with Bobby Hull and Phil Esposito. That line was the league's top scoring unit in 1966-67. Maki commented in the Schultz article:

The Third Triumph

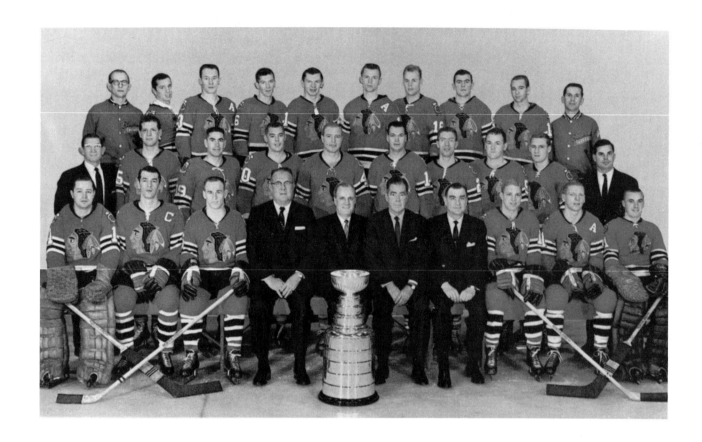

The 1960-61 Blackhawks brought home Chicago's first Stanley Cup in 23 years. Front row, l to r: Glenn Hall, Ed Litzenberger, Reg Fleming, Arthur M. Wirtz (president), Thomas N. Ivan (GM), James D. Norris (chairman), Rudy Pilous (coach), Bobby Hull, Bill Hay, Denis DeJordy. Second row, l to r: John P. Gottselig (PR), Eric Nesterenko, Dollard St. Laurent, Earl Balfour, Elmer Vasko, Ab McDonald, Al Arbour, Jack Evans, Wayne Hillman, Michael Wirtz (VP). Third row, l to r: Nick Garen (trainer), Murray Balfour, Pierre Pilote, Chico Maki, Ron Murphy, Wayne Hicks, Tod Sloan, Kenny Wharram, Walter Humeniuk (equipment mgr. and spare goalie). (Photo courtesy of the Blackhawks.)

On April 16, 1961, before 14,328 fans in Detroit's Olympia Stadium, the Chicago Blackhawks beat the Red Wings and took home their third Stanley Cup. It had been 23 years since the Windy City had been awarded the silver trophy. Explained former Hawk great Stan Mikita:

> "We weren't the best team in the League at that particular time. As far as the regular season goes, I think we finished in third place. However, we had some great goaltending from Glenn Hall and some good scoring from different people. That's what you need to win."

Before they beat the Red Wings for the Cup, the Hawks faced off with, and eventually passed the Montreal Canadiens in the semifinals. Glenn Hall's superior net-minding skills accented the team effort that was being put forth, and Chicago was able to beat them.

At the time, the Canadiens were HOT! They had won the Stanley Cup five years in a row prior to the 1960-61 season. However, their star, Boom-Boom Geoffrion, who had led the League in scoring, had his leg in a cast. Incredibly, he removed the cast and tried to play with his leg numbed by novocaine, but wasn't successful. Besides that, Rocket Richard had retired prior to the 1960-61 season.

Hall went ahead and held them scoreless for over two hours in the series, shutting them out altogether in the last two games. In the end, they beat Montreal four games to two.

In later years, Doug Harvey, a Montreal Canadien defenseman at the time, reflected upon the third game of the series in Stan Fischler's book *Those Were the Days*. Held in Chicago on March 26, the game went through three periods of sudden-death overtime: "We had it practically sewn up at least twice in the overtime. Once, when Henri Richard broke in the clear, I thought it was over." However, Hall made a close save. "After that," commented Harvey, "they had us." Although they beat the Hawks 5-2 in the next game, Hall shut them out in the next following two games, once in Montreal and once in Chicago.

Next came the series against fourth-place Detroit, who had beaten the second-place Toronto Maple Leafs four games to one in their semifinal series.

The first game, held in Chicago on April 6, brought a win to the series in favor of the burly Blackhawks. Beating the Motor City boys 3-2, Bobby Hull scored two goals in the first period at 9:39 and 13:15. Kenny Wharram also put one in during the first period at 10:10. The second and third periods were Detroit's. Len Lunde put one in during the second at 16:14. Al Johnson put in the other Detroit goal during the third at 19:18.

The second game, in Detroit, ended in a 3-1 Red Wing victory. In the first period, Young and Delvecchio scored at 8:10 and 17:39. In the second, Chicago defenseman Pierre Pilote scored the only Chicago goal, unassisted, at 0:41. In the third, Delvecchio scored once more for the Red Wings, at 19:22.

The third game was also a 3-1 game, but this time in favor of the Hawks. After a scoreless first period, the Blackhawks dominated the second on home ice with goals from Mikita, Ron Murphy, and Murray Balfour at 11:56, 14:19, and 18:17. In the third, Gordie Howe answered back with a goal at 9:28, but that was it for the Red Wings.

After traveling back to the Motor City, the fourth game was taken by the Wings, 2-1. After another scoreless first period of play, Bill Hay put one in for the Hawks at 7:34 and Delvecchio for the Red Wings at 8:48 during the second. Detroit's Bruce MacGregor broke the tie to tip the victory in their favor at 13:10.

Safely within the confines of 1800 West Madison Street, the Blackhawks whipped Detroit 6-3 in the fifth, action-packed game. Leo Labine answered first for the Wings at 2:14. Murray Balfour and Ron Murphy then scored two Chicago goals at 9:36 and 10:04. Howie Glover, at 15:35, put the final puck in the net for the Red Wings. Balfour scored for the Hawks at 16:25, and Stasiuk for the Wings at 18:49. After the close of the second, the teams were still tied. However, the third period brought momentum to the Blackhawks' efforts. Mikita scored twice, at 2:51 and 13:27, along with defenseman Pilote at 7:12.

The sixth game of the best-of-seven series turned out to be the proving grounds for Chicago. It was in this game that the team, described at the time by many experts to be the best that had ever represented Chicago in the NHL, would work their magic.

Glenn Hall, who minded the nets for that particular game, described it as one that will stick out in his mind forever. "I talked to Dennis Hull [Blackhawk forward, 1964-1977] yesterday," he commented recently. "He's got a radio show or something. He asked me if there was any particular game [that stands out]. I said, 'Yeah, I guess it would have to be the last game that we won the Stanley Cup.' We were in Detroit and we won. I think the final was 5-1. The 5-1 kind of sounds like a blowout, but it was late in the game that we won. But it sticks out, I played pretty well. Again, it sticks out simply because it was the final result of what you had been lookin' for all of your life."

Bill Hay, who was a Blackhawk forward at the time also gave his feelings on the victory: "It was enjoyable," he explained, "because that was what you worked hard at all year long. It isn't anything great or superhuman. Basically, it's winning the last game you played so the people, when you got back home, wouldn't criticize you for losing."

The game was dominated heavily by the Red Wings until early in the second period. At 15:24 of the first period, Parker MacDonald put Detroit ahead 1-0, scoring on a power play initiated by an interference call on Chicago's Al Arbour. Gordie Howe successfully executed a 40-foot drive that Glenn Hall stopped with his pads. However, MacDonald got the rebound and slipped it past Hall.

In the second period, Chicago gained momentum. Goals from Reg Fleming at 6:45 and Ab McDonald at 18:49 put the Hawks ahead 2-1.

The Red Wings went on the power play after Wayne Hicks, who was filling in for Chicago's injured Murray Balfour, was penalized. While the Blackhawks were concentrating on defense to kill the penalty, Fleming made an unassisted rush towards the Detroit goal and scored on Hank Bassen after poke-checking the puck away from Red Wing defenseman Pete Goegan.

Many believed that Fleming's shorthanded goal was the turning point in the game for Chicago. Although he agreed that particular goal was important, Glenn Hall gave his impression of the game:

"It's a combination of 20 guys or 18 guys, whatever you had in those days, and just getting a few good breaks. And believe me, you need the breaks."

Reg Fleming's unassisted goal was the turning point for Chicago in the sixth game of the 1960-61 season play-offs. (Photo courtesy of the Blackhawks.)

McDonald's goal came after Stan Mikita made a pass to Bobby Hull. Bassen came out of the crease to meet Hull and was knocked over into left-wing. McDonald, who was skating down left-wing, leaped over Bassen and slapped the puck into the empty net.

Although Chicago was powerful during the second period, the Red Wings weren't exactly asleep. Glenn Hall made several saves that were critical to the Chicago victory. While they were still on the power play, after Fleming had scored, Pete Goegan executed a hard, high shot from the blue line which Hall caught with his left, deep in the net. Three minutes later, Detroit went on the power play once again and Gordie Howe ripped a shot described as being almost identical to Goegan's at Hall, which bounced off his right arm and over his extended right hand. Hall made the save, once

again deep in the net. Also, after colliding with Hawk defenseman Ron Murphy, Detroit forward Howie Glover was sent to the hospital with possible internal injuries.

The third period was dominated heavily by Chicago, who scored three goals against the Wings, causing their confidence to slip. All of the goals were either the product of Detroit's defense giving up the chase or breakaways. Eric Nesterenko, assisted by Pierre Pilote and Tod Sloan at 0:57, put another point on the scoreboard. Then, although he had only scored two goals during the season, and only one in the previous two seasons, Hawk defenseman Jack Evans scored an unassisted goal at 6:27! Finally, Kenny Wharram put in the final goal that ensured a Chicago victory at 18:00. The final score: Chicago 5, Detroit 1.

When the smoke finally cleared, Hall had made 21 saves, and Bassen had made 20. NHL President Clarence Campbell presented the Stanley Cup to Ed Litzenberger, captain of the team. James Norris, then co-owner of the team, awaited the victors in the dressing room along with some of the men who had brought the cup to Chicago in 1934 and 1938. Mike Karakas, Alfie Moore, Carl Voss, Johnny Gottselig, and former coach Bill Stewart were all there. Also present, interestingly, were the two goaltenders that Chicago had beat for the cup in their first two victories; Wilf Cude and Turk Broda. Even Gordie Howe and goalie Terry Sawchuk, who had yielded his job to Bassen because of injuries, showed good sportsmanship by being present to offer their congratulations.

James Norris had become so excited he couldn't stand to watch the third period, commenting in the April 17, 1961 *Chicago Tribune*:

"Tommy Ivan and I went for a walk around the block when we got ahead 3 to 1. Our nerves were a little on the edge. I was pretty sure we were going to do it when Fleming got that goal, but somehow I didn't want to watch after we got two ahead. We're happy and proud tonight."

"This hockey team, I'd say, has improved 25 to 30 percent since the start of the season," commented coach Rudy Pilous after the victory in the same *Chicago Tribune* article.

"They're tired now. They have a right to be. Now they have the pride of champions. Both clubs had the heart, the spirit, the desire. The flesh was a little weak at the end, but we just had a little more left. You know we've played 93 games, and that's a lot of hockey, dating back to training games last fall."

Ed Litzenberger, then Team Captain, recalled the victory.

"When you grow up in Saskatchewan you never dream you're going to be playing in the NHL and or be

on the Stanley Cup winner, let alone be captain of a hockey club. So when those things happen to you, it's like, wow! I remember skating around Detroit with the cup on my shoulder and [afterwards] I was interviewed. Somebody said what did it feel like, and all I could say was 'Not bad for a little boy from Yorkton, Saskatchewan, is it?' That pretty much tells it all don't you think?"

The winning team received $1,750 per man, the losing team $750 per man. To keep the team motivated, Pilous explained:

"I raised a little hell. I just told them that tonight's game was worth $1,000 to the winner, and the loser gets nothing. If they didn't want it, I knew someone who did."

The team celebrated at the Metropolitan Airport cocktail lounge after they learned that, due to severe weather, their flight home had been cancelled. After leaving the airport for their accommodations, the party continued until 4:30 in the morning at Detroit's Leland Hotel, where Mr. Norris had rented an entire floor. Rudy Pilous described a humorous moment from that party:

"After the game, we went down to the airport. All the players were at the bar havin' drinks. Along comes Mr. Ivan and Mr. Norris. I said: 'We can't get outta here because of the snow storm.' So they said: 'Well, bring the cup,' we had the Stanley Cup with us, 'bring the Cup, and bring all the players and come on back to my hotel, we'll have our party there. [At the party, Norris] started to fill the Stanley Cup with a little booze. You'd go to pick it up and it's this big tall thing, ya know, pretty heavy. Ab MacDonald pushed him aside, and he'd never do that because they were pretty polite players, and he said: 'Just a minute Jim, I'll show

ya.' He screwed the bowl off the top and said: 'Now you can fill it up and hand it around.' Norris said 'How did you know that?' [MacDonald answered]: 'Don't you forget, you got me from the Canadiens and we won two of these before you!' So that was quite a joke."

Later, in Chicago, the team had a party at the Bismarck Hotel. Mayor Richard Daley presented a certificate of merit to Arthur M. Wirtz, James Norris, and captain Ed Litzenberger as the team was honored at City Hall, topping off an incredible accomplishment that has yet to be repeated in the Windy City. Litzenberger remembers that "morning after" ceremony. He recently explained:

"The next morning, of course, the season is over and everybody is bent out of shape… We fly back to Chicago and we have to go directly to City Hall, and they had a celebration with Mayor Daley. Needless to say, we weren't the most handsome bunch of guys sitting and standing at city hall. I had to give a speech, and I'm saying to myself 'I really shouldn't be here. I want to go home.' The job was done and we had won it. Now it was time to say good-bye and leave for our respective homes throughout the country and come back, and hopefully we'll all be together next year."

The Curse is Broken

In 1966-67, the Blackhawks topped off the decade by breaking the "Curse of Muldoon!" It was quite an accomplishment, considering the fact that they had never been able to reach first place since they joined the League in 1926.

In George Vass' book, *The Chicago Blackhawk Story*, coach Billy Reay gave his feelings at the time.

"I never dreamed as a youngster that I would ever coach the Chicago Blackhawks to their first league championship. This was a thrill for me that I just can't describe. It was a thrill because I knew exactly how much each player in our locker room had given to make this possible. We had wonderful spirit and willingness to achieve this goal. I give all the credit to the players."

Thinking back, former Chicago Blackhawk forward Bill Hay explained what was behind the Team's first Prince of Wales Trophy.

"That was the most exciting thing for me and that's really why I came back. I came out of retirement then. I had quit and I remembered that Jim Norris always said that to win the Prince of Wales Trophy, which the Blackhawks had never done; end up in first place, was as important as winning the play-offs. The Blackhawks had never done that and he had passed away and Tommy [Ivan] had called me. I thought if I could help I'd go back, which I did from January through April. That was a big thrill… What it took was good talent, and we really had a lot of talent."

Tommy Ivan observed that there was nothing like bringing up your players through your own system so they knew what was expected from them by the big club. The only thing Ivan expected was the best, and he most certainly got it!

At the time, Pierre Pilote commented that the entire "first-place thing" had been a monkey on their backs, and that it was a relief to finally win a championship and show everyone that they were the champions.

In the past, the team had depended a great deal on its star players. By the season's end these individuals would be worn out. However, during this particular season, the load was spread out in a more even fashion, which worked very effectively.

The 1969 Chicago Blackhawks, front row, l to r: Dave Dryden, Stan Mikita, Tommy Ivan (GM), Arthur Wirtz (chairman), William Wirtz (president), Bobby Hull, Denis DeJordy. Middle row, l to r: Nick Garen (trainer), Doug Jarrett, Tom Reid, Bill Orban, Michael Wirtz (VP), Coach Billy Reay, Howie Young, Eric Nesterenko, Jim Pappin, Don Uren (ass't trainer). Back row, l to r: Dennis Hull, Wayne Maki, Bob Schmautz, Gilles Marotte, Ken Wharram, Pat Stapleton, Pit Martin, Chico Maki, Matt Ravlich, Doug Mohns. (Photo courtesy of the Blackhawks.)

THE DEFENSE NEVER RESTS
THE 1970s

As the sixties slowly began to fade into history, and a new decade emerged, a period of change would present itself in Chicago. Coach Reay and Tommy Ivan began switching the team's emphasis from offense to defense, checking, and the importance of working together. The Hawks also moved from the East Division of the League to the West Division in 1970-71.

Commenting on this fact, former Blackhawk forward and assistant coach Cliff Koroll said: "I think that era was all defense. There was a real emphasis on defense. You know, you had your two-one, two-nothing, one-nothing, three-one games, where you don't see that in the game anymore. It's become real wide open offensively. If you couldn't play defensive hockey back then, you couldn't play in the League."

Early in the decade, Ivan and Reay acquired some excellent rookies like Keith Magnuson and Cliff Koroll from Denver University, as well as Gerry Pinder, also a college player, who had skated for the Canadian National Team. Pinder was a big scorer in the Western Canada Junior League.

After winning the NHL championship and taking home their first Prince of Wales trophy in 1966-67 (given to the team winning the NHL championship from 1938-39 to 1966-67. Given to East Division champs from 1967-68 to 1973-74. Now given to the play-off champion of the Wales Conference), the team repeated the feat in 1969-70. However, this time there were a lot more rookies on the roster. With great net minding from Tony Esposito and

a combined team effort, the Hawks beat out four other teams that were in the race for first place. They pulled the trigger in Montreal on April 4th, beating the Canadiens 4-1. Many thought that the 1969-70 team would fold before reaching this height, but they certainly didn't.

Cliff Koroll, who was one of those rookies, explained what was behind the achievement.

"I think the rookies had a lot to do with it," he said. "Three of us came out of Denver, where we had won the National Championship. We had a great coach in Murray Armstrong [at Denver] who really emphasized defensive play. So this was the one thing that the Blackhawks certainly needed...an emphasis on defense at that time. They certainly had the powerful offensive thrust with Bobby [Hull] and Stan [Mikita], and Pit Martin, Jim Pappin, and Dennis Hull. But, we had a lot of goals scored against us as well. So, [with] the three of us from Denver, our experiences playing defensive hockey, and Tony Esposito coming up and playing goal...four college boys really added to that [victory]."

Elaborating further upon the season itself, Koroll explained:

"We started off and we were zero and five, I remember that we went into New York and we got our first point; we tied the Rangers one to one. I scored my first NHL goal that night. It was a four against four situation. I'll never forget, Billy Reay threw Jim Wiste and I out there. Here are two rookies out there in that critical situation and we got a goal to tie the game. From then on, we didn't lose many hockey games. We just got better and better as the year went on. The final game was at the Stadium where we had to win the game, win or tie I think it was. We played the Montreal Canadiens who had to win to make the play-offs. We beat them 10 to 2. They pulled their goaltender in the middle of the second period. We were up five to two, and that's the only time I've ever seen a goaltender pulled that early. They had to win, tie, or score 5 or more goals to make the play-offs, and none of 'em happened. We just had a heyday icing the puck all night, trying to hit an empty net. So it was quite an exciting year."

Even playing for a Stanley Cup champion team in Montreal as a youth, and coaching the Black-hawks to their first Prince of Wales Trophy a few years earlier, in 1966-67, was incomparable to this particular championship victory in the heart of coach Reay. "To think that we lost the first five games of the season and then came on to achieve this," exclaimed the happy coach in George Vass' book *The Chicago Blackhawk Story* at the time of the victory. "It's unbelievable. We had to fight an uphill battle all the way. We had to play play-off hockey almost from the start. Nothing in my experience ever has matched this. This is the proudest moment of my life." As a matter of fact, Reay would also coach the team to a first-place division finish every season except 1974-75 and 1976-77 during the seventies.

Tony Esposito, Cliff Koroll, and Pit Martin (#7) pile up in front of the net with some Sesame Street characters. (Photo courtesy of the Blackhawks.)

During this decade, the Blackhawks also came close to bringing the cherished Stanley Cup back to the Windy City. However, they weren't able to pull it off even though they made it to the finals against Montreal in 1970-71, and again in 1972-73. That first loss, in 1970-71, is the game Pit Martin will never forget.

"I think the one game that sticks out the most was a loss; the seventh game against Montreal, in '71 I believe," explained Martin. *"We had the lead going into the third period and lost the Stanley Cup. Just before the end of the second period I remember feeding the puck to Bobby Hull in the slot and he fired a shot. He really got good wood on it, and it hit the crossbar. He hit the crossbar so square that the rebound ended up back at the blue line. If that had gone in, it would've made it 3-1 and it might have changed things."*

Cliff Koroll offered his view of what that first loss meant to him.

"The first one [1970-71 loss] we definitely should've won. We had a great team that year. We had great teams for a number of years, but that's one year that we definitely should've won it. Montreal upset Boston, we beat the Rangers. There was a perfect opportunity for us to win it.

Each team won the home game. We won the first two in Chicago and then Montreal won the next two. We won game five and [went] up to Montreal for game six. We were leading going into the third period and they came back and beat us. It was a freak goal. The puck jumped over Bill White's stick. Frank Mahovlich went in and scored. Then, the next, seventh game was back in the Stadium. We were winning 2-nothing in the middle of the second period. Back then, a 2-nothing lead was money in the bank. Bobby Hull just hit the crossbar and Jacques Lemaire picked the puck up in the cor-

ner and got to center ice and shot the puck in, and went off the ice for a line change, and Tony missed. It gave them a little momentum because they had quit at that point in time, because we controlled the game. Then Henri Richard scored two goals to beat us."

Elaborating further on the loss, Koroll explained that vivid memories of the event remain with him to this day.

"I still wake up nights after that one. It's a tough deal when you're so close. You were so close and you just didn't quite grasp on to it. I still have a lot of reminders of it. I still wake up occasionally from that one.

I guess it's something Billy Reay said to us before game six up in Montreal. He said winning a Stanley Cup is what we're all in the business for and a lot of people don't get that opportunity to even get that chance. You appreciate it at the time you do win it, but the times you really appreciate it is when you get a little older and ya' reminisce and look back and everywhere you go, people say you were on a Stanley Cup winner. Some of you may never get this close again to winning it. This was before game six. Those words just keep echoing in my mind all of the time because only one other time did we get close, and that was in seventy-three. Never had that opportunity to win the Cup again after that. It kind of haunts you a little bit."

Former Hawk forward Dennis Hull recalled what kind of a team the Blackhawks were during the seventies. However, the team's inability to take home the Stanley Cup on these occasions was something that immediately came to mind.

"[We had] great offensive power, great goal-scoring ability. We had, during that time, two of the greatest goaltenders to ever play; Glenn Hall

and Tony Esposito. Obviously, I'm prejudiced, but I saw them play every night that I played and they were magnificent. I don't know exactly what we lacked, because we'd get to the finals and go to the seventh game and just a break would keep us from going all the way...In 1971, it was a strange goal [that beat us]. We were outplaying the Montreal Canadiens by a long shot. In fact, we'd been in their end, if you've ever watched the tape, we'd been in their end so long, a little mist had formed on the ice. It [was] hot, a May day. When Jacques Lemaire shot the puck, Tony couldn't pick it up [out of] the mist that was right above the ice. It just jumps out of the mist right at the last minute, like Montreal had some secret play or something. Like they always do to find some way to win. It just jumps out of the fog and Tony doesn't see it until the last second.

"But it went to the seventh game in '64 and '73, so...we had great teams that went to the very final game. I don't know how you could ask for more of a team, except to win one of those series, but the Montreal Canadiens were tough."

THE MEN

PIT MARTIN

One of the Blackhawks' valuable forwards during the seventies was Pit Martin. Known for being a good two-way hockey player, Martin was a Chicago Blackhawk from 1967-68 to 1977-78. Playing with Detroit, Boston, and after Chicago, Vancouver, his NHL career, which began in 1963, spanned 17 seasons.

Pit, whose real name is Jacques, got his nickname from a comic strip in a French newspaper. Raised in a family of six children, he was skating at age five and playing organized hockey by the age of eight. During his career, in a *Maple Leaf Gardens Program*, writer Margaret Scott once described Pit as "a swift, powerful skater, quick and

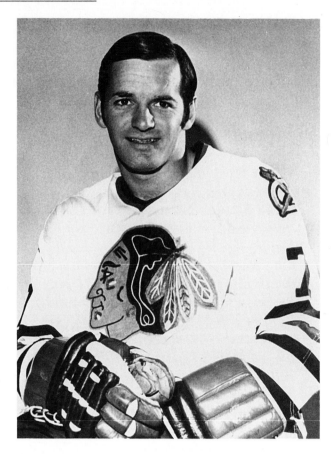

Pit Martin was an advocate of safety on the ice and felt that helmets should be compulsory. (Photo courtesy of the Blackhawks.)

adept around the net, and an insistent digger in the corners."

Wilf Cude, the goaltender that Harold March scored on in 1934, giving the Hawks their first Stanley Cup, coached Pit while he played for one of the Red Wing's midget clubs; the Noranda Oilers. It was he that, after his team won the Northern Ontario Hockey Association championship, recommended Pit be moved up to Junior. At the age of 15 he moved away from home to play for the Hamilton Red Wings of the Ontario Hockey Association. While there, he helped his team skate away with the Memorial Cup by scoring 42 goals and 46 assists.

After playing for about a month and a half for the Red Wing's minor league team in Pittsburgh, he turned pro with the Detroit Red Wings in 1963-64, when regular Alex Faulkner fractured his hand. He made such an impression after being placed on a line with Larry Jeffrey and Bruce MacGregor, that they later shipped Faulkner to the minors. Detroit later traded Martin to Boston, where he would be involved in another trade. That trade turned out to be one of the biggest, one-sided trades in NHL history.

Along with Gilles Marotte and Jack Norris, Pit came to Chicago in exchange for Phil Esposito, Ken Hodge, and Fred Stanfield. "I felt very good about the situation," commented Martin in the May 2, 1986 issue of *The Hockey News*, in an article by Randy Schultz. "Chicago had a winning team and was going somewhere. And I think if I remember correctly [and he did], Chicago had finished first the season before I joined them and I figured at that time that I was getting myself into a good situation."

When asked if he received any hostility from Chicago fans for coming to the Windy City in exchange for Esposito and Hodge, who became powerful hockey players with the Bruins, Martin explained:

> *"I don't think so. They had their fans, I'm sure. By the same token nobody cared all that much that I left Boston, I don't think all that many people cared that they left Chicago. They weren't superstars or anything at the time, neither was I. We were almost the same age, I suppose, and we were in the early years of our career. I don't think anybody thought anything more of it. I mean, I went to Chicago and they went to Boston. I really enjoyed Chicago and they probably really enjoyed Boston."*

Before reporting for duty in Chicago, Martin held out for a good part of training camp over a $1,500 difference in his contract.

> *"We were having a big argument as to whether I was going to make $18,500 that year or $20,000. So for $1,500 I held out for about 17 days; about half of training camp. Then he [Tommy Ivan] had old Jolly Jack Adams give me a call at home and told me he'd give me the $1,500, not to tell Clarence Campbell, and that I would have to sign a contract for $18,500 and he would give me the fifteen hundred*

> *bucks on the side...Mr. Campbell was the arbitrator of the case and said that since I was a lousy hockey player, $18,500 was plenty."*

Martin recently commented on his first game played in a Chicago uniform, an exhibition game in Montreal: "I'd only skated a few times since April [the previous season] and they dressed me anyway. I remember going out on the ice, my first shift. I got the face-off over to Bobby Hull and he gave it back to me. I shot and scored on Gump Worsley. The rest of the night I did nothing but go out there for 15 [or] 20 seconds at a time and get completely out of breath."

While playing for the Blackhawks, Martin skated on the M.P.H. line with Jim Pappin and Dennis Hull.

> *"They're two completely different guys," said Martin. "We, as a trio, worked very well together. We all got along. I think the biggest thing was that none of us were selfish, neither one of us was a selfish guy, and we had fun together off the ice as well. We hung together quite a bit off the ice. We had the same type of philosophy about the game. We were serious about it and we wanted to be recognized as good hockey players. Again, I think the unselfishness was the main thing. We didn't care who scored the goals as long as our line produced. That way the management would stay out of our hair and would keep us together, and we wouldn't have to fool around having to learn to play with different guys, so they kept us together for a long time. Of course Billy Reay had a lot to do with that. He was a pal of ours and we really liked him, and he liked us. [We were together] the better part of six years as I recall, and it made it real easy. We just went to training camp and we knew we'd be playing together. We'd play together the whole year, come back the next year, [and] it would be the same thing all over again. We*

didn't have to learn any new tricks or anything and it was just a matter of producing."

Being a professional athlete in the NHL was a little less high-profile during the days of hockey past than it is now. "Never more than a quarter of a page was given to the Blackhawks or hockey in general [in the newspaper]," explained Martin. "There was very little television coverage. Other than Bobby [Hull], Tony [Esposito] was recognized some, and Keith Magnuson a lot because he was a recognizable type. They're the only three guys I can think of who may have had to make their trips to the store when it was quiet, rather than any hour of the day or something like that. I could go to the grocery store or the bank or anything like that and absolutely nothing ever happened."

Martin has owned and flown his own airplane and has attended Windsor College and McMaster University, where he earned his B.A. He also received the Bill Masterton trophy for dedication, sportsmanship, and perseverance, in 1970. He was the third person to ever receive the award.

After getting the award, Martin commented in the June 11, 1970 issue of the *Montreal Star*: "This is quite a thrill for me. I don't think I could win one of the big five trophies and I'm grateful for the writers for starting this award. It's probably the most important trophy I'll ever receive." He explains today:

"It was kind of a low key thing at the time. There was really no publicity made about it. It was given to me at the draft meeting that June, I guess. I got a phone call saying I'd won the Masterton, would I come to Montreal and accept it. I went to Montreal and we went into this little room where there were a couple of photographers and I hoisted this trophy. They gave me some kind of a little replica that I still have that's, more or less, not falling apart, it's of such poor quality that I don't even have it out in my house. It's in the basement somewhere because people would ask me what it was and you couldn't even read what they had

engraved on it. It wasn't because I didn't take care of it, it was just because of the material it was made of."

At the time, Martin commented that he felt helmets should be compulsory. An advocate of safety, he claimed that players such as Bill Masterton could have avoided injury by wearing them.

Martin, who had eight 20 or more goal seasons, three 30 or more goal seasons, and one 90-point season, is also well known for something he did off of the ice. After the Blackhawks finished in sixth place in 1968-69 despite a star-studded line-up, Pit's words appeared in newspapers everywhere, as he blamed management for the state of things in a 1971 issue of *Hockey World*. "We finished last in the '68–69 season because management wasn't interested in winning," he said at the time. "They constantly made concessions to favored players and sacrificed the morale of the whole team in doing so."

The poor finish wasn't entirely management's fault, but was a failure by the team as well in the respect that they weren't functioning well as a unit. The next season, partly because Martin opened some eyes, the Blackhawks were able to bring the Prince of Wales trophy to Chicago as they finished first in the East Division.

Since his career with Chicago ended, Martin has been involved in several different pursuits. "Since I stopped playing I ... did some Hockey Night in Canada stuff, doing some commentary on television for a couple years," said Martin, who last visited Chicago Stadium to see the '91 All Star game. "Then I owned a restaurant here in Windsor [Ontario] for about three years and then I sold that. Since that time, since '86, I've owned a swimming pool servicing business here in Windsor...The longer you stay in professional sports, the less opportunities there are when you come out, I found anyway. Even though I have a university education and everything, nobody seemed very crazy about hiring me [after hockey] for anything because I was 35, 36, 37 years old."

Today, he continues to play for fun. "I just play with guys around here [Windsor, Ontario]. Mostly guys in their thirties who never really played pro hockey and they just like to go out for fun."

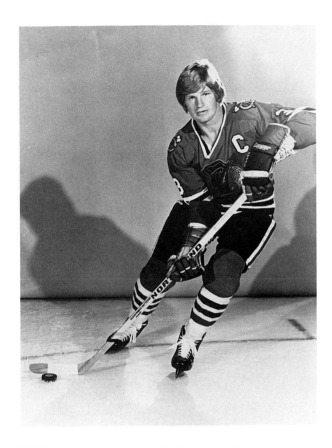

Keith Magnuson was known to drop the gloves on occasion.
(Photo courtesy of the Blackhawks.)

KEITH MAGNUSON

One of the most memorable Chicago defensemen of all time is, without a doubt, Keith Magnuson. Born the son of an insurance salesman on April 27, 1947, in Wadena, Saskatchewan, Keith played defense for the Hawks from 1969-70 to 1979-80. In 589 regular season games he racked up 1,442 minutes in penalties, and scored 14 goals and 125 assists. Including the playoffs, Magnuson racked up 1,606 minutes in penalties.

Magnuson commented years ago in George Vass' book *The Chicago Blackhawk Story* about playing in the big leagues.

"It is all I ever wanted to be from the time I knew what being a pro meant. Nothing else has ever appealed to me. When I was ten years old I'd go

with my best friend, Tim Gould, to the rink after school. We'd stay there until they threw us out, sometimes until 1:00 in the morning. Our parents would worry about where we were."

However, pro hockey wasn't the only height that he reached. Magnuson also attended Denver University where he played with longtime Blackhawk counterpart and friend Cliff Koroll.

At the time of Magnuson's retirement, Koroll gave his view of Keith and their friendship over the years in an article by Neil Milbert that appeared in the November 16, 1979 issue of *The Hockey News*:

"Keith and I go back to when we were 12-year old kids in Saskatoon. We played against each other in elementary school and high school—not only in hockey but in all sports. In football Keith was a [good]...quarterback. He threw the javelin and ran the mile in track, and he was a catcher with a lousy arm in baseball. No matter what sport it was, he had the same enthusiasm. When I was about 15-16, I was pretty close to the size I am now (6-1 and 195 pounds). And here was this little red-headed shrimp of about 5-2 and 130 pounds who kept taking runs at me when I'd get the puck in the corner. My senior year we won the NCAA Tournament and I was the captain. The next year, when I was playing minor league hockey in Dallas, Denver won the NCAA Tournament again and Keith was the captain. In college, Keith was a little more offensive-minded. He scored more goals in four years in Denver than he did in ten in the NHL."

Koroll recently elaborated further on the glory days he and Keith spent at Denver. "I guess I'll never forget that final game we played up in Duluth against the University of North Dakota. We were at the NCAA finals a couple of other years that I was there. We lost by a disputed goal another time, which I had scored. But this time [his senior year], it was ten minutes to go in the game and there was still no score. We ended up winning the game four to nothing."

Coach Reay had reservations about college graduates playing in the NHL, as far as their readiness and priorities were concerned. But in Magnuson's case, his desire, determination, and "all-out" attitude were incredible and quickly shot down any doubts about where he stood. He would spend his summers lifting weights and during the season would put in extra hours of practice, and always gave it his all during game time.

"I was lucky," he once explained in a *Chicago Tribune* article by Bob Verdi. "I came to the Blackhawks the year after they finished last in 1969, and they needed help on defense. I made the team, and we had a lot of us rookies, and Tony Esposito was fantastic, and we wound up winning the division. So I had to be fortunate to be coming up at just that time. I was lucky!" Magnuson would also often comment that he had to work extra hard at the game because he lacked God-given talent such as that found in Bobby Orr.

Something people used to make a big deal about was the fact that Keith took boxing and karate lessons during his career. "The business about my taking boxing and karate lessons has been blown up a little more than I care to see," he said at the time in an article by Bob Verdi that appeared in the January 29, 1971 issue of *The Hockey News*. "I won't back down from anyone and I'll go with anyone— that's the way you have to be. But I care a lot about kids, the young hockey fans. And I don't think they should get the impression that hockey is all fights, or the impression that you have to be more of [a] fighter than a player."

Off the ice, Keith Magnuson was known to be a gentleman and would often stay after games to sign autographs. In 1978-79, he appeared in only 26 games, and after undergoing his third knee operation, finally hung up his skates. "I wasn't helping anymore," he said in an unidentified source. "I knew I couldn't play every game because the knee wasn't getting any better. I knew that when we went with four defensemen, that I wasn't going to play, that I would only play when we went with six. I knew that even when I played, I couldn't do what I wanted to. I didn't have much ability to start with. I couldn't skate that well, or shoot that well, or pass the puck that well. I always had to

labor, even when everything was going all right. So when it wasn't all right…"

After quitting his on-ice duties, Magnuson became an assistant coach to Eddie Johnston. "His value doesn't show up in the stats," commented Johnston in the same source many years ago. "He had heart. When he played, when he practiced, he always had spirit. I wish I could spread it around to some of these other guys."

Keith later gave coaching a shot, but it didn't work out. Today, he resides in the Chicago area and works as an executive in the soft drink industry.

BILL WHITE

Another customary defensive pair during the early seventies was that of Bill White and Pat Stapleton. Bill White, who actually came to Chicago as a replacement for Stapleton when he injured his knee, later shared defensive responsibilities with him. The pair worked together well in that Pat was an excellent play-maker, and White didn't usually venture too far up the ice.

Bill White, known as a "defensive-defenseman," also coached one season for the Hawks. (Photo courtesy of the Blackhawks.)

In an unidentified source, coach Reay once commented on White: "He's not spectacular, but he does a solid, workman-like job. He doesn't make too many mistakes. He's not going to dazzle anyone, but he's just the steady, dependable sort of defenseman we need." White made the All-Star team three seasons in a row during his career (second team: 1971-72 '72-73, and '73-74).

Born in Toronto, Ontario, on August 26, 1939, the 6'1", 195-pound Bill White was often described as the League's best defensive-defenseman during his career, possessing defensive skills that were nearly flawless. While on the ice, he emphasized keeping things in order in the Hawks end of the rink, and feeding accurate passes to the forwards.

The fact that he wasn't a great goal-scoring defenseman wasn't because he lacked the ability to be one. Rather, it was because of the strict defensive system that coach Billy Reay emphasized, which included a lot of passing and the avoidance of getting caught too deep in the offensive zone.

White played junior hockey for the Toronto Marlboros. He turned pro in 1960 in the Maple Leafs system, dividing his first professional year up between Sudbury of the old Eastern League and the AHL Rochester Americans. He was then sold to Eddie Shore's AHL team in Springfield, where he was stuck for five years. The demand for NHL defensemen at the time reportedly wasn't great enough for teams to pay the kind of price Shore wanted for his players. "We tried to get him out of Springfield several times," explained Tommy Ivan to Dan Moulton in the April 20, 1979 issue of the *Sporting News*. "We thought he had the ability to help us, but Shore put a price on him that we just didn't feel we could pay. And I'm sure a lot of other teams had the same experience."

White is remembered for an incident that occurred while he was playing for the Springfield team. Shore fined the team for indifferent play the day after they had beaten Quebec 7-2! White, along with other players, went on strike and acquired the services of lawyer Alan Eagleson, who was practicing in Toronto at the time. Everything eventually got resolved before the players missed any games, and Shore's son took over the team, selling it to Jack Kent Cooke, who happened to be the new owner of the Los Angeles franchise in the NHL.

Despite his quarrel with Eddie Shore, White also had some respect for the man. "I am grateful to Shore for some things, though," he once commented in an April 20, 1979 *Sporting News* article by Dan Moulton. "He was a very patient coach and really taught his players what the game is all about. He'd have you do a certain thing over and over until it became automatic. I owe a lot to Shore's practices."

White played for Los Angeles before coming to the Hawks in 1969-70, where he remained until 1975-76. Including the play-offs, he scored a career total 57 goals and 247 assists, for 304 points in 695 games.

Bill White later gave coaching the Blackhawks a short trial in 1976-77. "That was hard to do," he explained in the same *Sporting News* article, "because I had played with a lot of those guys. We had Bobby Orr, but he was near the end of his career and his knee couldn't stand it anymore. And we had Stan Mikita, and he tried to help me as an assistant coach, but that didn't work out, and he just went back to playing."

In 1979, White replaced George Armstrong as coach of the Toronto Marlboros, and later worked as a sales representative for Cory Copy Systems in Toronto.

JIM PAPPIN

Jim Pappin played right-wing for the Chicago Blackhawks from 1968-69 to 1974-75. Including the play-offs, he scored 311 goals and 640 points in 859 games over the course of his 14-season NHL career.

Born in Copper Cliff, Ontario, Pappin grew up playing hockey for the athletic association in his home town. He was spotted early by scouts for the Detroit Red Wings, but in a twist of bad luck came down with the flu at their training camp and was forgotten. Later, a Toronto scout by the name of Bob Davidson spotted him and Jim ended up playing for the Toronto Marlboros.

In a humorous incident, Pappin and his Marlboro teammates played a game in top hats and tails against the Guelph Biltmores in 1959 after the Biltmore's coach, Eddie Bush, had said that they dress like a "bunch of bums."

Pappin turned pro in 1960 with Sudbury of the old Eastern League, and then played for the AHL

Jim Pappin–right-wing for Chicago from 1968 to 1975. (Photo courtesy of the Blackhawks.)

Rochester Americans. Jim's future coach, Billy Reay, was coaching the Sault Ste. Marie team of the same league at the time. In later years he commented in an Associated Press article by Ben Olan: "When you see a kid like that, you don't forget him, no matter who he's playing for. You just take his name and file it away somewhere. And if he ever becomes available, you grab him."

The fans in Rochester never did take to Pappin and were always all over him for making even the simplest of mistakes, despite two seasons in which he scored 28 and 34 goals. He spent quite a few seasons going back and forth between the Maple Leafs and their minor league Americans.

Eventually, he was brought up late in the 1966-67 season and he scored 21 goals for them. They sent him back to the minors, but called him back up in time for the play-offs. Once back, he led the Leafs to the Cup by leading the team in points with

15 in 12 games (7 goals, 8 assists). He also scored the winning goal that gave the Leafs the Stanley Cup over Montreal. At the time it was Toronto's eleventh Cup in franchise history, and the fourth in six years! It was the first time in nearly two decades that a member of the Maple Leafs had been a leader in play-off scoring since Ted Kennedy accomplished the feat in the play-offs of 1948.

"I was on the team in '64 when we won too," he recalls. "[In '64] it was the third time that [that particular] team had won [the Stanley Cup], but it was my first time. That's always the biggest one, the first time you win. But then in the second one, I led the scoring in the playoffs and I scored the winner. I remember we beat Chicago out, Terry Sawchuck played outstandingly in Chicago. Then against Montreal, Bower played the first few games until he got hurt, five games I guess, since Sawchuck came in and played the last game. All I remember is good goaltending the whole series. I scored the winning goal, but it was in the second period when I scored it, to give us a 2-nothing lead. So, it's not like you scored a winning goal in overtime. That's just the way it worked out. Anytime you win a championship it's a great thrill."

Surprisingly, after his sterling accomplishments, the Leafs shipped him back to Rochester the next season. Pappin refused to report and went on a ski trip instead. When he finally did return, he was traded to the Hawks for Pierre Pilote.

When asked what was behind his woes with the Maple Leafs, Pappin explains:

"Well, I never really got along with the coach. The year before, I had bonuses I got for winning the Stanley Cup and scoring the winning goal and being the leading scorer. I had a thousand dollar bonus for scoring 25 goals in the National League. I scored 22 but he sent me to Rochester. Even that [championship] year, he sent me to Rochester for a couple of weeks. I scored five or six goals down there and they didn't pay me the bonus because he said it wasn't NHL. But I was under an NHL contract. So, I argued with him all summer about that. Then I argued with him over a contract at train-

ing camp. Then, I never got along with him all winter so, he saw that the team wasn't gonna make the playoffs, and Rochester had a good chance of winning, so he sent me down to Rochester. He did that three times and we won three times in Rochester. I was on six championship teams in a row. Every time Toronto had a chance of winning I played for Toronto, and when Rochester had a chance of winning he sent me to Rochester. There were only six teams in the National League then, and only eight in the American League, there were only 14 pro teams. I was trying to get out of Toronto my whole career. I just got lucky and he sent me to Chicago. He [Imlach] could've sent me anywhere."

It was a shame that he was shuffled between the pros and minors for so long, because many believed him to be too good for the minor leagues. In 1965-66, he scored 36 goals and 51 assists in 63 games for Rochester. In the Calder Cup play-offs that season, he scored eight goals in 12 games, including a hat trick in one contest against Cleveland.

"If you talk to anyone that played with me, they know I was a poor loser," he said, looking back on the philosophy that helped make him an effective player. *"I was always hot. Wanting to win was the biggest thing, [I] couldn't stand losing. As far as an approach [is concerned], my goal was to get four or five goals a month, which would give me 35 a year. That's basically what I ended up with for my whole career, I averaged about 35 goals a year. That's the only goal I set, to score five goals a month. It's like when you go to the races, you get a racing form. Every time we'd play a game, I'd look at the other team to see who [was] playing and to see who we'd probably play against. [Then I'd] figure out what we'd probably have to do to beat them, that's all. Nothing's changed. Today*

they have video and all that stuff. We didn't have the video, we just had to go over it ourselves, game by game."

Recalling those who had the biggest influence on his career, Pappin said:

"I played junior for a good coach named Turk Broda, he used to be a goaltender for Toronto. He actually was the one that turned me into a hockey player. [Then], Billy Reay made me go from being just another hockey player to a better-than-average player. He knew how to motivate me. He knew how to use what I had to help the team, I guess. He used me in the right way. Imlach would always scream at you about not being able to check and all that stuff. I came here and Billy Reay made me a penalty killer. He made me learn how to check instead of just screaming about it. It [was] a whole different approach. He could read people a lot better, Billy was pretty sharp."

Before he was able to report to the Hawks training camp in 1970-71, he was struck with a case of Bell's Palsy. "I went to have a soft drink," he once commented in an Associated Press article by Ben Olan, "and the soda just dribbled out of the corner of my mouth. I looked in the mirror and the whole left side of my face was sagging ... dropping down. I thought I had polio. For almost four months, I had no movement in the left side of my face. The only good thing about it was that I didn't have to go to training camp. I watched a lot of baseball games while the other guys were getting in shape."

After he began playing for the Hawks, Jim was placed on the successful MPH line with Pit Martin and Dennis Hull. Hull once described Pappin at the time when he was first put on their line. "We're sure glad to have him on our line," he said in the January, 1969 issue of *Hockey World*. "He can really put the puck in the net. But he checks too; in fact, he's the kind of player who's concerned about checking. He doesn't want to go just one way."

Pappin recently commented about playing on the MPH Line:

"They [Chicago] actually made the trade with Toronto to get me to play with Bobby Hull and Pit Martin. In that training camp, Bobby Hull held out. He was in training camp, but he held out the first five games of the season, so they put Dennis Hull on my line with Pit Martin. We clicked right off the bat, so I never did play with Bobby Hull. We got to be good friends, we communicated well. Dennis had the big shot, he could shoot as hard as Bobby. He was just a kid then and all he needed was a little stability. Pit Martin had great speed and could move the puck. All my job was to make plays, try to set Dennis up, go to the front of the net. It just fluked out the way it worked, our three different styles complemented each other, so we ended up having a terrific line for about seven years."

Coach Billy Reay said the following of Pappin, who often received flak from Stadium fans, just as he did in Rochester in the same Ben Olan article.

"They don't appreciate what Jimmy's doing out there," he began. *"He's a tall guy and he doesn't waste any motion. So, sometimes I think the people confuse that for not working hard. But you've seen players who skate all over the ice, and what do they accomplish? You can't confuse all that motion for necessarily getting things done. I suppose if Jimmy weren't so tall and didn't take such long strides, he'd look like he was exerting himself as much as the guy who takes short, choppy strides. But Pappin has tremendous anticipation and reflexes. I can tell you that his defensive record pleases me, and show you that anybody he plays with will go well."*

Pappin recently shed some light on why he was not popular with Chicago Stadium fans, stating:

"I very seldom signed autographs, unless it was at the right time. I would never sign them before a game. Going into the building, I would never stop and sign them because I was too focused [and] didn't want to be bothered. Bobby Hull used to come in late all the time because he'd stand out there and sign autographs. It wasn't my mindset to do that. After games I'd sign. But when I'd see the same people getting autographs, it would just piss me off, so I'd just keep walking. By doing that, you get a lot of people mad at you because there are other people out there, but [oftentimes] it was always the same people over and over and over when you come out after [a game], so you just get tired of it after awhile."

Jim Pappin is currently a scout for the Blackhawks. After he finished playing for the Hawks, he played for Calgary and Cleveland before leaving the NHL. "I still work for the Blackhawks," he said. "[I've been doing that] basically ever since I retired. [I'm their] Pro Scout. I started doing the juniors and the colleges and after I found them Roenick and Belfour, they moved me up to Pro Scout. I didn't really do that, but they were in my jurisdiction. I saw them the most, and had the most to say about it, but a lot of the other scouts saw them too, so we got lucky."

CLIFF KOROLL

One of the most consistent wingers for the Hawks during the seventies was Cliff Koroll. Koroll, like his former roommate Keith Magnuson, is an alumnus of Denver University. During his career he was one of the few collegiately-experienced athletes in the League. Before breaking into the NHL with the Blackhawks, Koroll spent a year playing pro hockey with Dallas of the Central League.

Thinking back to his childhood, Koroll recalled his beginnings in the world of ice hockey. "I had

Cliff Koroll played 10 seasons with the Blackhawks as a winger. (Photo courtesy of the Blackhawks.)

three older brothers," he said. "They used to build a rink in the back yard all the time, each winter, give me a pair of their old skates, and shove me out there. I started at the age of three, skatin' in the back yard, and away I went from there. I had somebody to play with all the time and try to teach me what had to be taught. I guess it must've worked."

While playing for Denver, where he served as team captain, Koroll helped his team win the NCAA Championship his senior year.

"I think, number one, if it weren't for going through the college ranks, I would've never made professional hockey," he explained. "I made that choice when I was about 14 or 15 years old, that I wanted to get an education. I bypassed playing junior hockey in Canada to pursue an education. So, right off the bat, if you were gonna make it, you were coming in the back

door anyway. There were four of us that came together at that same time. I think breaking the barrier, so to speak, wasn't that difficult because there were four of us and we were successful that first year when the team went from last place the previous year to first place. So I think having that success really helped. It showed the people that college hockey wasn't so bad after all."

Recalling what it was like to play his first professional game in Chicago Stadium, Koroll described what kind of an experience it was.

"I remember my legs were numb. It's pretty tough walkin' up those stairs to get on the ice. I had a few exhibition games before that, so it kind of broke you in a little as to what to expect. But it really was a great thrill. I remember I couldn't sleep the night before, and had trouble eating all that day before the game. It was really a great experience. It's something I've never forgotten and probably never will. You finally realize your boyhood dreams, and that was to play in the National Hockey League."

Koroll came to the Hawks as a replacement for Kenny "Whip" Wharram who had experienced heart trouble that forced him to hang up his skates. Doctors once caused Koroll some worry when they thought he also had a heart condition after he went in for a check up. When Koroll arrived home from the physical, the doctor phoned him, explaining that he wanted to see Cliff right away because they thought he had an enlarged heart.

"I nearly drove my car off the road returning to the hospital, my hands were so sweaty," said Koroll at the time in a January 10, 1973 *The Hockey News* article by Bob Verdi. "I couldn't stop thinking about Kenny Wharram. I was in a daze. Only when I got back and they checked me again did they realize that it was a defect in the x-ray, that there was nothing wrong. I can't tell you what a relief that was."

Cliff, who spent 10 years with the Hawks (1969-70 to 1979-80), once played with Dan Maloney on a line with Stan Mikita. Stan once gave this impression of Koroll in the February, 1974 issue of *Hockey World*: "I had a bad back for most of the time Cliff was breaking in [stemming from an incident in which he was cross-checked in the small of his back]. He knew this and did more of the dirty work in the corners than anyone realizes. And he listens and learns and works hard, harder than most people believe. He practices longer than many and never stops trying to improve his shot and other phases of his game."

Koroll attributed much of his success as an athlete to Mikita, once explaining that playing with Stan was the greatest thing that ever happened to him.

Koroll gave his opinion of what type of an athlete he was during his NHL career.

"I think I was the type of player that could do a lot of things," he began. "I was an offensive player. I scored quite a few goals in college. I can't remember exactly what I had in Dallas the first year. So, the offensive abilities were there. But I think the strong point was the defensive play which, like I said earlier, was taught to us by Murray Armstrong. I think that really helped me make it in the National Hockey League. I always played the power play and I killed penalties all the time so [I was] sort of an all-around type player. I wasn't going to be a 50 goal-scorer by any means, but I certainly had some great years. Thirty-three goals, I guess, was the highest I had the one year [1972-73]. But, I had several 20+ seasons."

Continuing the description of his playing career, Koroll stated that he focused more on defense in his later years with the Blackhawks.

"As my career went on, I got into more of a defensive mode, our line having to play the top lines on other teams, becoming a checking line so to speak,

and spending a lot of time penalty killing. So, the goal production dropped off because of more emphasis on stopping the opposition as opposed to doing all the scoring. Stan [Mikita] and I would always end up playing on the top line on every team. So, eventually you get in that defensive shell."

Vic Hadfield, who used to play left-wing for the New York Rangers and Pittsburgh Penguins, once gave an opponent's view of Cliff in a January 2, 1976 *The Hockey News* article by Bob Verdi: "I'll tell you what he reminds me of. You know those big table hockey games where you pull the knob and the players just go up and down the wing? Well, that's Cliff Koroll. Up and down, never strays, always there, nothing flashy."

The ever-consistent winger, who scored 208 goals and 462 points in 814 games, later coached Milwaukee of the IHL and spent seven years as assistant coach of the Blackhawks.

"After I retired, I was assistant coach for seven years with the Hawks," he said. "I enjoyed it. It's a lot tougher than I realized as a player. You kind of take for granted everything the coach did until you really got in the situation yourself. There's a lot of work involved, a lot of responsibility. It was enjoyable."

Cliff Koroll also worked in the Hawks' front office for two years, doing public relations work, as well as sales and marketing. He also did computer work for the draft, among the many other things he did within the organization. He worked for an independent company that works with suppliers to McDonald's restaurants. "They're an extension of McDonald's and they're part of the McDonald's family," he explained. "At McDonald's direction, they control about five suppliers to McDonald's worldwide."

DENNIS HULL

One of the Blackhawks' better forwards during the 1970s was Dennis Hull. Born on November 19, 1944 in Pointe Anne, Ontario, he played left-wing for Chicago from 1964-65 to 1976-77. Later he spent a season with the Detroit Red Wings before retiring. Including the play-offs, Dennis scored 336 goals and recorded 385 assists for 721 points in 1,063 games over the course of his 14-season NHL career. He was a second-team All-Star in 1973 and played for Team Canada in 1972.

Some called Dennis "The Silver Jet" only partly in fun. Many believed his shot to be slightly harder than his older brother Bobby's.

Reminiscing about days long ago, when he learned to play the game with his brothers, Hull said:

"I grew up in a small town in Canada. It was a cement factory town. I used to play [hockey] on the Bay of Quinte; it was a body of water right in our town that boats used to come in [on] to pick up the cement. My brothers and I used to shovel off a patch of ice as big as a rink. For some strange reason, as soon as we finished getting it shoveled off, there were enough kids around there for a game. Just playing there with my brothers on the Bay of Quinte [stands out in my mind].

"We played all of the different sports. But in Canada, hockey is the number one sport. Everybody plays, but I'm not sure everybody thinks about playing in the NHL. Although, I guess almost everyone does. Hockey Night In Canada is what everyone [watches] on Saturday night there; [watching] the game of the week.

"So, we played all the sports. Bobby was obviously better than everyone else when he was playing minor hockey and playing baseball and football and all those things. He's just a great athlete. My other brothers and I obviously weren't that good, but we loved to play just as much. I ended up playing with my other two brothers in Junior hockey in Belleville, [Ontario], that was Junior B. Then, the Blackhawks asked me to go to St. Catharines and unfortunately, my other two brothers didn't get a chance to go."

Dennis Hull was on the "MPH Line" with Pit Martin and Jim Pappin. (Photo courtesy of the Blackhawks.)

Dennis played Junior A hockey for the St. Catharines Tee Pees, just like Bobby. After a slow start there, he scored 48 goals in his fourth season, 15 more than Bobby had during his best season with St. Catharines.

He was only 16 years old when he came to the Tee Pees in the fall of 1960. Just as it would be when he finally moved up to the Blackhawks, he was overshadowed in some aspects by his older brother. Many of the St. Catharines players were older than Dennis, and because of his name, they were extra hard on him.

"Bobby had already left home and began his great career when I was just starting out," he said in Bill Libby's book *Pro Hockey Heroes of Today*, recalling those early years. "When I played near home, my dad kept me informed on Bobby's exploits. When I got to St. Catharines, my coach there kept me up to date on him. He did so much every step of the way that it was hard to live up to."

Today, looking back over his career in a different perspective, Hull sheds a new light on that situation, commenting:

"If you think about it there was no problem until I did get to Chicago, simply because Canadians understand the game of hockey and they understand how one person is obviously better than the other and how most Canadians realized the difference in our talent. So, it was never really a problem until I got to Chicago, and it really wasn't a problem there. It was simply the fact that people thought that I should play like Bobby. Of course, the players on my team and my coach obviously knew that that wasn't possible. So, I think as players and coaches we laughed at it more than anything else. The fans are the ones that sort of thought that I should play like Bobby. I wish I could've; I wasn't the only one who couldn't play like Bobby. But,…as I mentioned, I really didn't become Bobby Hull's brother until I got to the Chicago Blackhawks."

"[Dennis took a lot of heat for being Bobby's brother] earlier when he was a kid, but he came into his own about the time I got there," said former teammate Jim Pappin. "He gave me credit for turning him into a hockey player. The fans used to get on him all of the time and boo him. So one day in the paper, I got mad and said, 'I wish the fans would boo me instead of him.' So they turned around and started booing me for the rest of the time that I played here and didn't boo him anymore. But at least it got them off his back. It never bothered me because I wasn't a fan-type person anyway."

When asked if this situation changed after Bobby jumped to Winnipeg of the WHA, Hull said: "No, I don't think so. That never changed in Chicago. I did get a chance to play more on the power play after Bobby went to Winnipeg, you can see that in my statistics. I made the All-Star team the year Bobby went to the WHA as well. But, it's just the fact that I got a chance to play more."

Former coach Billy Reay remembers Hull as one of his favorite athletes. "It's a strange thing, but Dennis Hull, he was one of my projects that I enjoyed very, very much because there was so much pressure on the kid because he was Bobby's brother. He didn't have a lot of confidence and I used to tell him, 'Dennis, as long as I'm here, you'll be here, so quit worrying.'"

In the 1973 play-offs, Hull was a powerful force in the Blackhawks race for the Stanley Cup against Montreal. It was he who scored the game-tying goal in the fifth game of that final series, which allowed them to eventually win 8-7. However, the Hawks lost 6-4 in the sixth game, and the Cup went to Montreal. Scotty Bowman, who was coaching the Canadiens at the time, admitted that they had to shadow him quite a bit in order to be successful.

Former teammate Bill Hay gave his impression of Dennis: "Dennis Hull was a favorite of mine when he came into the League as a rookie," he said. "[He was overshadowed by Bobby] a little bit, but it didn't affect him. He's a good-natured fellow and he had some good talent."

Former coach Billy Reay explained what type of an athlete Dennis was in Bill Libby's book *Pro Hockey Heroes of Today*:

"Dennis is an honest, hard-working player who can take the tough going. He's durable. He's smart. He plays his position. He plays what we call positional hockey. He makes very few mistakes. He shadows his man. He takes the openings as they present themselves. He has nearly as hard a shot as his brother. If he has a fault, it's a tendency to try too hard. When he starts to slump, he worries and he presses. That's why he has a good year, then a bad year scoring-wise. But he always has a good year playing-wise."

Gary Edwards, who spent 13 seasons minding the nets in the NHL for various clubs, gave his impression of Hull in Libby's book:

"He has a good short shot, but he really hurts you with his slap-shot. He gets it off fast, on the move, before you can get set for it. It comes in hard and high. It's not as hard as Bobby's, but seems heavier. Maybe because of the sort of shot a player has, the sort of spin he puts on the puck, some shots seem heavier than others. Dennis makes that little rubber disk seem like a heavy hunk of steel. If you get in front of it, it hurts you wherever it hits you."

Today, looking back over his career, Hull describes himself as a player: "I'd say [I was] pretty average. Maybe [I had a few]…little ups and downs. I had a couple of ups that I'm pretty proud of; being the leading scorer in the play-offs a couple of times, and assisting on Bobby's 500th goal, making the All-Star team, and scoring 40 goals."

The "downs" Hull went through were in part attributed to the critical fans at Chicago Stadium:

"The disappointing thing for me is the fact that I scored 300 goals, and I scored 200 of them on the road. If you score 200 goals on the road, you should at least score that many at home. So, I was a 400-goal scorer on the road and a 200-goal scorer at the Stadium. It was disappointing not being able to perform at the Stadium, simply because of what the fans wanted, and how they reacted to my play. A lot of times, when we were winning or losing, Billy Reay would sit me on the bench just so I didn't have to go through that. It was difficult to play there, for sure. The numbers don't lie. It would've been nice to be a 400-goal scorer instead of a 300-goal scorer. I was a 400-goal scorer on the road, so I was pretty proud of that."

Dennis Hull was a linemate on the MPH line, along with Pit Martin and Jim Pappin. The line was quite a scoring combination for the Blackhawks during the 1970s. Recalling the days when the trio was together, Hull said:

"Jim Pappin and Pit Martin were the perfect linemates for me, and they were also my best friends. It's hard to ask for anything more than that. I

think if you talk to anyone who's on a line, the most important thing is that you're friends, [that] you like each other. I think it's very difficult to play with someone who you don't really see eye to eye with. Ya know, we did everything before the games and after the games together, so that's the number one, important thing. When you're out there on the ice and you're playing with your friends, that's number one.

"But, to get to the hockey part of it, Jim Pappin [was] probably one of the best play-making right-wingers, one of the smartest players to ever play. If you want to talk about underrated guys. Ya know, he knew how to play hockey as well as anyone that I'd ever played with or had seen play.

"Pit Martin had a lot of speed, and Jimmy and I were fast as well, so it ended up that we worked perfectly together. One of the things Billy Reay always used to say in the paper [was that]; 'You have to stop Stan's line,' or he'd say; 'You have to stop Bobby's line,' when we went into another team's rink. He was just setting them up and we would do a lot of the damage; Jimmy and Pit and I in the visiting rinks. All you have to do is check our numbers to see that.

"We would work on lots of things in practice, not that we were great practice players. Billy Reay said we were the worst practice players he'd ever seen. But once the game started, we could perform."

Recalling the one game he'll never forget, Hull regrets that it wasn't with Chicago. "I had a chance to play for Team Canada in the World Championships in 1972," he said. "We beat the Russians with 32 seconds to go in the final game in Moscow, so that was pretty special."

Dennis was traded to the Red Wings in the 1977-78 season, after which he retired from professional play. Commenting on what he has pursued since leaving the NHL as a player, Hull said:

"I went back to school [at] Brock University in Canada [St. Catharines], and I got my degree in history. I taught at a private school and coached the hockey team. Then I came back to Chicago and I was the athletic director at the Illinois Institute of Technology for ten years. I now help out in their development office, raising funds. I did the color for San Jose in their first year. It was a great experience to see a new team formed; see the first game, the first goal, the first win on the road, the first of everything. It's a whole bunch of firsts that will never happen again, so it was a lot of fun."

JOHN MARKS

Born in Hamiota, Manitoba, John Marks played left-wing for the Blackhawks from 1972-73 to 1981-82. During his career he broke Glenn Hall's record of consecutive games played [now held by Steve Larmer] on December 16, 1979, the 50th anniversary of Chicago Stadium.

Marks moved to Winnipeg at the age of 12 where his father ran a restaurant and general store after his mother passed away. He later attended the University of North Dakota before turning pro. After that, he spent two years with Dallas of the Central League.

An intelligent hockey player who always made the right moves when it counted most, Marks possessed good puck-handling skills and strong skating ability, as well as a hard shot from the point. Including the play-offs, he scored 117 goals and 289 points in 714 games.

Marks would rather have played defense during his days in Chicago, as he did during his childhood, at the University of North Dakota, and up until his second year in the minors. "When I came up to the Hawks in 1972-73, I was a defenseman until the semifinals of the play-offs. The team felt I was effective at forward and I've liked it well enough," he said in a January 4, 1980 article by Bill Libby, which appeared in *The Hockey News*, "but within me I think I might have been better at defense and might be a pretty good defenseman by now if I'd stayed there."

John Marks was the first Blackhawk player to break Glenn Hall's record for consecutive games played. (Photo courtesy of the Blackhawks.)

"That Johnny Marks was a guy that we drafted years before and then he went to college...," Billy Reay recently explained. "[He] was a kid that we had when he was 15 years old. I can remember tellin' him that if he went to college, that when he finished that I'd do everything I could do to help him out. He turned out to be a pretty good hockey player for the Hawks. He played left-wing and he played defense."

Although never a big goal-scorer who attracted enormous amounts of attention, 6'2", 200-pound Marks possessed remarkable endurance and made his contribution to the team. Veteran referee Andy vanHellemond recalled: "John Marks couldn't score well, it wasn't easy for him to score goals. He wasn't a gifted goal scorer. He worked hard and in his prime there were some other teams like the Flyers who tried to trade for him because he was their kind of player. He worked hard, worked the boards hard and in the corner. He could play forward and defense. He was on the line with Mikita and Koroll for awhile."

Until the 1992-93 season, he served as the coach of the Indianapolis Ice of the International Hockey League, and coached in Pittsburgh's farm system as well.

GRANT MULVEY

From 1974-75 to 1982-83, 6'4", 200-pound, Grant Mulvey played right-wing for the Chicago Blackhawks. Born in Sudbury, Ontario, on September, 17, 1956, Grant Mulvey played junior hockey for the Calgary Centennials of the WCHL, where he scored 31 goals in one season before reporting directly to the Blackhawks' training camp at the age of 17.

He was the Windy City's number-one amateur draft pick in 1974. After reporting to the Hawks, he was never sent down to the minors during his first season. It was his size and physical style of play that caught the attention of scouts.

"There was a little bit of time when I kind of wished that I would've been able to learn at a slower pace," said Mulvey. "However, the rules at that time indicated that a player had to stay with the big team or go back to his junior team, and Chicago wanted me to stay with the big team."

When asked about what it was like for him, as a young rookie, to report to the Chicago Blackhawks, Mulvey said:

"First of all, the excitement and the nostalgia that was behind the Chicago Blackhawks was incredible. They had just come off of a couple of great seasons in 1971-72, '72-73. Chicago was at an all-time high in excitement. Channel nine, WGN, was our TV station at the time and [they] covered all the games. There was just a nice fever for hockey in Chicago at that time. However, it was dwindling away because Bobby Hull had left and the World Hockey [Association] had come in. Chicago was unable to acquire anybody as great as Bobby Hull was, to be able to electrify the fans."

In an April 9, 1980 *The Hockey News* article with columnist Neil Milbert, Mulvey once offered a bit of his philosophy on making it to the Black-

hawks. "From the time I broke in I knew I could play in the National Hockey League," he explained. "Guys I'd held my own against in the juniors were in the NHL and if they made it there was no reason I couldn't. I was big and strong and dedicated."

Mulvey is remembered for a feat that still remains a Blackhawk team record. In a February 3, 1982 game against the St. Louis Blues, ten minutes into the first period, he scored a goal. Then, in less than nine minutes time he scored four more, and also managed to assist on another goal. In the second period, he was awarded with another assist. He had broken the record of most points in one game that was previously held by the legendary Max Bentley, who scored seven points on January 28, 1944, and had scored five goals in one game!

"Terry Ruskowski was the recipient of, I believe, four of the five goals," he explained several years ago, "and I was just able to whack it in. Terry was everything that night. It seemed to work for

Grant Mulvey broke Max Bentley's 38-year-old record of most points scored in one game. (Photo courtesy of the Blackhawks.)

both of us. You don't realize it's happening at the time. However now, ten years later, actually it's gonna be eleven now, there's been some great players; Al Secord and Denis Savard and Steve Larmer. Great goal scorers, and yet they haven't done that. Even in the NHL, there haven't been a whole lot of guys that have scored that many goals in one game."

Mulvey played on one of the NHL's better lines during his career; the RPM (Ruskowski, Preston, Mulvey) line. "Naturally, when you're a young boy growing up, you'd like to make the NHL and when you make the NHL you want to strive to be the best at your position," he stated. "When you're able to do that on your team, you work towards being the best at your position in the League. At one point...we were one of the better lines in the NHL and I led the team in scoring [39 goals in 1979-80]. We also led in leadership. We did very well on the team, so playing with those guys was definitely a highlight."

In the late 1970s, the Blackhawks began to slump a little. "I believe we were always a contender in the division," explained Mulvey when asked about it. "In fact, for the most part we were always up there, high enough [so that we] always made the play-offs. We always did quite well, however, we weren't an exciting hockey team in the late seventies. Until Denis Savard and Terry Ruskowski and a few other players came in, Denis being the number one guy [and] Al Secord. They came to the forefront and Denis was electrifying."

Mulvey also offered a description of what the atmosphere of the team was like while he played in the mid-seventies and early eighties.

"I've never met a bad hockey player yet," he said. "The guys were straight-up guys and I was very fortunate that I played with some very, very, nice people. Even the times when we struggled, we still all were a pretty close-knit bunch of guys and we had a lot of fun together. There was always one guy, or two guys, that would ease the doldrums, you could say. However, most of the time the guys were very, very, very, good and enjoyable to live with."

When asked if the teams were falling away from cohesiveness and the dedication to team purpose, Mulvey explained:

"It's a business today. When I played, you didn't look at your occupation as a business, you looked at it as just a bunch of big boys playing hockey, and that's really what it was...It's just that business has entered into the economics of the game and, on the player level, you have to treat it very much like a business. They still love to do it. The studies have been made that the players, the camaraderie, is really what they strive for. What we were all about is we were a close-knit bunch of guys, we had a lot of fun together, and the only difference [is] they've got more zeros on the end of their paychecks. Owners are shrewd businessmen. The players are the ones that sacrifice their bodies to be able to entertain the measure that they do entertain. So the players should be given equal opportunity to make a fair living, and a fair living in that entertainment world is a nice dollar."

Including the play-offs, Mulvey scored 159 goals and 299 points in 628 games over the course of his 10-season, NHL career. He spent nine of those seasons with the Blackhawks, and his last with the New Jersey Devils.

Grant currently lives in the Chicago area, where he is involved in both hockey and business. "Since I retired, I've been very active in the game of hockey," he said recently. "I own a hockey school. The name is Midwest Elite Hockey School, and we teach kids that are five years old all the way up to adults."

Grant also explained that his school allows him to develop as well. "I'm very active in it and spend a lot of time learning and trying to polish my skills as a teacher. It's terrifically rewarding for me. I enjoy it an awful lot."

Mulvey has been involved with DRL Enterprises, where he has created NHL-licensed, removable tattoos and patches that resemble trading cards.

"They're called Seasons Action Player Patches, and children can have them signed by the players and wear them on their jerseys or jackets." His major pursuit, however, is his presidency over the Chicago Wolves of the IHL.

Chicago also had other talented athletes on the roster during the seventies. Among them were men like Jerry Korab, a product of the team's farm system, who played both defense and left-wing, and Phil Russell. Chicago lucked out when they picked up Russell 13th in the 1972 amateur draft. He turned out to be a solid, tough, talent for the Blackhawks for six seasons. "He was a very, very good defenseman for us, and probably the best fighter in the club," said former coach Billy Reay. "He was tough, but he was just an all-around pretty good defenseman."

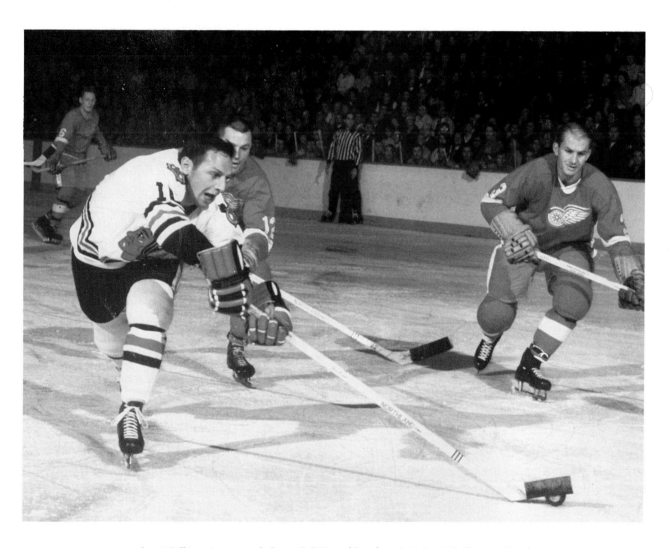

Dennis Hull in action against the Detroit Red Wings. (Photo from the Hockey Hall of Fame Archives.)

Pit Martin, Jim Pappin, and Dennis Hull—the infamous MPH Line against the Montreal Canadiens. (Photo from the Hockey Hall of Fame/Frank Prazak Collection.)

The legendary Tony Esposito blocking a shot during a game with the Canadiens. (Photo from the Hockey Hall of Fame/Frank Prazak Collection.)

Pat Stapleton, Tony Esposito, and Bill White — a defensive force for the Blackhawks in the early 70s shown here playing against Montreal. (Photo from the Hockey Hall of Fame/Frank Prazak Collection.)

THE ELUSIVE 80s

The eighties, like the late fifties, were a time of rebuilding after the strains of League expansion and the creation of the World Hockey Association. Under then Coach and General Manager Bob Pulford, new talent began to flow into Chicago Stadium. Because of Pulford, Chicago acquired such talent as Denis Savard, Steve Larmer, and Troy Murray, resulting in the development of badly needed offensive power. The Blackhawks managed to make the play-offs every season during this decade, and had a 104-point season under coach Orval Tessier in 1982-83, earning him coach of the year honors. Hawk forward Al Secord recalled:

"During the eighties, I think we were probably in one of the better decades the Blackhawks have had since the early sixties when they last won the Stanley Cup. I mean, they've had some great hockey players come through like Stan Mikita, Bobby Hull, and Dennis Hull, all those

Blackhawks 1982-83 team. First row, l to r: M. Bannerman, B. Pulford (GM), William Wirtz (president), B. Murray, A.M. Wirtz (chrman.), D. Wilson, T. Ivan (VP), M. Wirtz (VP), T. Esposito. Second row l to r: J. Davison (asst. GM), D. Savard, C. Mulvey, T. Lysiak, O. Tessier (coach), A. Secord, R. Preston, D. Sutter, C. Koroll (asst. coach). Third row l to r: S. Thayer (trainer), R. Preston, T. Murray, B. Gardner, P. Marsh, T. Higgins, D. Feamster, L. Varga (trainer). Fourth row l to r: K. McCudden, K. Brown, D. Crossman, G. Fox, S. Ludzik, S. Larmer. (Photo courtesy of the Blackhawks.)

guys...Pit Martin. But I think as a team, the Blackhawks were very much more of a team. I don't know, we just had more sense. We just seemed to have it together more than, I think, in the past.

"I came in December of 1980 and that year we actually finished pretty strong. Then from 1980 on, we had some great seasons. We went to the semifinals, I think, six times. We might've been just a player or two away from getting into the finals for the Stanley Cup. Those were the years that Edmonton was playing well with Gretzky and Messier and those guys."

Former Chicago Blackhawk forward Terry Ruskowski, who played on the RPM Line with Rich Preston and Grant Mulvey during the early eighties, feels that the team was good defensively at that time, but admits that they really did not have great offensive power. However, the Hawks did have Denis Savard during the eighties. Besides his performance as an athlete, his presence also helped the team in other ways. Said Ruskowski:

"With Savard coming, it changed the whole aspect of our team. I tell ya, when you get a goal-scorer and a guy that can do that with the puck, it takes the pressure off other players, and then the other players respond a lot better. All of a sudden, the burden of scoring is not on them, they don't have to worry about scoring, it just comes more naturally to them because the pressure's off. I think that when Savard came, it was probably one of the best draft choices [the Hawks have] ever had."

During the 1980s, the Blackhawks had several coaches guiding the franchise through the seasons, some more successful than others. Among them were Eddie Johnston, Bob Pulford, and Orval Tessier. Keith Magnuson and Bob Murdoch also enjoyed short stints behind the Chicago bench during this decade.

EDDIE JOHNSTON

Eddie Johnston, who coached the Hawks in 1979-80, used to play goal for them in 1977-78. He also minded the nets in Boston, Toronto, and St. Louis. His career spanned 16 seasons in all. He posted a 3.25 GAA in 592 games played. Before stepping up to coach the Hawks, he coached their minor league affiliate, the New Brunswick Hawks.

Johnston was born into a poor, western Montreal family. He had to work hard for everything. Besides delivering papers and hanging wallpaper, he worked in a bowling alley at night. Every now and then, he would pick up some money boxing in area penitentiaries under false names.

In a January 11, 1980 *Chicago Tribune* article by Skip Myslenski, Johnston once commented: "[If] you work hard for something, and then accomplish something, it means something. I've seen it all. I've had hard times and good times. I traveled buses coast to coast. I made $3,500 a year. I was on a Boston club when it won 10, 12 games a year. That's the only way you appreciate good times. I know. When I was growing up, nothing was given to me."

In comparison to his predecessor, Bob Pulford, Johnston was more easy going with his players. Around the time he became coach, Johnston told the *Chicago Tribune's* Bob Verdi: "When I came here as a player two years ago, the dressing room was a morgue. When practice was over, players couldn't wait to get out. It was like somebody yelled 'Fire!' But to win you've got to be together. Now, it's like my old days in Boston. One guy goes for a beer, all 20 guys go."

Even though he could relate to his players, Johnston wasn't a softy. Discipline and the basics were the elements he stressed with his athletes, keeping their respect at the same time.

Johnston emphasized offense and aggressiveness during his stint as coach. At the time, Chicago wasn't one of the most offensive teams in the NHL. He did bring the Hawks to a first place, Smythe Division finish. However, in the play-offs they folded in the quarter-final. Keith Magnuson went on to replace Johnston for the next season. Magnuson was replaced during the following season by Bob Pulford.

Johnston coached the Pittsburgh Penguins from 1980-81 through 1982-83. After that, he served as their General Manager for five seasons, after being named to that position on May 27, 1983. During that time the Penguins drafted such players as Mario Lemieux, Craig Simpson, Doug Bodger, Bob Errey, and acquired defenseman Paul Coffey in a trade. In 1988-89, Johnston served as Pittsburgh's Assistant General Manager, after which he went to the Hartford Whalers, where he served as General Manager and Vice President for three seasons. Today, he has returned to Pittsburgh and now serves as head coach, filling the vacancy left by the departure of Scotty Bowman in 1992-93.

ORVAL TESSIER

In 1982-83, Orval Tessier took over the reins of the Chicago Blackhawks. Before becoming a coach, he played wing for various teams. He played for strict Coach Hap Emms on the Barrie, Ontario Junior Flyers, and turned pro in 1953 at the age of 20. Once a pro, he led the Quebec Hockey League in goals and, after playing in four games with the Montreal Canadiens in 1954-55, he went to the Boston Bruins. After playing in 23 games for the Bruins, he was sent back to Quebec, where he became the QHL's scoring champ in 1957.

Because he wasn't a fast enough skater to play in the NHL, and because of family obligations, Tessier chose not to pursue an NHL career. After playing in the minors for some time, and undergoing back surgery, he hung up his skates in 1964, retiring from pro play with the now nonexistent Portland Buckaroos of the WHL and became a sales representative for Molson's Brewery.

In 1971, Tessier began coaching the Cornwall Royals of the Quebec Junior League, which at the time was a team in poor shape. The previous season, they had only won six games. Astonishingly, under his wing they went on to win the Memorial Cup.

Former Blackhawk defenseman Bob Murray, then 17 years old, was the captain of that team. "He took over a rotten hockey club, but there was never any doubt in his mind that he knew what he was doing," Murray commented in an April 3, 1982 *Chicago Tribune* article by Skip Myslenski. "As a player, you knew he knew how to coach, and I found then that he knew when a guy needed a pat on the back and when a guy needed a kick in the rear."

Coach Orval Tessier was known for his sometimes intimidating coaching methods. (Photo courtesy of the Blackhawks.)

After coaching Junior Hockey for ten years, Tessier took a coaching position with the New Brunswick Hawks of the AHL, then co-sponsored by the Blackhawks and Maple Leafs. Many considered New Brunswick to be the worst team in the AHL. He forged the team into champions, leading them to the AHL League title. This accomplishment earned him AHL Coach of the Year in 1981-82.

The Blackhawks, who had struggled under coach Keith Magnuson, named Orval Tessier as their coach on June 16, 1982. Almost one year after he was hired, he revealed a little of his philosophy to *Chicago Tribune's* Skip Myslenski in an article entitled "The Iceman," which appeared in the April 3, 1983 issue.

"I came to Chicago not to win popularity contests but to win hockey games without hurting anyone. If you wanted to win a popularity contest, you'd take 20 guys at the beginning of the season and say: 'We're not going to trade any-

body, so go out and buy a house. Enjoy yourselves. We'll have light practices and try to win as much as we can.' At the end of the year, those players will say you're the best guy they ever played for, that you were nice to them and their wives and their kids, but that we didn't make the play-offs. When players say their coach is such a great guy, that's an easy guy to beat. He doesn't have any gumption. Now I'm not always right but, if I feel I am, I'll say it at the top level [to his bosses] or at the low level [to his players]. I'm by no means a fence sitter. I'm by no means a yes man. The world is filled with those, and they're not successful. I respect my players. I respect the people I'm working for. But a human being worth his salt should be able to stand up for himself.

"Remember Leo Durocher's statement that nice guys finish last? The statement doesn't end there. I think what Mr. Durocher meant is if you're afraid to step on toes, if you're afraid people will react badly to what you say and do, then you can't do your job."

Because of his intimidating coaching methods, many players had a distaste for Tessier. In May of 1984, Tony Esposito commented that Orval frequently intimidated younger players. He also said that many players didn't speak their minds about Tessier out of fear of being traded or sent to the minors.

When asked about Tessier, former Blackhawk forward Terry Ruskowski said:

"I don't think [anybody] respected him. Nobody respected him because he was a liar. He was a liar, he was a two-faced...there's two things I didn't like about him, his faces, because he was two-faced all of the time. In front of you he was a nice guy, but then all of a sudden when you turned your back he was the type of guy that [said]: 'No we can't play him, he's no good, he's too slow, he's too old.' He thought I was too old to play and [I] went into L.A. and played three

more years, two in Pittsburgh, and one-and-a-half with Minnesota. So that's how much he knows about bein' old and a player bein' through.

"He had no respect for his players. His players hated him. Once a player hates a coach, they're not gonna play for him. They're not gonna put out. Behind his back they're gonna start making fun of him...I mean, when he comes back from Edmonton and said he wants to go to the hospital for the guys to have a heart transplant [an unpopular statement of Tessier's that made it to the press], what is that? These are professional players getting good money, and they're playing hard. They did very well to get where they are. I think he's a two-faced back-stabber, and I don't like him at all. He's probably the least favorite of the coaches, no, he is the least favorite coach I ever had."

In a November 15, 1982 *Sports Illustrated* article by Jack Falla, Blackhawks Al Secord and Doug Wilson offered their opinions of Tessier, revealing a different perspective.

"You work for Orval, you play for him," said Wilson. "That was the first thing he told us. He got our respect right away because he made a lot of moves and sat some people down. That takes guts for a rookie coach."

"I played for Don Cherry in Boston," commented Secord when asked about Tessier, "and in one way they [Tessier and Cherry] are alike because they stress hard work. But where Don wanted us to be physically intimidating, Orval emphasizes skating, coming back with your check, [and] playing good position in our end."

Today, looking back upon his former coach, Secord still views him in a positive light:

"I think what happened with Orval [is], the year before Orval came, we had

a good hockey team and we knew it, but we weren't playing consistent. We were fairly new together and the good teams we played well against, the poor teams we played on the same level. So that showed a lack of maturity [and] a lack of consistency. And then finally, when Orval came, it was a new guy coming into town and he demanded a lot from his players. When he demanded a lot, that made us pull up our bootstraps and we had a great season. I think we played well up until about February and then we kind of petered out for the rest of the season."

When asked about the famous comment Tessier made concerning the heart transplant his players needed, Secord said:

"Yeah, well, the way I look at that is, I've been called worse. That particular statement just made it to the press. I think if you're a professional, you take those kind of comments and you just apply [them] in a positive way. I mean, that didn't bother me whatsoever, it didn't change my play. That might have been used maybe as a crutch for not winning. But when it comes down to it, we're the guys on the ice that do the job. When you get to that level, you went through a lot of ups and downs in your career to get to be a professional, and something like that shouldn't alter your play."

Billy Gardner, who also played for Tessier said the following of his former coach:

"Well he came from Moncton...the year after I was there. They won the Calder Cup, they won the championship, so he had a lot of respect in that regard, being a winner and winning in the American Hockey League, which was a pretty big deal...We jelled so well at the start when he was there, it was the year that we had 104 points. You know, things went well. He was the kind of

coach that used motivation more than tactics. Roger Neilson was our assistant coach, he was more [of a] behind-the-scenes, knowledge-of-the-game sort of guy. Orval was the kind of guy that liked to try and get under your skin at times, a motivator, a type of Mike Keenan in that regard. The problem with Orval was that it just sort of wore off. He kind of got over his head a little bit saying a few things. That's probably why the second year, he didn't make it through it."

Tessier had a way of being mysterious with his players in the sense that he didn't want to show his emotional side. Some of his players felt that he believed he wouldn't be an effective coach if his players got to know that side of him.

Former Blackhawk forward Tom Lysiak once offered his opinion on Orval's approach to coaching in an article by Skip Myslenski, which appeared in the April 3, 1983 issue of the *Chicago Tribune*:"I think he wants us to have an 'I'll show you, you s.o.b.' attitude," he said. "He doesn't want you to sit back. He wants you hungry all the time. He wants you trying all the time. He makes us shoot for No. 1. He makes us want it."

In his first season (1982-83), Tessier brought the Blackhawks to a 104-point, first-place, Norris Division finish. He was awarded the Jack Adams Trophy that season, which is given to the NHL coach who has contributed the most to his team's success. However, in the play-offs, the Hawks lost the Conference Championship. The next season (1983-84), Chicago slipped to a fourth place Norris Division finish. Bob Pulford once again stepped in as coach during the 1984-85 season.

BOB PULFORD

Pulford is a man who has donned many hats (Coach, G.M., Senior Vice President) within the Chicago Blackhawks organization. A graduate of McMaster University, Pulford played professional hockey with the Maple Leafs, and later the Los Angeles Kings. During his 16-season NHL career, which spanned from 1956-57 to 1971-72, he scored 281 goals and 643 points in 1,079 games. He played on four Stanley Cup teams while he was with Toronto (1961-62, '62-63, '63-64, '66-67), and was known for his penalty-killing ability. Pulford was an NHL All-Star six times during his playing career. On June 21, 1991, he was inducted into the Hockey Hall of Fame.

After playing for the Kings, Pulford stepped up as their Coach in 1972-73 and remained so until 1976-77. He was named Coach of the Year in 1974-75 for bringing Los Angeles to a 105-point season, and posting a 42-17-21 record.

In July of 1977, the Blackhawks named Pulford Coach and General Manager. That season, *The Hockey News* voted him Coach of the Year. Since that time, Pulford has served as the team's Coach on several occasions (1977-78, '78-79, '81-82 [with Keith Magnuson], '84-85 [with Orval Tessier], '85-86, and '86-87). He was General Manager of the team from 1977 until 1990-91, when Mike Keenan assumed the title of G.M. along with his position as coach. With Keenan gone, Pulford has assumed the position of G.M. once again, in addition to serving as Senior Vice President of the Chicago Blackhawks.

Bob Pulford has a reputation for being a strict disciplinarian behind the bench. However, as a coach he knows how to relate to his players, preserving and boosting their confidence when needed. While Pulford was coaching the team in 1981-82, after Keith Magnuson stepped down, former Blackhawk forward Ted Bulley once commented on Pulford in the April 25, 1982 issue of the *Chicago Tribune*: "Pully knows how to motivate. In meetings he looks at you, stares at you. If you have a meeting in the morning, you're ready to play right then. He knows how to do it. In other meetings, you'd just go over the lineup and that was it. Pully gets you going, he has you scoring goals before games. You're sitting in the locker room, seeing yourself scoring. It's a great feeling right there."

In the same article, Pulford offered a bit of his philosophy on coaching:

"If a person falls off a horse, you put him right back on. I thoroughly believe in that," he said. "It goes right back to effort. If you don't make the effort, you won't make the mistake. All I ask for is effort, and to criticize for making a mistake while giving effort would go against

all I stand for. A mental error is something different. But an error of effort should be complimented almost. More than anything, you have to show them you have confidence in them. These are basically young people. Say your 11-year-old son is being coached by someone who's not playing him. What's that coach saying? He's no good. That's a very dangerous thing to do."

Former Hawk forward Terry Ruskowski still holds a lot of respect for Pulford, whom he played for during his days in Chicago.

"I really liked Pully as a coach. He coached me for just part of the year when Keith Magnuson was gone. He's the type of guy the players respect, and I respect him highly…He was a disciplinarian on the ice, you worked hard for him. But that's what I wanted to do anyway. That's what you're supposed to do. You're supposed to work hard all of the time. So I loved that attitude; work hard in practice and in the game you'll get more ice time and do what you have to do. I really liked playing for Pully!"

Veteran referee Andy vanHellemond recalls Pulford in a positive light as well:

"Pulford was a very knowledgeable hockey person. He was an excellent player, worked hard all his life and I guess he expects that from his players or employees. I never saw him be overbearing. He always gave us the time to say why we did things. He has a temper like anyone else, so sometimes he's going to blow his cork. I find over the years a lot of these people who get upset at a call in a game have had a lot of things building inside whether it's the way their teams played or their record and it's just something that that particular night sets off and it's just an accumulation of a lot of things that have built from day to day or week to week before that and if you're in the

wrong place at the wrong time, you're there when the volcano goes off. Some of them have said afterward that it's not you personally, it's just the game itself made me mad and a couple of calls pissed me off and the players are playing, so it's not always you it's just everything building up and I just finally let it all out. We are the ones in the spot it ends up being dumped on. He's done that in that hallway and if walls could talk there would be a lot of stories there. It's a forgotten thing, and I respect a person for that. If he can display his anger and how upset he is, but then not carry a grudge, I think that's important, and that's the way Pulford was."

Besides being Head Coach of Team USA in the 1976 Canada Cup Games, Pulford was the Co-Manager of Team USA in the 1991 Canada Cup. He was also the first NHL Player's Union President in 1967. Today, besides being the Blackhawks' Senior Vice President, he is also their Alternate Governor. In his spare time, he likes to restore old cars.

THE MEN

During the 1980s, the Blackhawks had a number of quality players on their roster. Among them were goalie Murray Bannerman and defensemen Bob Murray, Doug Wilson, and Keith Brown. The better forwards were Tom Lysiak, Rich Preston, Terry Ruskowski, Billy Gardner, Darryl Sutter, Steve Larmer, Denis Savard, Al Secord, Eddie Olczyk, and Troy Murray.

MURRAY BANNERMAN

Murray Bannerman was one of Chicago's main goaltenders for seven years (1980-81 to 1986-87), although Esposito was still with the team until 1983-84. He became their top goalie in 1982-83, and his career took off after a successful 104-point season, during which he manned the nets about half of the time, along with Esposito.

Describing Bannerman, former teammate Terry Ruskowski said:

"Murray was a guy that started off as a real good goaltender. He was in the shadow of Esposito for a number of years,

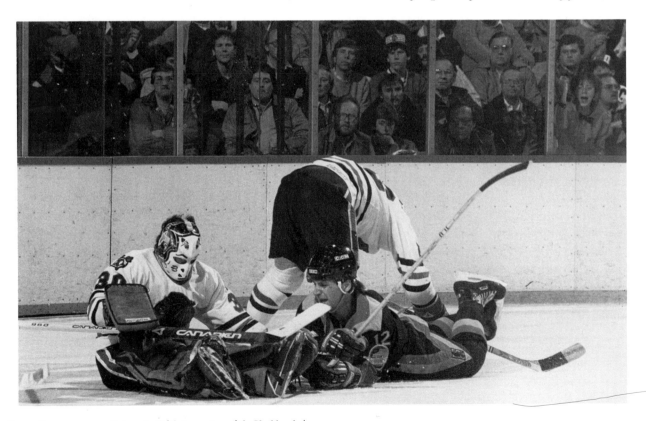

Murray Bannerman – goalic in action!! (Photo courtesy of the Blackhawks.)

but when it was his time to play, he played, and he played very, very well...I think if Murray Bannerman would've stuck to playing hockey and was really concentrated about hockey, he wouldn't have had to worry about being out of hockey now. I think that he had the qualities to be a goalie for a number of years, a very good goalie. I know that he was a quality goalie, but it seemed like his mind was not totally focused on hockey all the time."

Veteran Chicago Blackhawk forward Al Secord also gave his view of former teammate Murray Bannerman. "You'll probably laugh at this," he said, "but I think all goaltenders are weird. I think anybody that puts himself between two pipes and a net and has something at over a 100 m.p.h. fired at them is crazy. But Murray played very well for us and he was a good goalie."

After seven years with the Hawks, Murray was sent to Saginaw of the IHL early in the 1987-88 season, and then to the AHL Baltimore Skipjacks, who won only 13 of their 80 games. After that, he ended his professional hockey career. Bannerman commented about his departure from Chicago:

"I knew they [the Blackhawks] were going to get some other goaltenders. The only thing I was upset about was when I talked to them all summer [in 1987], they told me to come to camp, work hard and, 'We'll give you a good chance to be a member of the team again.' Obviously, when you don't play one league game, that's not much of a chance. It's their right to make changes. But is it really so much to tell a guy you're not in their plans? I don't feel they ever really did it. Judging by the way many things have been handled, I guess you can't expect it."

Bannerman's NHL career spanned eight seasons. Before coming to the Hawks, he also played in one game for Vancouver. Posting eight shutouts, he holds a career GAA of 3.83. Today, he resides in the Chicago area.

BOB MURRAY

Bob Murray played defense for the Chicago Blackhawks from 1975 to 1990. During his 15-season career, he scored 151 goals and 419 assists in 1,120 games (including the play-offs). Bob is only the fourth Hawk player to reach the 1000 game mark, and in the 1990 play-offs he became the first player in Blackhawk history to play in over 100 play-off games. A skilled athlete, Murray was known for his determination and skill as a player. In an article by Ross Forman that appeared in the March 3, 1993 issue of *Hockey Digest*, Murray expressed his feelings on his playing days. "I was a steady player," he said. "I could skate and move the puck. I read the play very well. My only problem was my size. I had trouble with certain teams that were bigger. I had trouble with the bigger guys, and that's how it's always going to be with the smaller defensemen."

In that same article, Murray also described the one thing from his career that bothers him to this day.

Bob Murray played defense for the Blackhawks for 16 seasons. (Photo courtesy of the Blackhawks.)

"The nagging thing from my career is that I got to the semifinals several times, but never got to the Finals of the Stanley Cup," continued Murray, who played center and right-wing during his junior hockey days in Quebec. "It bothers me that the group of guys I was with didn't take that step. Sure, we can make excuses. We hit Edmonton during their dynasty, and they were the best team, no doubt about it. But the fact of the matter is we didn't do it. I'd call us underachievers. I have some close friends from that group, and it really bothers me that we didn't win the Stanley Cup. We were a pretty good hockey team during the mid-80s, and there was a lot of talent, but we just didn't do it."

Billy Gardner, a former teammate of Murray's, gave the following description of him:

"Murph was a difficult guy to really get to know unless you [were] able to really get to know him, and I was one of those few who was able to. I got along with Bob and I think he was sort of like the father figure in my time. I think he appreciated people that could understand the game, which I thought I could, and we had extensive talks sometimes about what was going on in situations...As a player, he was always there, played the same way every game, was very good, very steady. [He was] another guy who probably wasn't appreciated enough by his teammates, but game in, game out he was always there and look where he is now, his knowledge of the game is obviously very good because of his position now [director of player personnel]...I think he makes a lot of decisions on what happens and I think his position gets stronger all the time."

Murray became a scout for the Blackhawks in 1990, and is currently their director of player personnel, a position to which he was appointed in 1991. In addition to his duties with the Blackhawks,

Murray has served as the director of the Northern Illinois Hockey League and has coached for the hockey teams that his sons play on. Murray is also an assistant pro at Kemper Lakes Golf Course in Long Grove, Illinois.

DOUG WILSON

Another talented blue-liner who played for the Hawks during the eighties was Doug Wilson. Born on July 5, 1957 in Ottawa, Ontario, Wilson played defense for the Chicago Blackhawks from 1977-78 to 1990-91. He was a dedicated, polished player and a very classy individual.

Wilson established himself as a top-rate defenseman over the course of his distinguished pro career, which spanned 16 seasons. He was also a big contributor offensively, leading Blackhawk defensemen in scoring nine seasons in a row (1981-82 to 1989-90).

Known for his speed and agility on the ice, Wilson was a finesse player. He played a strong positional game, and possessed a hard, accurate slap shot.

At the close of the 1994-95 season, Wilson ranked ninth in goals (225), fifth in points (779) and third in assists (554) on the Blackhawks' lifetime leaders list. He holds numerous franchise records, and is the Hawks' all-time highest scoring defenseman in goals, assists, and points. He also holds records for most goals by a defenseman in a season (39 in 1981-82), and most points by a defenseman in a season (85 in 1981-82). He also shares with Grant Mulvey the Blackhawks club record for shots on goal by a single player in a game. He tied Mulvey's 1980 record on November 6, 1983, with 12 shots against the New Jersey Devils.

Wilson started school in England when he was three years old because his father was in the Air Force at the time. When he returned to Canada at the age of six, he was more advanced than the other kids, and skipped a few grades.

Doug played junior hockey in Winnipeg. He later played for the Ottawa 67s of the OHA for two seasons, scoring 51 goals and 167 points in 101 games. While there, he was named to the OHA's first All-Star team in 1977.

In 1977, he was drafted number one by the Blackhawks (sixth overall), and after a good training camp he made the team. Wilson had wanted to

Doug Wilson another defenseman who played for the Blackhawks from 1977 to 1991. (Photo courtesy of the Blackhawks.)

be a hockey player his whole life. "I never really thought about anything else," he once commented in an article by Neil Milbert that appeared in the April 11, 1980 issue of *The Hockey News*. "I put all my marbles in one basket and I realize now that was taking a big chance. I didn't put very much effort in my school work."

Discussing his arrival as a rookie with the Blackhawks in the same *The Hockey News* article by Neil Milbert, Wilson once said:

> *"I feel I was kind of fortunate. Bob Pulford was just coming in as general manager and coach and was installing a new system. The other guys all had to learn a new system and impress a new coach, so I was starting out even. That was the year Bobby Orr sat out to try to rest his knee for his comeback and he also was a big influence. He kept telling me*

not to get down on myself and to play with confidence and not worry about making mistakes."

In the November 20, 1992 issue of the *Toronto Sun*, Wilson commented on another early influence on his career to columnist Lance Hornby. "I roomed with Stan Mikita my first year," he said. "He was like a second father to me. He taught me a lot about hockey and a lot about life, namely to treat other people with respect."

Commenting on what makes Doug Wilson such a first-class guy, on and off the ice, his former teammate, veteran Hawk forward Terry Ruskowski said:

> *"Doug Wilson is a good friend. You can rely on Dougie. He's an excellent hockey player and has had...one of the best shots in hockey. When it comes to play, you didn't look at Dougie to say; 'What kind of a game are you going to have?' You knew Dougie was going to be there.*
>
> *"He's a very, very dependable guy, and he's a class guy. He's the type of guy that, when he talked, he didn't say much. But when he talked, everybody listened. He had that respect from his teammates. He had a lot of respect and I respect him. I was the captain of the team, but when Dougie talked, I respected him and I really listened."*

Because he came into the NHL before 1979, Wilson, played without a helmet during his career. At the end of his career, he was only one of a handful of veterans allowed to do so until the League reversed its mandatory helmet rule for the 1992-93 season. The League did this so players would be more careful about using their sticks, and to "make players more recognizable and the league more marketable," according to an article by Tom McMillan and Steve Dryden in the September 11, 1992 issue of *The Hockey News*. In that article, Wilson said that he didn't think marketing should come before safety, and that he would not recommend playing without protection to anyone.

On Saturday, November 21, 1992, Wilson played his 1,000th game in San Jose, where he ended his professional career. As fate would have it, that game turned out to be one against the Blackhawks. Wilson was honored in a ceremony before the game, and was given a trophy by former teammate Keith Magnuson. Magnuson gave a moving speech about Wilson's many attributes and accomplishments, and presented him with a jersey from the Chicago Blackhawk Alumni Association.

Moving around is a fact of life when playing professional hockey. A trade can send a player across North America in the blink of an eye, creating the need for total readjustment. Wilson feels that it wasn't easy to make the transition from Chicago to San Jose, especially with his children.

In the March 1992 issue of *Hockey Digest*, in an article by Ken Rappoport, he discussed his first visit to Chicago as a member of the Sharks.

"[Playing in Chicago as a member of San Jose] was tough. You go over all the games you played there, a lot of memories and times. I was concerned about going to the wrong bench. It would have been a natural reaction after playing 1,000 games there. It was nice to go back. The fans were super, and Chicago will always have a place in my heart."

Wilson's career highlights included his game-tying goal that allowed Team Canada a victory over the Soviets in the 1984 Canada Cup, and an 85-point, Norris Trophy (outstanding defenseman) season in 1982. He received First Team All-Star honors in 1982, and Second Team All-Star Honors in 1985 and 1990. He also played in the NHL's All-Star game from 1982-86, and 1990 and 1992. During his career, Wilson scored 237 goals for 827 points in 1,024 games.

While he lived in Chicago, Wilson worked as a salesman and did public relations work for Coca-Cola. On Friday, September 12, 1993, Wilson announced his retirement from the National Hockey League. At that time, he also stepped down as the president of the NHL Players Association. Wilson stated that his back problem, a degenerative disc, was a factor in his decision to hang up the skates.

KEITH BROWN

Defenseman Keith Brown played for the Blackhawks from 1979-80 until late September, 1993, when he was traded to the Florida Panthers for rightwing Darin Kimble. Only two other individuals (Dave Taylor and Ray Bourque) have played longer for one NHL team. Before coming to Chicago, Brown played for Portland of the WHL, where he shared Rookie of the Year honors with John Ogrodnick in 1978. He was honored as the WHL's top defenseman in 1979, and was named to the League's First All-Star team that season as well. Brown was the Blackhawks' first choice (7th overall) in the 1979 Entry Draft.

Keith is best known for his compassion and humanitarian spirit. In 1992, the Blackhawks nominated him for the King Clancy Memorial Trophy (awarded to the NHL player who is a leader on and off the ice, and who has made humanitarian contributions).

In a *Chicago Tribune* article with Tim Tierney, Denis Savard commented on Brown. "I've always liked Keith Brown," he said. "I'll never forget what

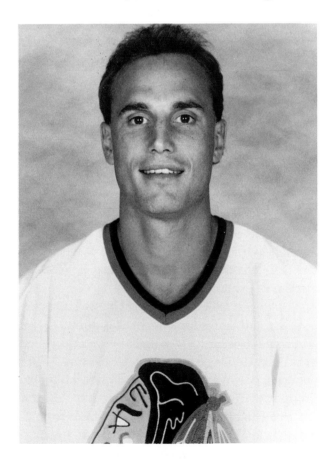

Keith Brown played for the Blackhawks from 1979 to 1993. (Photo courtesy of the Blackhawks.)

151

he did for me. I was a French kid in town, and he moved me into his place. That's the type of guy he is. He'd do anything for you, and not only me."

Former teammate Al Secord reinforced Savard's statement, and offered a glimpse into his hockey abilities as well.

"Everyone knows he's very dedicated to his family and to his hockey," said Secord. *"He was a good team leader. He wasn't a real talker, but he led through example. He was very well respected. I think the thing that stands out in my mind is when young guys would come into town, Keith always had an open door at his house and kept them there until they got straightened away; either in a hotel or a place [of their own]. So, he's very generous in that way, and that's a team leader type of thing he used to do.*

"I think he was a defensive defenseman," continued Secord. "He was very consistent, very strong. [He] did his job [and] he came to play every game."

Keith scored 68 goals for 342 points in 863 games (through the 1993-94 season). He retired from the Florida Panthers in 1995 because of bad knees. He will stay in Florida and take business classes.

TOM LYSIAK

Another one of Chicago's key forwards during the eighties was Tom Lysiak. A native of High Prairie, Alberta, Lysiak played center for the Blackhawks from 1979-80 to 1984-85. If it weren't for hockey, Lysiak once commented that he would've become a game warden.

"It wasn't till I was about 13 that I became a rink rat and started taking hockey seriously," he once said in an article by Neil Milbert in the October 19, 1979 issue of the *Chicago Tribune*. "When we went out of town for games, it was a long haul from 25 to 180 miles. Somehow, another kid from my town and I got the attention of scouts from the Edmonton Oil Kings and they sent us an invitation to go to their Junior hockey training camp. We were getting ready to go when we read we'd been traded to a new team, Medicine Hat."

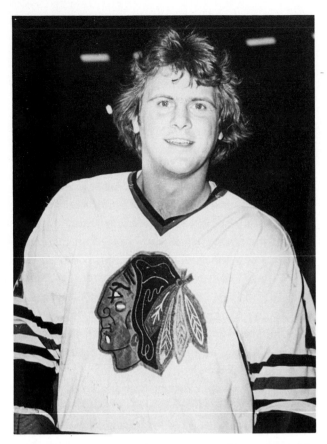

Tom Lysiak, one of Chicago's key forwards in the '80s. (Photo courtesy of the Blackhawks.)

Medicine Hat, which was over 600 miles away, had received Lysiak, his friend, and another player in exchange for a player the Oil Kings had lost to them sometime before. The coach there, Jack Shupe, made a prediction that startled Lysiak, who had done well in their training camp. He said that Lysiak would make it to the NHL in three years. "I respected his knowledge and I thought to myself, 'If I work hard, I know I'm going to make it,'" he said in the same Milbert article. Lysiak played junior hockey with Lanny McDonald, with whom he became close friends. Later, the two of them would go on to be picked in the top five of the 1973 draft.

After his second season with Medicine Hat, Lysiak had become one of Junior hockey's best players, scoring 96 points that year (including one 10-point game vs. Edmonton). The next year, also with Medicine Hat, he scored 58 goals and 96 assists for a total of 154 points.

This farm boy went on to become the Atlanta Flame's first draft choice in 1973 (second overall behind Denis Potvin). He would later become the highest scorer in that club's history. His NHL career, which ended in 1985-86, spanned 13 seasons in all. Including the play-offs, he scored 317 goals and 906 points in 997 games.

Although his production slipped after he left Atlanta for Chicago, Lysiak was a key player for the Blackhawks during the eighties. In 1980-81, he led the team in points with 76, a point ahead of second-place Denis Savard. He was a seasoned veteran while he played for the Hawks, and saw a lot of action on the power play. His line was often pitted against the best lines of opposing teams.

Tony Esposito once gave his opinion of Lysiak in an article by Neil Milbert in the February 8, 1980 issue of *The Hockey News*. "If Lysiak isn't a hockey player, then I've never seen one," he said. "I see the way he's always playing for the team and not himself, the way he works both ends of the ice and gives it all he's got. At home or on the road, it doesn't make a bit of difference. He puts out."

Lysiak was also known for his leadership skills. A year after his point-leading season, Doug Wilson described Lysiak in an article by Skip Myslenski, which appeared in the December 26, 1982 issue of the *Chicago Tribune*.

"He's our leader by example, and he could be the most important hockey player on this team. He probably is," said Wilson. "He's not as flashy as Denis Savard, but he dominates when he's out there. He does a lot of things that require sacrifice, things that aren't the glamorous part of the game, but are important. I think he could be the most underrated player in the league. I think he's as important to this team as any other player on any other team is to his...He's so unselfish, a fine person, you really can't say too much about him. I just feel lucky to play with him."

Looking back, former Hawk Billy Gardner commented on Lysiak:

"He was just sort of a happy-go-lucky guy. He enjoyed what he was doing and was never real serious until he was on the ice. He was the kind of guy who was fun to be around in the dressing room.

In fact, the other day I was listening to Ruuttu talking about being in Vancouver, and he said the atmosphere is so much different, so much looser. The Blackhawks have always had that label of being too serious and so a guy like Tommy was fun to have, he was kind of a prankster and jokester and loosened everybody up. Talent-wise he was awesome, and he probably displayed as much as he probably could have. He was just an easy-going guy and to really see him everyday in practice, you [had] to love what he could do, but when he got on the ice, [it was a] he did it when he wanted to sort of thing, and he probably could have done it a lot more."

A low point in Lysiak's career occurred when he was given a 20-game suspension for tripping linesman Ron Foyt during an October 30, 1983 game at Chicago Stadium against the Hartford Whalers. Lysiak was one of the Hawks who was especially skilled at face-offs. The incident happened after Foyt took him off of a face-off, as he had done several times before during the game. Lysiak's action resulted in an immediate game misconduct from referee Dave Newell.

RICH PRESTON

Rich Preston was another one of Chicago's better forwards during the early eighties. While playing professional hockey, he was known for his penalty-killing abilities, and was a decent two-way player. He will be remembered for playing on the famous RPM Line with Grant Mulvey and Terry Ruskowski.

Preston was the property of the Hawks when he graduated from Denver University in 1974, but instead of settling for a seat with their Central Hockey League team in Dallas, he jumped to the WHA with future Hawk teammate Terry Ruskowski. "We were sure we would play there right away, and playing with Gordie Howe was a big attraction too," he said in an October 26, 1979 *The Hockey News* article. "When the merger talks [between the WHA and the NHL] cropped up last season, four or five teams were interested in me, and I was a free agent, so I could talk with them. I signed with Chicago because I like the city, and I know Cliff Koroll and

Rich Preston was a member of the famous RPM Line with Grant Mulvey and Terry Ruskowski. (Photo courtesy of the Blackhawks.)

Keith Magnuson from Denver. We all went to college there, and that meant something to me."

Preston got his start in the pros with the Houston Aeros, spending four seasons there on right-wing. After Houston, he spent a season with the Winnipeg Jets before Chicago claimed him in the 1979 expansion draft.

Around the beginning of his first season with the Blackhawks, Preston once described himself in an article by Bob Verdi, in the October 26, 1979 issue of *The Hockey News*. "I'm a jack of all trades and a master of none," he said. "I go up and down the wing, and I play the corners that's a big part of my game. I want to score at least 25 goals this year [1979-80] if I can and be a 'plus' player if I can. I just want to be able to contribute." Actually, Preston had a 61 point season in 1979-80, scoring 31 goals. However, that was the best season he would have, as his production slipped after that. Including the play-offs, Preston scored 131 goals for 313 points

in 627 games during his 8-season NHL career that ended with the New Jersey Devils in 1986-87.

The 1992-93 Chicago Blackhawk Media Guide said "Preston garnered everyone's respect by coming to the rink prepared, by helping younger players cope with the grind of an NHL season, and by playing tough, intelligent hockey." He served as the Blackhawks' Assistant Coach through the 1994-95 season.

TERRY RUSKOWSKI

Terry Ruskowski, Preston's linemate on the RPM Line, was born on December 31, 1954, in Prince Albert, Saskatchewan. Ruskowski grew up on a farm, where he learned to skate on a pond. He began playing junior hockey in Humboldt, Saskatchewan, at the age of 15. From there, he played hockey in Swift Current for three years before ending up in Houston of the WHA.

Just like his teammate Rich Preston, the Hawks drafted him in 1974 and told him if he played for them, he would be sent to Dallas of the Central Hockey League. Instead, he went to play with Gordie Howe and his two sons for the Aeros, who offered him a three-year, no-cut, no-trade contract.

"It was an absolute thrill playing with Gordie," said Ruskowski, now the head coach of the ECHL Columbus Chill. "Mark [Howe] and Marty [Howe] and myself and the guys who first came in as rookies got along very well because we were all the same age…and playing with Gordie was just an absolute dream come true. He taught us little things, but just his presence and how he handled himself taught all of us what to do and how to do it."

After the Houston franchise dissolved, Ruskowski went to Winnipeg, like Preston. Howe and his sons went to play in Hartford. In Winnipeg, he led the Jets to the WHA title in 1978-79. Glen Sather called him the heart of the Jets club and the League's most valuable player.

The next season (1979-80) Ruskowski found his way to the Chicago Blackhawks, where he played his first game in Chicago Stadium on September 22, 1979, tying the Canadiens 5-5. It was there that he played on the famed RPM Line with Preston and Mulvey. Ruskowski said that he contributed his physical style of play and passing skills to the line, and Preston and Mulvey took care of most of the goals.

"Grant Mulvey set himself in a position where he could just one-time it. We worked on it a long time; just passing and one-timing it. He was a goal-scorer. It was just a combination of three. I passed it to him, and he put the biscuit in the basket as we say. Preston was great in the corners. He had very strong legs, [and a] strong upper body. He really dug the puck out. So, it was a combination of three people [doing] what they do best."

Ruskowski also explained that the RPM Line was a very close knit trio off the ice as well as on it. He and Preston had played together in Houston and Winnipeg, and in Chicago, the coach roomed he and Mulvey together. Said Mulvey: "We roomed together, we played together, and we went out after games together. It was a close-knit line. We always cared for each other. If one guy was in trouble, two other guys were there to help him out. If you want to have a successful team [and a] successful line, you've got to have that kind of camaraderie in the line."

Terry Ruskowski, another member of the famous RPM Line–Ruskowski, Preston, and Mulvey. (Photo courtesy of the Blackhawks.)

Although he wasn't a superior skater, Ruskowski possessed excellent puck-handing skills, and was known for his ability to set up scoring opportunities for his teammates. As in the WHA, he proved to be an aggressive player. He wasn't a goon, however. He once commented that he didn't feel fighting was in the spirit of the game, but that he wouldn't stand around and allow any of his teammates to be roughed up.

After only 12 NHL games, coach Eddie Johnston named Ruskowski team captain for his leadership qualities. At the time, in a March 21, 1980 *Chicago Tribune* article by Skip Myslenski (1980), he commented: "The only thing I worried about was bad feelings among the players. Four, five different guys deserved it, and I didn't want to cause any friction. I would have given it up. If there had been any bad feelings, then you can't play well as a team, and because of that I would have handed it back, even though it meant so much to me. Being captain is a great honor, but I think there's greater honor in winning the Stanley Cup."

In the same *Chicago Tribune* article by Skip Myslenski, Ruskowski once commented that he relied largely upon hard work to make it to the pros instead of natural talent. "When you can't rely on talent—and I'm not really a good skater, a good shooter, a good stick handler—when you can't depend on talent, you have to depend on working harder. It's my natural response, reaction; my natural instinct is to try and do the best I can, to do things right. I think I've felt that way since I was a kid."

"When you see the things that Terry does, how he prepares, and the way he never stops working, you can't help but work harder yourself," Ruskowski's former linemate Grant Mulvey once explained during their career in a March 28, 1980 *Chicago Tribune* article by Neil Milbert.

Today, Ruskowski feels the same way, explaining: "I wasn't a fast skater, didn't have a great shot, but I was physical and I worked hard, I really worked hard. I thought, 'that's what got me here, and that's what's gonna keep me here.'"

Terry lists Bill Dineen (former NHL forward with Chicago and Detroit), his former coach in Houston, as a favorite coach in a long line of good coaches he had the opportunity of playing for. Besides Dineen, Ruskowski played for Tom McVie, Pat Quinn, Bob Berry, and Herb Brooks. Said

Ruskowski, "I've been very, very fortunate to have quality people that taught me the game, taught me to be not just a great hockey player, but...to be a good person, period."

Thinking back, Ruskowski recalled the most memorable games of his career.

"Truthfully, two things come to mind. Grant Mulvey, when he scored the five goals in one game; [it was an] amazing game! We were playing together. It was incredible to watch, it was a great feat.

"But, I think the game that really stuck out in my mind more than anyone else in Chicago was the game that we played in the semifinals [one year], the first game against Vancouver. The place was packed and we went out. This was when the transformation from the older guys going out and the younger guys coming in [was taking place]. We went to the semifinals, and we went out for warm-ups. There were 18,000 fans in the warm-ups, and they were giving us a standing ovation; yelling all through the warm-ups. We went down in the dressing room and they were still cheering and going crazy. We came [out] for the game and there was 19, 20,000, and they were even louder! I went up to Pully [coach Bob Pulford] and I said: 'Pully, start me and don't ever take me off!' I was so pumped that they had dropped the puck and it was all over. I wouldn't have come off the ice, I was just so pumped!...We didn't win the series, but I think we won the game. It was just a tremendous feeling. I [haven't] had a rush like that in a long time.

"Of course, winning the Avco Cup in the World Hockey Association, [was memorable]. Especially in Winnipeg, [because] we were more a part of it. In Houston, we were the fourth line. We got a little bit of ice time, but not a whole bunch. In Winnipeg, we were more of a part of winning the Avco Cup, [that] was a great feat also."

Terry was with the Hawks from 1979-80 to 1981-82. His NHL career spanned ten seasons in all. Besides Chicago, he played for the Los Angeles Kings, Pittsburgh Penguins, and Minnesota North Stars. Including the play-offs, he scored 114 goals and 433 points in 651 games, at the same time racking up 1,440 minutes in penalties. It is quite possible that Ruskowski has been captain on more NHL teams (Chicago, Los Angeles, and Pittsburgh) than any other player.

After playing, Terry started coaching hockey. First, he coached junior hockey in Canada (Saskatoon Blades), and has since coached in the East Coast Hockey League.

BILLY GARDNER

Billy Gardner played for the Hawks from 1980-81 to 1985-86. After a short stint with Hartford, Gardner returned to end his NHL career with the Hawks, appearing in eight games overall during the 1987-88 and 1988-89 seasons. Gardner's best seasons for the Blackhawks were 1983-84 and 1984-85. During the former season, Gardner was third on the team in goals, scoring 27 for 48 points in 79 games. During the latter, he scored 17 goals for 51 points in 74 games.

When asked who has been most influential upon his career, Gardner said: "I would say first and foremost, Gary Green. Because when I was drafted to Peterborough Petes, I was a defenseman. He was the coach and G.M. for two years, and we ended up winning a World Cup my second year, and [losing] in the finals my first year. He had me in and said he thought I had all the capabilities to make it, but [that] I was too small as a defenseman, and [he] moved me to center. So I would say maybe that transition helped me make it [to the NHL]."

Gardner's fondest memory of playing for the Hawks dates back to the earliest moments of his career, before he had officially made the squad. Said Gardner:

"Usually, all the young guys [at training camp] get all those 55 and 50 numbers on their jerseys when they're playing. [It was the] first game in my second training camp when I knew I was gonna make it. I had number 14 in the

Billy Gardner—remembered for his penalty-killing duties with teammate Rick Patterson. (Photo courtesy of the Blackhawks.)

first game, an exhibition game, and I ended up scoring three goals against Montreal. So I went from 51 to 14 and scored three goals. I remember Louie Varga [the team assistant trainer] saying 'you've made it.'"

Many remember Gardner for his penalty-killing duties with teammate Rick Patterson. Someone once commented that the unit was similar to that of Eric Nesterenko and Chico Maki. Responding to this, Gardner replied:

"First of all, to be put into the same sentence with those two guys. I know Eric. We've been around [him] a lot the last couple of years. He comes to the alumni functions, and we've played in a couple tournaments and games with Eric. He's a great man. To be in that high regard with that name, I know that those two guys were great players. I just think

we took a lot of pride in it. Our main focus in the game was probably the penalty kill, and we didn't get a lot of regular playing time for a couple of years. We knew that's what our job was. I think when you have people put into a situation like that, you take pride in it. When a penalty was called, we knew we were going to be up there and we wanted to do our best to keep them off the sheet. I think that had a lot to do with it. We knew what our job was, it was outlined pretty much to us and we tried our best and our hardest every time we went out there."

Gardner scored a total of 73 goals for 188 points in 380 games. He currently works as a commentator for Sports Channel.

DARRYL SUTTER

Another one of Chicago's more remarkable forwards during the eighties was Darryl Sutter, who was the head coach of the Blackhawks. Darryl grew up with his brothers on a 640-acre farm in Viking, Alberta.

Amazingly, five of his brothers made it to the NHL. Ron, Rich, Brent, Brian, and Duane have all played for different NHL teams. Ron plays for Quebec. Brian has been head coach for the St. Louis Blues and the Boston Bruins. Brent is with the Hawks as a center.

The boys all learned to play on a frozen pond on the farm, and when that thawed out, they moved their games to the barn, using a tennis ball instead of a puck.

In the January 11, 1987 issue of *The Sunday Star*, in an article by Frank Orr, Duane Sutter, who spent two seasons playing for the Hawks as well, offered some insight into those games of long ago.

"There would be six or seven of us and four or five neighbor kids in a small space playing what could be called a very competitive game," he said. "Those games are the reason why we're not afraid to operate in traffic on the ice now. When you've played in a loft game with Brian, Darryl, and Brent Sutter, you're well pre-

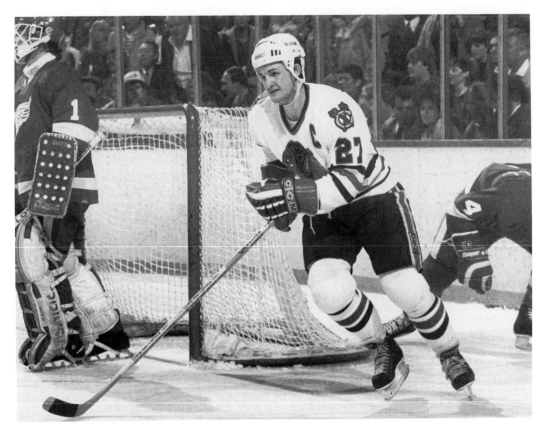

Darryl Sutter in action against the Red Wings. (Photo courtesy of the Blackhawks.)

pared for what happens in a corner in the NHL.

"Cripes, did we take it seriously? The losers wouldn't speak to the winners for days. I can remember a few times when things got so hot in the barn games, that our dad would take the tennis ball away for a few days until it cooled off."

As with all of the Sutter brothers, Darryl played junior hockey for the Lethbridge Broncos of the Western Hockey League. In 1978, Darryl was drafted by the Hawks in the eleventh round (179th overall). He spent a season playing in the Japan National League where he was named Rookie of the Year, before making the NHL. In 1979-80, he played for New Brunswick of the AHL, then the Hawks farm team, and was named Rookie of the Year there as well. His first full NHL season was 1980-81, when he led the team in goals with 40. In 1982-83, he was named team captain.

Darryl's 8-season, NHL career was spent solely in Chicago. Including the play-offs, he scored 185 goals for 322 points in 457 games. While a player,

he was known for his ability on the power play. As stated in the *1993-94 Chicago Blackhawk Media Guide*, "Darryl ranks eighth among All-Time Blackhawk play-off goal scorers with 24. He shares two Blackhawk play-off records: most goals in one play-off year with 12 (1984-85) and most overtime goals in one play-off series with two (against Minnesota 1984-85)."

Billy Gardner, who played with Sutter, described him in the following way:

"As a player, [Darryl was] a guy with very limited talent. But [he was] a great leader because of his desire to win and take his best attributes, with his limited talents...to the best possible scenario, and that was to work hard and score goals. He was a natural goal scorer and played with Tom Lysiak, who was a great player. They sort of complimented each other because Tom was so great with the puck and Darryl just went to the net and scored a lot. You have to admire the guy. Out of all the Sutters, he probably had

the least amount of talent. But when he played, he had a lot of stats to show he was contributing. To look at him, you have to admire what he did for the amount of talent that he had. That's why he was a great leader and motivator also. He was injured a lot, and that's what actually shortened his career. Definitely that's why he's a coach. You hear him in the paper sometimes and you wonder why he said what he said, but that's probably the reason why, because he always played hurt. Maybe if he didn't, he would have played longer, but things add up and it took its toll eventually, on the end of his career."

Sutter was quite an iron-man, holding onto the philosophy that you play for your money. During the 1984-85 season, he had arthroscopic surgery on his knee in September, tore rib cartilage in October, and to top it off, suffered a concussion in November. Amazingly, he remained in the lineup and continued contributing. He scored a goal in a game four nights after his concussion, helping the Hawks defeat the Rangers 6-4.

In the November 30, 1984 issue of *The Hockey News,* in an article by Neil Milbert, Sutter said:

"If they play me regularly, I darn well better produce. The concussion is no problem. It's just a slight concussion. I had a bad head for a day or so, my neck was a little stiff and my mouth hurt. Nothing major. I was lucky the knee was hurt early in training camp, so it really hasn't hampered me. When the ribs got hurt you had to wonder. Injuries like that are tough. But you just try not to think about it."

In the end, it was injuries and painful knees that ended Sutter's professional career. Since then, he has turned to coaching, but recently retired due to family matters. During the off-season, Darryl and his five other brothers each spend a week serving as instructors at Sylvan Lake Summer Hockey School each year. The camp is halfway between Edmonton and Calgary.

THE PARTY LINE

When it came to offensive power in Chicago during the eighties, three players in particular were a powerful force. In 1982-83, those three men, Denis Savard, Steve Larmer, and Al Secord, formed a line. Between the three of them, they scored 132 goals and 297 points in their first season together.

When asked about his experiences playing with Savard and Larmer, Secord explains:

"I think you could call it [the line] a three-fingered glove. Stevie Larmer had his particular style of play, I mean, he could shoot the puck, he worked hard in the corners, [and was] very consistent. Denny had most of the talent on the line, or all of the talent on the line [with a laugh]. He could handle the puck, draw guys to him, dump it off, you know, make the tough passes. Myself, basically staying on my side, working up and down the wing, working the front of the net. I think the three styles complemented each other and we had a lot of successful times."

Occasional line changes aside, Secord said the Party Line was together for about three or four years. He also said that the line, along with the entire team, was a close-knit group off the ice.

Veteran Blackhawk forward Terry Ruskowski offered an in-depth look into what made the Savard, Larmer, Secord combination such a success.

"Secord was very strong in the corners. He intimidated a lot of people [and] because of his presence, he got the puck. Denis Savard was a wizard with the puck. He'd get the puck, [and] move it around. Larmer was a guy where, he always got open for these types of people and boom, in the net. If they [the opposition] keyed on Larmer too much, then Secord would come in and deflect a lot of shots or get one of those empty-net goals that Savard used to get and pop in. It's a combination, again, of three people doing their jobs very well.

"Secord intimidated people. In front of the net he got a lot of deflections. Guys were scared to move him out because if they cross-checked him or hit him too hard, Al was coming back to get revenge on them. That way, he got a little extra room goin' around the net. A lot of people thought Al was just a tough guy [who] couldn't play, but Al was a very skilled person. He worked hard in the corner, he had a very good shot, and he was strong on his skates. In front of the net [he was good at] getting those rebounds and reflections.

"With Savard, he handled the puck so well that if you keyed on him, then the other two people were open [and] he just dished it off. It was a good combination of people, good passing, good puck control, and a guy in the corner that could really work the puck.

"And of course, Stevie Larmer, everyone knows the kind of player he is. He's a character player that comes to play every game and you can tell what kind of a player he is. It doesn't matter, on the road or at home, he's there to show up."

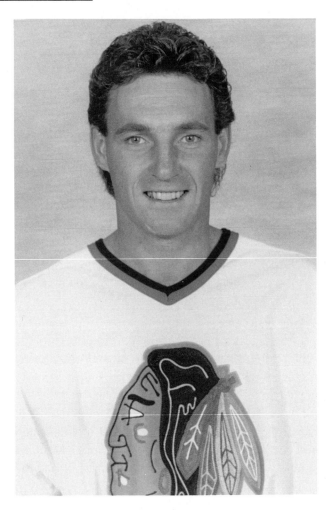

Denis Savard was Chicago's most electrifying player in the 80s. (Photo courtesy of the Blackhawks.)

DENIS SAVARD

Looking individually at the three linemates, it's fitting to begin with the man who, without a doubt, was Chicago's most electrifying player during the eighties. A 5'10" center from Pointe Gatineau, Quebec, Denis Savard is now back with the Blackhawks after short stints with the Tampa Bay Lightning and Montreal Canadiens. He played for the Blackhawks from 1980-81 to 1989-90, and returned to the Windy City late in the 1994-95 season.

Savard's best season was 1987-88, when he was placed third in scoring in the NHL, behind Mario Lemieux and Wayne Gretzky. That season, he accumulated 131 points, which to this day remains a franchise record. He was the leading scorer for the Blackhawks for seven consecutive seasons (1981-82 to 1987-88), and led them in goals in 1983-84, '85-86, '86-87, and '87-88).

Born on February 4, 1961, Savard was raised in Verdun, Quebec. Savard's older brother, André,

recalled Denis' beginnings in hockey in a 1990 *Sports Illustrated* article by Michael Farber:

"The first game Denis ever played was at Notre Dame de Lourdes school when he was seven years old," he said. "It was the first time he'd been on skates. He'd been on ice before, but only wearing boots. My parents hadn't bought him skates because the rink was outside and it was cold and they weren't sure he would like it. He wore [brother] Luc's old skates, which were pretty big for him, and scored eleven goals. My mom and dad went to the next game to see for themselves. That's when they bought him his own pair of skates."

As a boy, Savard played for his future coach Orval Tessier at a summer hockey school. Tessier predicted Savard would play in the NHL someday because of his exceptional skating abilities. Soon, he would be on his way there as his play improved with experience.

An odd thing about Savard are his days with the Montreal Juniors, a team owned by the Canadiens. While there, he played on a line entitled Les Trois Denis (the three Denis's) because his two linemates were Denis Cyr and Denis Tremblay. They were not only the best of friends, but they were also all born on the same day, February 4, 1961. They started playing together at the age of 13, and after five years together, scored a combination of over 400 goals.

While playing Junior, Savard was named to the QMJHL First All-Star Team in 1980, and was also the League's Most Valuable Player that season.

Soon, days of working in his uncle's restaurant as a bus boy and dishwasher and playing Junior hockey were over. In 1979-80, Savard was chosen by the Blackhawks with their number-three pick. It came as a big surprise to everyone, since many believed the Habs would choose the local superstar with their number one pick. The Canadiens went with a bigger player instead, choosing 6'1" Doug Wickenheiser of the Regina Pats, who had led the WHL in scoring. Winnipeg chose defenseman Dave Babych of the Portland Winter Hawks with their number-two pick.

"We knew Wickenheiser, Babych, and Savard would be the first three players to go in the draft," Bob Pulford commented at the time in a *Toronto Star* article by Rick Matsumato. "We would have been happy with any of them. But as fate would have it, we got Savard and it couldn't have turned out better for us." Savard wasn't upset over not being selected by Montreal, commenting that he was just glad to have made it to the pros.

Tony Esposito gave his impression of Savard at the time of his rookie debut in the same *Toronto Star* article. "He's very fast and shifty," he said. "He has all the moves. But he's also an all-round player. He has one of the best plus marks on the team. He does his part defensively as well as doing his thing offensively. A lot of kids with his offensive ability simply try to beat everyone and score. But not Denis. This is a team game and he's a team player."

Savard was a shifty skater, quick and agile, while he played for the Hawks. A wizard with the puck, he possessed very good ice vision, and had a deadly wrist shot. His exceptional ability enabled him to play on the 1982-83 second All Star team, and set the Blackhawk club record for most playoff goals in a game. He accomplished the latter feat on April 10, 1986, when he scored four goals against the Toronto Maple Leafs.

Many compared Denis to former Hawk great Stan Mikita. While serving as the Blackhawks' assistant coach, Cliff Koroll stated in the same *Toronto Star* article:

"There are two undeniable similarities between Stan and Denis. One is between the ears and the other is between the arm pits. Denis is a smart hockey player, just as Stan was. He also knows where the other end of the rink is. He comes back to check. He has a lot of heart, just like Stan. Denis always puts the team's performance ahead of any individual accomplishments. He possesses a lot of fine characteristics."

To help him relax, Savard enjoyed horse racing while he lived in Chicago. He owned several of his own horses, once commenting that racing was the only thing that got his mind on something other than hockey.

Denis didn't prosper under Coach Mike Keenan as he had under Bob Murdoch. In the *Sports Illustrated* article "Return of the Native," by Michael Farber, Savard said:

"I even changed as a person [under Keenan]. Instead of a guy who laughed all the time, I became quiet. I had become too intense. I couldn't figure Mike out. I could never do what I wanted to do. I'm a gambler. In the offensive zone, sometimes I'd like to try a move that is everything or nothing. That doesn't mean if I lose the puck I won't be back for defense. But if the move works, I might be clear to the net. I couldn't do that with Mike. If I didn't throw the puck in deep, he said I wasn't going to play. For his system and style, I was worth nothing."

In an early November 1988 practice, Savard got angry at Keenan after he put the team through a grueling session that consisted of over an hour of hard skating and very little else. Before the practice was over, he took off for the gate, as if to leave the rink. However, Doug Wilson and Keith Brown stopped him and persuaded him to remain on the ice. The next day, Savard apologized to the entire team, in a meeting. Some of his teammates were angered by his actions.

Savard was team captain for part of the 1987-88 season, but he resigned in 1988-89 after he was injured in the middle of the season. Savard and former coach Mike Keenan didn't get along with one another, to put it mildly, and Keenan ended up trading him to the Canadiens on June 29, 1990 for Chris Chelios and a second-round draft choice.

Savard was named to the Second All-Star Team in 1983, and made appearances in NHL All-Star games in 1982-85, 1986, 1988, and 1991. Upon his return to Chicago, he showed flashes of his youthful days with the team during the play-offs. While playing with the Canadiens, Savard learned to play a more defensive game, turning him into a more well-rounded player.

Pro Scout Jim Pappin commented on Savard's return, saying:

"He's 34 years old. But people forget that he was a great player here, and he still has speed and he can still play, but he's been playing with a bad team for the past couple of years. Coming back to the Blackhawks, I expect him to score 20 goals. I don't know why, I mean next year. Twenty or 25 goals because he's playing with better players, he still has the speed, he's gonna play with somebody decent here and shoot the puck. He was coming back here to live anyway when his career was done. Everything is right now. He's gonna end his career here. He actually was responsible for the Blackhawks for ten years. He carried the team for a good seven of those ten years anyway. People went to the Stadium to see Denis Savard because the teams weren't that good then. So basically, it's one of those both ends watch your face type of deals. I mean, we owe him, but we don't owe him. You don't owe anybody anything, you owe it to yourself. So that's a way for him to finish his career. He can set up shop here in Chicago, and ya know, a lot of these smart companies can use him as a punt person or a sales type of person when his career is done and he can make himself a lot of money. He's already in the door. There's not one person in sports who you can ask, 'who is Denis Savard,' and they [won't be able to] tell ya. You ask them who somebody else is and they'd have to think. I think he'll do well, Savvy. We'll get two good years out of him for sure."

In an April 10, 1995 *Chicago Sun Times* article by Brian Hanley, Savard said: "Putting that [Blackhawks] sweater on again—I can't explain it—but I felt more energy. I don't know if it's the crest or what, but I felt as if I never left." As of the close of the 1994-95 season, he boasted an impressive 15-season career total of 451 goals and 1,263 points in 1,063 games. Although he spent $4^{1}/_{2}$ seasons away from the Hawks, Savard is firmly recorded among the Blackhawks lifetime leaders in assists (2nd), points (3rd), and goals (4th).

STEVE LARMER

Another one of the greatest Chicago Blackhawks of the 1980s was right-wing Steve Larmer. Referred to by his teammates as Grandpa, 5'11" 185-pound Larmer played in 891 consecutive, regular-season games for the Chicago Blackhawks. At one time, he was third in consecutive games played in the League behind Garry Unger (914) and Doug Jarvis (962).

The key behind Larmer's iron-man streak was his endurance, perseverance, and tolerance for pain. Even in junior hockey, he was tough. After breaking his wrist, he missed one game, but after that returned to the ice and played in a cast for four months. In the 1991-92 *Chicago Blackhawks Official Yearbook*, in the article "Someone You Can Depend On," by Ian Hutchinson, Mike Bullard of the Toronto Maple Leafs said: "He's in an elite group. He plays with pain. No one ever knows if he's hurting or not. He plays in a small rink so you know he's taking his licks, but he's always been able to put the numbers on the board."

Where's the party? Steve Larmer, as a member of the Party Line, was one of Chicago's greatest right-wingers in the 80s and on into the 90s. (Photo courtesy of the Blackhawks.)

In that same source, the Hawks' head trainer Mike Gapski commented on Larmer's toughness, saying: "One time, he fell face first, came over to the bench and handed me a whole tooth from the top to the root. He just turned around and skated back out."

Born on June 16, 1961 in Peterborough, Ontario, Larmer played junior hockey in Niagara Falls, Ontario. During his final two seasons in the OHL (1979-80, & 1980-81), he scored 118 goals for 247 points in 150 games (including the play-offs). In the OHA, he received Second Team All-Star honors in 1981. In the sixth round of the 1980 draft, he was chosen eleventh by the Hawks (120th overall).

In 1981-82, under his future NHL coach Orval Tessier, Larmer helped the AHL New Brunswick Hawks to a Calder Cup victory. While in the AHL, he received Second-Team All-Star honors in 1982.

In 1982-83, he became a Chicago Blackhawk regular, winning the Calder Trophy as the League's outstanding rookie with a 43-goal, 90-point season. It was a super season for Larmer during which his new coach, Orval Tessier, lined him up with Denis Savard and Al Secord. In 1983, he also received NHL All Rookie Team honors.

In the October 6, 1992 issue of the *Chicago Tribune*, Darryl Sutter and Rich Preston offered their comments on Larmer at the time he came up to the Blackhawks. "What we saw initially was somebody who was very capable of being able to put the puck in the net on a regular basis," said Sutter. "But I don't think you anticipate the longevity or the success."

"We knew he was a good player, and a smart player both offensively and defensively," commented Preston. "But I

don't think anybody [thought he] would have the records he's had. The most amazing thing is his durability. As much as he plays, to have 800 straight games is amazing to me. It's a long season. You have a lot of nagging injuries. But I think that's where he's a true pro, in the sense that he said, 'I get paid to play hockey and I'm going to play it. I'm not going to let a minor injury keep me off the ice. You're going to have to take me off on a stretcher.'"

Larmer is a very dedicated two-way player who practices and plays with everything he's got. His strong work ethic is second to none.

Early in his career, many held the opinion that Larmer was overshadowed by linemate Denis Savard, who played the puck more than he passed it. However, Larmer's consistency and scoring ability are proof positive that he's one of Chicago's most valuable athletes.

In the June, 1991 issue of *Beckett Hockey Monthly*, in an article by Tom Wheatley, Larmer offered a bit of his philosophy on playing in the pros: "There's a lot more to playing than just scoring goals," he explained. "There are a lot of little things that you've got to do. People just see the end result. ... The one thing that you play for is respect from your teammates. I hope I've always had that. What other people think, what their opinions are, really doesn't matter."

Larmer's best season was 1990-91, when he scored 44 goals and led the team in scoring with a career-high 101 points. He also led the Hawks in scoring in 1988-89, and 1989-90. Since he came to Chicago, he has had five 40 or more goal seasons (1982-83, 1984-85, 1987-88, 1988-89 and 1990-91.)

At the conclusion of the 1994-95 season, Larmer ranked third in goals (406), fifth in assists (517) and fourth in points (923) on the list of Blackhawk Lifetime Leaders. In 1990-91, he was awarded with *The Hockey News/Inside Hockey* "Man of the Year" award. He has been voted to the All Star team twice (1990, 1991). In addition to this, he scored Canada's winning goal against the United States in the 1991 Canada Cup.

At the age of 32, Larmer, who served as Alternate Captain of the Blackhawks, requested to be traded in May of 1993. The Blackhawks wanted him to stay, and were willing to pay him a fair amount to do so. However, Larmer was adamant, and refused to play in Chicago under any circumstances.

In the September 3, 1993 issue of *The Hockey News*, in an article by Mike Brophy, Larmer gave an explanation for his trade request. "I really don't want to go into why I want to be traded publicly because that wouldn't do anybody any good," he said. "Nothing ever gets accomplished that way. Besides, how long can you spend in one place before it's time to move on? To get stimulated and excited again, I feel a change of scenery is necessary."

Later, Larmer also said that he wasn't very happy in the Windy City, and that a trade would make things easier on both him and his family. Sadly, the trade he longed for came after the 1993-94 season had gotten under way. This meant that his "Iron Man" streak of 884 consecutive games played had come to an end.

"Grandpa's" wish finally came true on November 2, 1993. The Blackhawks sent him off to the Hartford Whalers in exchange for defenseman Eric Weinrich and forward Patrick Poulin. The Whalers then proceeded to trade Steve, a draft pick, prospect Barry Richter, and forward Nick Kypreos to the New York Rangers for forward Darren Turcotte and defenseman James Patrick. All in all, it was quite a deal.

The deal worked out well for both sides. The pre-trade tension felt by many of the Hawks was gone, and the team was able to focus on the season at hand. Once he arrived in the Big Apple, Larmer got off to a hot start, with three goals and three assists in his first three games. He was also reunited with his old coach, Mike Keenan, with whom he helped the Rangers win the Stanley Cup in 1993-94.

Larmer is missed by many. As Bill Wirtz was quoted as saying, in a September 30, 1993 *Chicago Sun Times* article by Herb Gould, "He's one of the finest people ever to wear a Blackhawk sweater, somebody you'd love to have as a brother or a son." Larmer retired at the end of the 1994-95 season.

AL SECORD

The last member of Chicago's powerful scoring trio of the eighties was Al Secord. Secord played minor and Junior B hockey in his home town of Espanola, Ontario. He played Junior A for the same team (the OHL Fincups) in two different cities, Hamilton and St. Catharines, Ontario. Commenting on the things that allowed him to make it to the pros, Secord said:

"Everybody needs work in different areas, and everybody has their strong points. Mine was playing physical. I think what helped me in my career towards starting to score some goals, as well as playing physical was the conditioning. I had always worked out, but I went to hockey school when I was 23 and 24 years old. Going to that hockey school in the summertime taught me how to be in better shape… Basically, when I told the body to do something, the body did it because it was in shape to do it. I think the tools were there, but the physical and [strength] conditioning helped bring it out a little bit more. I think playing the physical part of the game created more room for me on the ice, which helped me score some goals. Playing with two guys like Savard and Larmer and Timmy Higgins, we just complemented each other."

Secord came to Chicago in a December 18, 1980 trade with the Bruins, which sent defenseman Mike O'Connell to Boston. He played left-wing for the Hawks until 1986-87, and again in 1989-90, his last season in the NHL. Before returning to Chicago to finish his last professional season, Secord played in Toronto and Philadelphia. Including the play-offs, Al scored 294 goals for 550 points in 868 games. He also racked up 2,475 minutes in penalties over the course of his 12-season NHL career.

Playing on the line with Savard and Larmer in 1982-83, Secord became the second player in Blackhawk history to score 50 or more goals in a season, when he scored 54.

He led the Blackhawks in scoring twice (44 goals in 1981-82, 54 goals in 1982-83).

Al Secord holds three Blackhawk club records, including an NHL record for scoring the fastest four goals in one game. (Photo courtesy of the Blackhawks.)

Describing what it took on a personal level, beyond the ability to score goals, to lead the team in scoring those two seasons, Secord said:

"I think the biggest part of being a good professional is consistency. If you notice rookies that come up; they'll play maybe one or two good games, and then maybe three or four mediocre [games]. Then they have to fight back to play that good game again. Well, the good pro, through experience and ice time, learns to be more consistent, instead of being on an emotional roller coaster; being up and down all the time. They learn to even out and maintain that mental attitude and play consistently all the time. That way, overall, you're going to get a

better season. I think that was [behind my ability to score]. Just through maturity and being in top physical shape helped reduce injuries and [allowed me to] stay on the ice. Plus, the combination of playing with two really good hockey players."

Secord holds three Chicago Blackhawk club records, the first of which equaled an NHL record originally set by Harvey (Busher) Jackson in 1934. On January 7, 1987, in a 6 to 4 victory over the Maple Leafs, Secord put the biscuit in the basket at 0:31, 3:36, 3:46, and 8:55 of the second period, setting the record for the fastest four goals in club history.

In the January 8, 1987 issue of the *Chicago Tribune*, Eddie Olczyk, who set up the goals for Secord, explained to reporter Tim Tierny: "That second period, I've never experienced anything like that. From playing in Moscow to the Olympics, nothing like it. Everything he touched was golden."

Secord's performance allowed the Hawks to beat the Maple Leafs 6 to 4, putting an end to a 9-game losing streak against Toronto. It was Al's fifth career hat trick, and his second career 4-goal game. It ended a short personal slump, as he had only scored one goal in the previous 12 games. Unfortunately, he ended up watching the last half of the third period from the bench after he hyperextended his elbow. The record has since been matched by Calgary's Joe Nieuwendyk, in January of 1989 when he scored four goals in an 8 to 3 victory over Winnipeg.

The 6'1", 205-pound Sudbury, Ontario, native also set a team record for minutes in penalties during a season (now held by Mike Peluso, 408 in 1991-92), when he racked up 303 in 1981-82. Also, in an April 9, 1983, 2 to 1 Blackhawks play-off victory against the St. Louis Blues, Secord set the club records for penalty minutes in one play-off period (35) and penalty minutes in one play-off game (37) when he was given a major misconduct, and two game misconducts in the second period.

Describing his philosophy on being such an aggressive player, Secord explains: "My skills were not as good as a lot of other players that made professional. I think early in junior I had to realize what my strengths were and use them to the best of my ability to play. Being physical was what got me to the NHL and I had to remember that throughout my career."

In an article by Neil Milbert in the March 26, 1982 issue of *The Hockey News*, Secord said: "I want to be thought of as a hockey player, not a fighter. Fighting takes a lot out of you. If I didn't fight, I probably would have more goals. It's not just the time you spend in the penalty box; it's also the physical abuse your body takes. But my game has to be physical. I can't forget what got me here. You've got to be realistic; you can't live in fantasyland."

While he played for Chicago, Secord took boxing lessons at a south-side gym. "I started boxing, actually, when I was an early teenager. I had found a boxing club on the south side. I went there and trained a little bit, just to keep a hand in it." Al spent time training under a coach by the name of Ray Murray while he was there. "I was the only white guy in the club, but I tell ya, everybody treated me very nice. Very nice people there."

Secord didn't pursue boxing just because of its aggressive nature. It was very good conditioning as well, something he was a big student of. "It was good training," he said. "I was treated very well. They taught me a lot. It was good conditioning. Boxers are some of the best conditioned athletes in the world. So, I used that for my training for hockey. I was not only taking care of myself, but being a heavier guy, it taught me to be light on my feet and help quicken my reflexes, things like that."

In the previously-cited Neil Milbert article, Secord once commented that another benefit he received from boxing was mental control and discipline. "Boxing teaches you how to control your head, not to get excited, and not to do something stupid," he said at the time. "It gave me discipline."

Thinking back over his career, Secord related the one fight he'll never forget.

"Probably the one I had with Dave Hutchison [1550 career penalty minutes] in Toronto. I was a new member of the Bruins and hadn't quite made the team yet; it was only the second or third game into the season. We were in Toronto and Don Cherry had sort of bribed me to take my helmet off and he would start me in

the game and put me on the first power play. So, my first shift out there, I guess I was running around a little bit and Dave Hutchison and I met up in the corner and we had a fight. I guess Don was a little worried about me because Dave was such an established tough guy. But I did really well in the fight and the fight pretty well made the team for me. Not dirty [fighting], just stand-up, rock'em, sock'em fist fighting."

When asked to recall his most memorable game, two things came to mind. "Scoring the 50th goal was memorable," he said. "That, and I can remember scoring a winning goal against Hartford when I was with Boston with Gordie Howe hooking me while I was scoring the goal. So that was a memorable goal."

On September 3, 1987, Secord was traded to the Toronto Maple Leafs with teammate Ed Olczyk. In return, the Leafs sent Rick Vaive, Steve Thomas, and Bob McGill to Chicago. Some people felt that Toronto coach John Brophy was after Secord for his aggressiveness, not his playing ability.

"I think he was looking for both," said Secord. "I think when I came from Chicago, he didn't want me to change a thing. I honestly think I could've done better in Toronto. I wasn't producing the numbers or playing the way that I think I should have. But, like I said, all you can do is go out there and give your best effort and take what comes."

After playing in Toronto, Secord went on to play for the Flyers. He returned to Chicago and finished up his last NHL season there in 1989-90. Today, Al lives in Michigan where he works as a commercial airline pilot.

"I basically took six months off after I announced my retirement and went to school and finished up my airplane ratings," he said. "I was a private pilot since 1984. I used to fly, basically, in the summertime. I was what they called a V.F.R. [Visual Flight Rules] pilot; I would just fly on the nice days. A couple of years before I retired, I was going to school in the summer, getting my commercial ratings, [and] my instrument ratings.

"When I retired I went to Philadelphia and flew cargo at night with a pharmaceutical company. Basically, that's where I built up my time, which qualifies me for the job I'm doing now. Now I work for a company called Great Lakes Airlines, and we fly under the United Express colors. We're a commuter for United Airlines, we're in agreement with them. We fly out of Sault Ste. Marie, Michigan and we stop in the various cities throughout Michigan. [We] bring the people into the major hubs like Chicago O'Hare and Detroit every day."

When asked how he would describe himself as a player, Secord, now 33, said: "How would I describe myself? Oh, let's see. Well, I hope I gave the impression of being a hard-working, honest player that, when I went out, I gave a 100–150 percent whether it was a good game or a bad game. That I showed that I was there to play and I was out there to win, doing the very best while I was out there." Today, Secord plays for the Chicago Wolves of the IHL.

EDDIE OLCZYK

A native of the Chicago area, Ed Olczyk played right-wing for the Chicago Blackhawks from 1984-85 to 1987-88. The son of a Polish immigrant from Germany, Olczyk was born on August 16, 1966, and grew up in Palos Heights, Illinois. He spent a successful season playing Junior B hockey in Stratford, Ontario, before (along with Al Iafrate) becoming the youngest player on the 1984 U.S. Olympic Team in Sarajevo at the age of 17. In six Olympic games, he racked up nine points.

After the Olympics, where the Americans failed to make the medal round, Olczyk turned down an offer to play for the Toronto Marlboros and was chosen first by the Hawks (third overall) in the 1984 Entry Draft. Because he was a local, Olczyk was an instant hit with Chicago fans. In a January/February 1988 *Inside Hockey* article by Steve Dryden, Eddie commented: "In my first game, I scored a goal and the fans started chanting my name like they used to for Tony Esposito. I'd never felt better in my whole life."

Eddie Olczyk–a Chicago native and son of a Polish immigrant, whose career is still going strong. (Photo courtesy of the Blackhawks.)

While with Chicago, Olczyk played on the "Almost Clydesdales Line" with Troy Murray and Curt Fraser. In the same Steve Dryden article, Eddie recalled playing on the line during his second season [1985-86] with the Hawks, commenting: "Troy almost got 100 points (45-54-99), I almost got 80 and Curt almost got 70 (29-39-68). My confidence was so high. And then all of a sudden it happened—Toronto [then in fourth place, 29 points behind first-place Chicago] sweeps us in three straight." That second season, when he scored 29 goals for 70 points in 79 games, was Olczyk's best with the Blackhawks.

Being a Chicago native was a source of stress for Olczyk. Reportedly, some of his teammates were envious of all of the special attention he received. In the same Dryden article, former Blackhawk Rick Patterson said: "I think there were one or two players who were envious of him. But I don't think they caused him a problem...He is really emotional. And he believed the guys really didn't like him when something happened...but it didn't happen very often."

Former teammate Billy Gardner said the following of Olczyk, shedding some light on Olczyk's overall situation:

"It's a funny situation, Eddie being a Chicago kid when he made the Olympic team back in '84. In the summer, in July, the Blackhawks called me to go represent the Blackhawks and give Eddie a token of appreciation for making the Olympic team. I was the guy they called. I took Eddie a sweater with the number 16 on it. This was before he was even playing with Chicago. I got to meet him and his family even before [the] time when he was drafted. So it was kind of neat to have him drafted in the first round and to have him as a teammate. I think Eddie was misunderstood too. He was a great guy and he had time for everybody and had a lot of talent. I think he just got into the position here where he had a lot of pressure on him because

he was the hometown kid. Maybe getting out was ... good for him. He had a couple good years after that, and I guess he's playing o.k. now. Overall, he was a very nice guy, and a great human being who had a lot of talent."

On September 3, 1987, along with Al Secord, Eddie was traded to the Toronto Maple Leafs for Rick Vaive, Steve Thomas, and Bob McGill. He had the best seasons of his career with the Leafs, scoring 42 goals for 75 points his first season there. In 1988-89 and 1989-90, he scored 38 goals for 90 points and 32 goals for 88 points, respectively.

After spending a little over three seasons in Toronto, Olczyk has since gone on to play for the Winnipeg Jets and the New York Rangers. He was with New York in 1993-94 when they won the Stanley Cup. Because he and teammate Mike Hartman did not play 40 games during the season, the League ruled that their names not be included on the Stanley Cup. Due to a fractured thumb, Olczyk played in 37 games, and Hartman 35. Ironically, the names of Oilers' owner Peter Pocklington's wife, and Oilers' public relations man Bill Tuele appeared on the trophy in previous years.

In an October 7, 1994 *Toronto Sun* article by Dave Fuller, Rangers general manager Neil Smith commented on the decision: "I think leaving Eddie O's name off the Cup is a tragedy," he said. "He was with us from the start of training camp all the way through June 14."

In the same article, Olczyk said: "Twenty-five years from now, I'd love for my kids' kids to be able to go to the Hockey Hall of Fame to see the Cup with their Grandfather's name on it, but I guess that's not going to happen."

Still with the Rangers, Olczyk's career total, as of the close of the 1993-94 season, stands at 263 goals for 626 points in 718 games. Some of Eddie's other career highlights include playing for the United States in the 1984, 1987, and 1991 Canada Cup tournaments, appearing in the 1987, 1989, and 1990 World Championships, and serving as the captain of Team USA at the 1993 World Championships in Munich, Germany.

TROY MURRAY

Troy Norman Murray was Chicago's sixth choice (57th overall) in the third round of the 1980 Entry Draft from the Tier II St. Albert Saints. He played center for the Chicago Blackhawks from 1981-82 to 1990-91, and after spending a season-and-a-half in Winnipeg, returned to the Windy City in 1992-93. After staying only a short while, the Hawks put Murray on waivers on February 16, 1994, and sent him to the Indianapolis Ice. On March 11, 1994, he was traded to the Ottawa Senators with the Hawks' 11th round choice (Rob Mara) in the 1994 Entry Draft.

Born on July 31, 1962 in Calgary, Alberta, Troy played hockey for the University of North Dakota prior to his arrival in Chicago. While in the WCHA, he was named Freshman of the Year in 1981, and was elected to the WCHA Second All-Star team in 1981 and 1982. During Christmas vacation, he served as Captain of Team Canada and his team went on to win the World Junior Championship.

After he returned from the Christmas holidays, he led the Sioux to the NCAA Championship in March of 1982. That tournament was held in Providence, Rhode Island. One of his thundering checks sent a University of Wisconsin player off of the ice on a stretcher. In 1982-83, after his sophomore year at the University of North Dakota, he came to the Chicago Blackhawks.

Commenting on his development as a player in the February 14, 1986 issue of *The Hockey News*, in an article by Mike Perricone, Murray once explained: "I was always a goal scorer. Gino Gasparini is the coach who really stressed playing in the defensive end. I give him more credit than anybody that I've gotten even as far as I have gotten." Playing defensively is what got Murray the Frank J. Selke Memorial Trophy in 1986 for being the League's best defensive forward.

Murray's former teammate Al Secord gave his impression of Troy: "When he first came to the club, I guess the biggest thing that stands out with me [is] how he used to throw out these real hard body checks. He used to nail guys and straighten 'em up. He's a very, very strong guy. He's very dedicated in the off-season in conditioning for the following season. He comes to play."

Murray has played a physical game since the beginning. During the 1982 World Junior Championships, Murray showed the type of play that Secord described. That season, he and his Canada teammates took home the gold medal.

Terry Ruskowski, also a former teammate of Murray, gave his impression of Troy:

"I didn't play with him [that] much. To me, Troy Murray was one of the sturdiest guys on the skates that I've ever seen. In practice, in scrimmage, I tried to hit him and man, it's like hitting a brick wall! He made some checks that, at that particular time, I hadn't seen in a long time. Because he was so strong on his skates and had such good balance, when he hit somebody, the guy was hit. To try to knock him off his skates was almost impossible. He was very sturdy on his skates. [He was] another kid that I really liked; a quiet guy that came to play hockey. He wanted to play and he came to play hockey. He was another real good asset to the Chicago Blackhawks, real good asset. He's the type of guy that, on the road or at home, Troy was counted on. In fact, he wasn't very aggressive fighting-wise, he didn't do that. But, nobody intimidated him either. He just kept on hitting and playing hard. He was a very strong skater. He was a good shot, and he handled the puck well."

Troy Murray played center for the Blackhawks from 1981 to 1991. (Photo courtesy of the Blackhawks.)

Along with Warren Rychel, Murray was traded to the Winnipeg Jets on July 22, 1991, for Bryan Marchment and Chris Norton. As fate would have it, he was traded back to Chicago for a draft pick and minor-league defenseman Steve Bancroft after two seasons there, because the Jets were in the market for younger players. However, as previously mentioned, Murray's career with the Blackhawks quickly came to an end during the 1993-94 season. At the close of the 1993-94 season, Murray had scored 219 goals for 547 points in 806 games.

Terry Ruskowski seeing some game action in the 80s against the Maple Leafs. (Photo from the Hockey Hall of Fame/Miles Nadal Collection.)

COLD STEEL ON ICE

THE 1990s

The decade of the 1990s has introduced a great deal of hockey excitement to the city of Chicago, along with some great achievements. However, it has also introduced some disappointing moments. Things got rolling early on with a little of both.

In 1990-91, the Blackhawks rocked and rolled their way to the top of the League, taking home the President's Trophy (team finishing first overall during the regular season) with 106 points and a Norris Division championship. This was quite an accomplishment. However, the sweet taste of victory turned sour in the postseason when the Hawks were eliminated in the first round by the Minnesota North Stars.

1992-93 Chicago Blackhawks—Top row, l to r: Ed O'Brien, Mark King, Randy Lacey, Mike Gapski, Cal Botterill, Lou Varga, Pawel Prylinski. Third row, l to r: Cam Russell, Rod Buskas, Christian Ruuttu, Brian Noonan, Dave Christian, Jocelyn Lemieux, Rob Brown, Greg Gilbert, Bryan Marchment, Frantisek Kucera, Mike Hudson. Second row, l to r: Stephane Matteau, Keith Brown, Ed Belfour, Jeremy Roenick, Jim Pappin, Rich Preston, Darryl Sutter, Paul Baxter, Bob Murray, Jimmy Waite, Michel Goulet, Igor Kravchuk, Stu Grimson. Front row, l to r: Brent Sutter, Steve Smith, Jack Davison, Mike Keenan, Peter Wirtz, William W. Wirtz, Dirk Graham, Michael Wirtz, W. Rockwell Wirtz, Thomas Ivan, Robert Pulford, Chris Chelios, Steve Larmer.

The team had a strong chance of taking home Lord Stanley's Cup. It was a little embarrassing, since the Hawks had made it to the third round of the play-offs the previous season, even though they hadn't been as successful in the regular season.

The next season brought even more excitement as the Blackhawks made it to the Stanley Cup finals for the first time since 1973, after they eliminated the Edmonton Oilers 5-1 on May 22, 1992, taking that series 4-0. At the time, they had won 11 straight play-off games in a row. However, the Penguins were unstoppable. They were also on a roll, and went on to swallow up the Hawks in four straight games, tying the record for most consecutive victories in one play-off year (In 1992-93, Montreal also tied this record).

It was hard to accept what had happened when the Penguins battled back from a 4-1 deficit in the second period and ended everything with 13 seconds to go. Even though Eddie Belfour criticized himself for not playing well, the fact that Pittsburgh played a superb series cannot be denied.

Actor Jim Belushi, then the Blackhawks' Celebrity Captain, recalled the final game in Pittsburgh: "All I remember is the first period," he explained. "My buddy Rob Curtis and I, [an] old hockey fan, we sat in the crowd. And that first period, when they scored like four goals, we were screamin' and shovin' it down their faces! The crowd was dead silent and you could hear me and Rob screaming through the whole place. When they [the Penguins] came back and won, we had to get out of there before they killed us!"

A diehard Hawks fan, Belushi also got wild earlier in the play-offs, when Chicago eliminated the Red Wings from the postseason play. "In Detroit, when we beat Detroit..., Mrs. Wirtz [wife of owner Bill Wirtz] handed me a broom and I threw it over the glass, onto the ice when we swept Detroit. They caught it on camera. No one will ever let me forget it. They don't understand why I haven't been fined."

After being swept by the Blues in the first round of the 1992-93 postseason, experiencing a power play in bad need of repair and a weakened offense, management emphasized youth going into the 1993-94 season. Change was evident everywhere as the team lost Steve Larmer, who demanded a trade, and new faces (Tony Amonte, Paul Ysebaert,

Robert Dirk, Gary Suter, Randy Cunneyworth, and Matthew Oates) were circling everywhere about the Chicago Stadium Ice. Coach Sutter commented on this in a March 25, 1994 *Chicago Sun Times* article by Brian Hanley, saying: "I told my captains that...[one] night I looked down the bench and realized there were only six players there who finished the season here last year—Chris Chelios, three centermen, Joe Murphy, and Ed Belfour. And Murph came here at the end of last season. That's a tremendous change."

The same system of play governed the Hawks' game style during the 1993-94 season, even though some alterations were made for the offense, mainly Jeremy Roenick. In a January 12, 1994 *Chicago Sun Times* article by Brian Hanley coach Sutter described the Hawks "system," commenting: "Our system is one of contact and contain similar to football coverage really. And playing physical doesn't always mean running people over. Guys just have to be more responsible for their performance defensively. Not locking out [costs us goals]."

Despite all of the changes, and some spectacular postseason net-minding by the Eagle, the Blackhawks were once again defeated in a hard-fought, opening round of the Stanley Cup play-offs by the Toronto Maple Leafs. During the regular season, they had very impressive penalty killing, and ended up with an overall sixth-place finish. Their power play was very flimsy, which worked against them in the play-offs.

The goal by Mike Gartner that eliminated the Blackhawks from the play-offs in 1993-94 was historic for several reasons. First of all, it was the very last scored in Chicago Stadium. Secondly, it caused the Hawks to be the first team in League history to lose 1-0 three times. It also caused Toronto net-minder Felix Potvin to become the second goalie in League history, next to former Maple Leaf Frank McCool in 1945, to shut out the opposition three times in postseason play. Despite the historical significance, it was not a memorable game for Chicago.

Prior to the 1994-95 season, Jeremy Roenick said: "You can expect a more offensive team [this season]. We have a tremendously talented team. We haven't seen a team like this in Chicago on paper in a long time. I would expect to see a lot of urgency and a lot of excited faces come the start of the season."

Roenick's statement was somewhat correct, especially when one considers all of the inconsistency and adversity the 1994-95 season presented. The team's offensive production was much improved, especially when they faced Pacific Division foes. After returning from the NHL's lockout and getting back into shape, the Hawks experienced a much-improved power play, and managed to stay afloat after Jeremy Roenick was injured and the team fell into a bad slump, going winless for 13 games. In the end, however, the Hawks bowed out of the play-offs in an intense, hard-fought battle for the conference title with the Detroit Red Wings in the fifth game. Thirsty to end their Stanley Cup drought, the Red Wings had more depth and offensive power than the Hawks, and were able to capitalize on their edge to advance to the finals, despite great goaltending by Ed Belfour.

One interesting move the Hawks made was the acquisition of Bob Probert from the Detroit Red Wings in the preseason for $6.6 million. Probert had been let go from the Detroit Red Wings because of his long history of drug and alcohol abuse, which involved near deportation by the U.S. Immigration and Naturalization Service and numerous arrests.

In an August 1, 1994 *Chicago Sun Times* article by Brian Hanley, Red Wings senior vice president Jim Devellano commented: "To think they [the Blackhawks] can do in one month what we've been trying to do for ten years. We had an assistant coach, Colin Campbell, whose only job was to look after Bob Probert. He did as terrific a job as he could, but in the end he couldn't do it. I don't have any axes to grind, and there is no bitterness. I like Bob personally. I've had so many dealings with him; he's almost like a son to me. But at some point you have to say enough is enough. And we reached that point."

The Blackhawks put Probert through a lengthy rehabilitation program at the ASAP Family Treatment Center in California, which he completed. "It's his life, not just his career we're talking about now," said Darryl Sutter in the September 16, 1994 issue of *The Hockey News*, in an article by Tim Sassone. "The organization he came from can say what it wants, but the fact is he didn't have much direction. I wish he didn't have this problem, but he does and he needs help. He can't do it on his own."

Probert was cleared by commissioner Gary Bettman to play again in the NHL for the 1995-96 season. Hopefully, he will be able to stay clean and will step into his role as the team's new enforcer, especially with the birth of his new daughter Brogan. Only time will tell.

Hawk centerman Jeremy Roenick gave his feelings on the acquisition, commenting:

> *"Bob's gonna be a big asset to our team. Obviously he's gonna be a big asset for me, personally. I'll have someone on the side that if someone's gonna come hit me they're gonna have to think twice about it. Ya know, I'm gonna get a little bit more room. I think people aren't gonna be as brave to go after me at times because, I mean, Bob Probert's gonna be right there. That's not saying I can't handle myself, because I've proven year after year that I'm not going to back down to anybody, I don't care who it is. I've shown that by fightin' Bob Probert, I've done that by fightin' [Craig] Berube, I fought Marty McSorley, so it's not like I can't handle my own battles. But it just puts a little question mark into other people's heads before they make something, and that indecision could mean whether I beat somebody or not."*

When asked if there were any concerns over past entanglements some of the Hawks might have had with Probert over the years, several teammates explained that the situation posed no problem. Said Roenick: "Oh, everything goes out the window. Unless you do something that blatantly, obviously jeopardizes someone's career. A fight, or a big hit or anything that happens in the game, it's usually pretty much forgotten about. I mean, we do what we have to do on the ice, but a lot of people can go out after the game and be friends and go out for a beer too. Everything is based on the game, not so much on people's personalities."

MIKE KEENAN

In the coaching department, the Hawks began the decade with Mike Keenan behind the bench. Born on October 21, 1949, Keenan has acquired a reputation for being a harsh, intimidating, discipline-oriented coach whose methods can be unpredictable at times. In Chicago, he earned the

Mike Keenan—nicknamed "Captain Hook" for pulling goalies and the team's best players when he felt the urge. (Photo courtesy of the Blackhawks.)

While there, he and the Flyers were very successful. Beginning in 1984-85, "Iron Mike" took the team to a league-best 53 wins, for a total of 113 points. That season, and once again in 1986-87, he took the Flyers to both the Patrick Division Title and the Wales Conference Championship, as well as the Stanley Cup finals. In 1986-87, the Flyers were defeated 3-1 by the Oilers in the seventh and final game. Keenan's authoritarian coaching methods didn't sit well with the players, especially the younger ones, in Philadelphia, and in May of 1988 General Manager Bobby Clarke fired him.

Two months later, on July 9, 1988, Keenan was named Head Coach of the Blackhawks. In the Windy City, Keenan continued to find success as a coach, even though his style wasn't accepted by many. In 1989-90 and 1990-91, he coached the team to Norris Division Titles. In the latter season, he was named *The Hockey News'* NHL Coach of the Year, as he coached the Blackhawks to a League-best, 106-point season, for which they took home the President's Trophy.

Commenting on his style in *The Hockey News* article by Damien Cox, which appeared in the October 2, 1992 issue, Keenan said: "You have to remember, I wasn't a former player when I first started coaching and I was going into an industry which did not have much patience for coaches. So my survival instincts took over early in my career. There are some things I look back on and wish I was more polished. I wish I hadn't been as tough on guys as overtly as I was."

Former Blackhawk veteran Troy Murray, in a *Sports Illustrated* article by Jay Greenberg, spoke positively of Keenan. "What Mike expects from us, we never expected from ourselves," he said. "I never realized how much more of an effort I had to put in. He's always challenging us to go to a higher level. When you reach that one, you get pushed to another one."

In 1990-91, Keenan took on the duty of General Manager in addition to his coaching responsibilities. In June of 1992, he then put coaching aside to focus solely on his duties as General Manager. He was relieved of his position on November fifth of that year. According to an article by Al Morganti, which appeared in the November 20, 1992 issue of *The Hockey News*, the Blackhawks made Keenan a generous offer to continue as their General Man-

nickname "Captain Hook" for his habit of pulling goalies and the team's best players whenever he felt the urge. Although he is still a demanding coach, his style has toned down since his earlier days in the National Hockey League.

Keenan graduated from St. Lawrence University, where he played hockey. He later coached Junior B hockey in the Metro Toronto League, before earning his Masters in Education from the University of Toronto. In 1980, he coached the OHL Peterborough Petes, beginning a very successful coaching career. In 1982-83, he coached the AHL Rochester Americans to the Calder Cup. Then in 1983-84, he coached the University of Toronto to the CIAU Canadian College Championships.

Keenan's NHL debut came with the Philadelphia Flyers in 1984-85, where he remained until 1987-88. In Philly, he became the first coach in NHL history to win 40-or more games in each of his first three seasons, and won the Jack Adams Trophy (NHL coach judged to have contributed the most to his team's success) in 1985.

ager, but they would not allow him to negotiate contracts; a common responsibility of most G.M.s. According to the article, he was also supposedly seeking to be named an alternate governor, and wanted to be able to start all trades.

On April 17, 1993, Keenan was named Head Coach of the New York Rangers, who hadn't won a Stanley Cup for 53 years. Supposedly, he has worked on his shortcomings as a coach. In the April 4, 1993 issue of *The Hockey News*, he commented: "I think [the] abrasive stuff is overstated. From time to time, I will openly admit, I went close to or over the line. But I've grown and matured as a coach and I think you'll be surprised to see that development as far as my ability to relate to players."

More recently, in the May 29, 1994 issue of the *Chicago Sun Times*, Keenan commented on the hardships he has experienced prior to the 1993-94 season.

> *"When I was fired in Chicago, I had time to reflect upon some of the things I should have processed before. I have had a lot of hardships, a lot of losses. I lost my brother, then my parents were divorced, then Rita and I had six miscarriages.*
>
> *"I was fired in Philadelphia, without what I believed at the time to be just cause. I was fired in Chicago with even less cause. I have come to an understanding of why the people in Philadelphia would fire me, but in Chicago it was a complete power struggle, inexcusable. Then, after that, I lost my family [separating from his wife, Rita, and 15-year old daughter, Gayla, last spring]. So I am now in a different place in my life."*

After the Rangers hired him, Keenan became the highest-paid coach in NHL history. Prior to the 1993-94 season, his cumulative coaching record was 343-228-69, 62-52 in the play-offs. His arrival in New York was accompanied by an incredible regular season record, and the Ranger's first Stanley Cup victory in 54 years! Keenan proceeded to jump ship to the St. Louis Blues the following season, where he was able to secure the job of coach and G.M. once again.

In addition to his regular coaching background, Keenan has also succeeded in other areas of coaching as well. In both 1986 and 1988, he coached the Wales Conference to All-Star victories. In addition to this, he has coached Team Canada to two Canada Cup Championships (1987 and 1991).

DARRYL SUTTER

After injuries ended his playing career, Darryl Sutter turned to coaching. He served as the Blackhawks' assistant coach in 1987-88, and then went on to coach their minor league team, the Saginaw Hawks, in 1988-89. He led Saginaw to a 102-point East Division finish. The next season, he coached the Hawks' new minor league team in Indianapolis, leading them to a first-place division finish (second in the league) with 114 points. Darryl received the Commissioner's Trophy for Coach of the Year that season as the Ice won the Turner Cup. In 1990-91, he again served as the assistant coach in Chicago until 1992-93, when he was named head coach. At that time, he became the youngest coach in the NHL at the age of 33. At the close of the

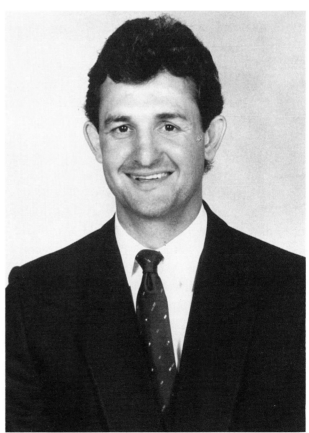

Darryl Sutter—turned to coaching after injuries ended his playing career. (Photo courtesy of the Blackhawks.)

1994-95 season, with tears in his eyes, Sutter made a decision to resign as the Hawks' head coach so that he could spend more time with his wife and children. His 2-year-old son Christopher has Down's syndrome. "It wasn't a hard decision," he said in a June 19, 1995 *Chicago Sun Times* article by Brian Hanley. "I think I had other priorities. And sometimes what's best for you is not what's best for everyone else."

Continuing, he explained some of the pressures he had to deal with as head coach in more detail. "Let me tell you something about being a head coach," he said. "It's a miserable thing to be. It eats you up and consumes you all the time. Even when you are sitting with the kids at home, you're not thinking about the kids, you're thinking about how to get more out of a guy in the locker room." Sutter said that he would remain with the Blackhawks in some capacity. He also said that he would never work for another hockey club, as his loyalty remains with the Hawks organization.

Darryl coached because he loved the game, not for money or fame. As he said several days before his retirement, in an article by Brian Hanley in the June 14, 1995 issue of the *Chicago Sun Times*, "I've said it before, I don't coach for ego or money. My background is still what drives me in whatever I do, and with that goes the importance of my family. I didn't come from a material world where you need $1 million or are judged on how much you make, so that's part of it. I still don't have hockey out of me…But as much as I want to do it and all that…Let's put it this way, they [the Hawks] would get along without me just fine."

Blackhawk defenseman Cam Russell, who played for Sutter in Indianapolis, gave his opinion of him in the June 26, 1992 issue of *The Hockey News*, in an article by Tim Sassone. "Darryl's one of those people who commands respect," he said. "He's the kind of guy you want to go through a wall for. Darryl doesn't rant or rave or do a lot of yelling, but he's intense. He hates to lose."

In the same article, Sutter commented on his philosophy as a coach. "I think one of my strengths is being able to sit down and go one-on-one with a guy," he explained. "But I'd rather not talk to you at all if I have to lie to you. The truth hurts, but the truth helps."

One of the obstacles Sutter faced as Head Coach of the Blackhawks was coaching his younger brother Brent (for a time, he coached Rich as well). Although many may feel that because they were brothers, Darryl went easy on him, Sutter insisted this was not true, pointing out that the opposite is often the case.

Hawk forward Joe Murphy gave his feelings on Sutter prior to the 1994-95 season, commenting:

"Darryl's fair and up-front and honest from my dealings with everybody on the team. He gives no preferential treatment to Richie or Brent, I mean, that's just blown out of proportion. He's the coach and those guys are the hockey players. I know they're brothers, but when we hit the dressing room and the ice, it's business. I've very much enjoyed playing for Darryl. I think it's a good situation. He knows the game real well. I'm just excited to come back in again. We basically turned over the whole team last year, I mean, 10, 12 new guys. For the whole coaching staff and for the whole team, that's like building a whole new team from scratch. I'm excited."

CRAIG HARTSBURG

The man that now serves as the head coach of the Chicago Blackhawks is Craig Hartsburg. The Hawks' 30th coach, Hartsburg spent ten years in the NHL as a defenseman with the Minnesota North Stars. A native of Stratford, Ontario, he was an assistant coach with the Flyers. The 1994-95 season was Hartsburg's first as a head coach at any level. He was most successful in his debut, leading the Guelph Storm to a first place finish in the OHL, with his team finishing late in the finals against the Detroit Junior Red Wings. The season earned him coach of the year honors by both the Ontario and Canadian Hockey Leagues. Hartsburg named Dirk Graham, with whom he played with in Minnesota, as his assistant coach in addition to Lorne Henning.

Hartsburg was known as an offensive-defenseman and was the North Stars' captain for six seasons, until injuries forced him into retirement. He was chosen Minnesota's first choice (sixth overall) in the 1979 NHL draft. Hartsburg played in 570

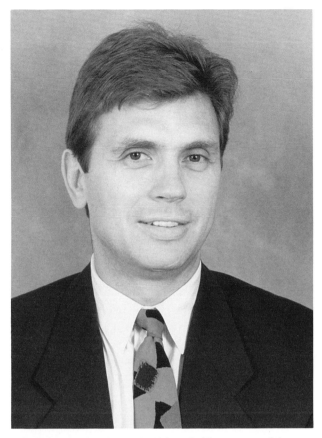

Craig Hartsburg is the Blackhawks' 30th coach. (Photo courtesy of the Blackhawks.)

games during his NHL career, recording 98 goals, 315 assists (413 points), and 818 penalty minutes. On November 1, 1986 versus the Blackhawks, he became the only North Star defenseman to score a hat trick.

Hartsburg lists winning the Canada Cup Championship in 1987 as his most memorable hockey moment. He participated in three NHL All-Star games (1980, 1982, and 1983) and also competed in three World Championship tournaments for Team Canada—and was chosen best defenseman of the 1987 World Championships. In February of 1992, Hartsburg was voted to the North Stars' 25th Anniversary Dream Team by Minnesota fans.

THE MEN

One plus is that the Blackhawks of today are a close group of individuals who pull for each other both on and off the ice. Said Hawks center Jeremy Roenick: "We're very close knit. We have a lot of guys who are very close. They are good friends.

There is not anybody on our team who anybody dislikes, which I think is very important. We're willing to go to war, go to battle every night for each other. Off the ice, the guys get together a lot and go out on the town or go together and shoot pool, or just go to the bar and watch the football game. It's a lot of fun. When we go out on the road we go for dinners. A few groups of like five or six, seven guys [go] instead of like one and two and three people at a time, so it's a lot of fun."

Among the Blackhawks on today's roster are some phenomenal athletes. Fortunately, Chicago has been home to many of them for the entire decade of the nineties. Others, like the remarkable Michel Goulet and dependable Steve Larmer, are no longer with the team. However, their contributions will most certainly not be forgotten. Among the 1990s' best are Ed Belfour, Chris Chelios, Steve Smith, Cam Russell, Jeremy Roenick, Bernie Nicholls, Tony Amonte, Joe Murphy, Steve Larmer, Michel Goulet, Dirk Graham, and Brent Sutter.

ED BELFOUR

Looking at goaltending in Chicago, several quality net-minders have donned the Indian-head sweater during the nineties. Among them are Jimmy Waite, Dominik Hasek, Greg Millen, and Jeff Hackett. However, without a doubt, the main attraction in Chicago's goaltending ranks is Ed Belfour. Labeled by Hall-of-Famer Vladislav Tretiak as one of the best goalies in the world, Ed Belfour was signed as a free agent by the Chicago Blackhawks on June 18, 1987. Since that time, he has emerged as one of the National Hockey League's top net-minders. He is the definition of intensity and determination.

Born on April 21, 1965, in Carman, Manitoba, Belfour played for the Carman Cougars as a youth in his home town. He began playing hockey at the age of five, and at the age of 12, he started playing goal when his coach decided that he was racking up too many penalty minutes as a center. In 1985-86, he was voted the MJHL top goaltender while playing for Winkler, and was a First Team All-Star. He never played Junior A hockey, but instead went on to play for the University of North Dakota, where he received a hockey scholarship. While there, he was a WCHA First Team All-Star, and helped the Fighting Sioux beat Michigan State in 1987, resulting in a NCAA Championship victory.

In the Spring of 1987, Belfour was acquired by Chicago. He soon received All-Star honors in the IHL while playing for Saginaw, then Chicago's minor league affiliate. Also, in 1987-88, he shared the Longman Memorial Trophy as the IHL top rookie. Since Chicago already had good goaltenders in Jacques Cloutier and Alain Chevrier, along with Jimmy Waite tending goal in Indianapolis, Belfour became a more seasoned goalie by manning the pipes for the Canadian National Team before earning a regular seat in the NHL in 1990-91.

It was the Blackhawks' Pro Scout Jim Pappin who largely discovered Belfour. Pappin explains:

"My son went to college up in North Dakota, that's how I found him. He kept tellin' me 'Dad, we got a good goaltender up here, and he's a Blackhawks fanatic. He just wants to play for the Blackhawks, doesn't want to play for anybody else. You have to come up and look at him.' So I went up to see him, and the first time I didn't like him that much because of the different style that he's got - he's always had the same style that he uses now. It looked like he had a lot of holes in him. But, the more I kept watching him [the better he looked]. They won the championship that year, before they got there.

I finally talked our Head Scout, Jack Davison and Bob Pulford into goin' to see him in Detroit, the last weekend they played. So [we] really only got to see him twice, once in the practice and once in the game. Everyone was [trying to sign him]. There were about ten other teams trying to sign him, so I kept telling them, 'He wants to play for the Blackhawks, make him a decent offer. He wants to be a Blackhawk.'

They said, 'Well, what if he's not good enough?' I said 'Don't worry about that.' Because I knew he was an athlete. He ran triathlons, I knew all those facts on him from when my son went to school with him, and how hard he competed. John Marks, who played for the Black- hawks, was his coach up there. So he got on the phone and started telling them

Ed Belfour—one of Chicago's best net-minders of the 90s. (Photo courtesy of the Blackhawks.)

that they'd better take a serious look at him. So between all of us, we ended up getting lucky and getting him anyway. But then he had to go and learn to play. He had to go on the Canadian Olympic Team. We screwed him around for two or three years in the minors. He made himself good, anyway. We knew that going in, that he was going to make himself a good goaltender because he had the desire."

When it comes to net-minding style, the Eagle's is a bit unorthodox, something that his critics give him heat about on occasion. Like Glenn Hall and Tony Esposito, Belfour is a butterfly-style goalie. He has a flopping, sprawling style, and isn't afraid to leave the crease. Because he plays the puck more and is more adventurous, he tends to become involved in altercations more often than other goalies.

However, the Eagle's style works for him. In the January 8, 1993 issue of *The Hockey News*, Eddie commented on his style, saying: "I'm not a pretty goalie and I don't ever want to be called one, to tell you the truth. I'm not a show goalie. I'm not like that and I never will be. I just get the job done."

Belfour is an intense individual, and during the off-season he spends his time participating in triathlons. After running track in high school, he began running in these events during the mid-eighties. "Triathlons are tough," he explained in the September, 1991 issue of *Triathlete*. "I like that aspect. Once you've completed a race, it's very satisfying; you feel good inside. You know you did it and can do it again. And you compete against yourself rather than other people."

Belfour's intensity and dedication have enabled him to succeed in the NHL. His former high school coach, Ernie Sutherland, commented on his traits in the July 1991 issue of *Beckett Hockey Monthly*. "Eddie is the same in nearly every aspect now as he was in high school," he said. "He hasn't changed his work ethic, his attitude on the ice, his concentration, his will to win and his demeanor if he's pulled from the net. They're all the same. Any player worth having has got to want to be in the game. No one wants to be there more than Eddie. I've never seen anybody put any more into the game as a player than Eddie has."

Former Hawk Billy Gardner, a good friend of Belfour's, comments:

"To see Eddie perform—I mean I'm an Eddie backer—I don't know if you ever hear me, but I'm always for him just because of his work ethic. He wants to be the best all the time and if he has a bad night he stays behind for about an hour-and-a-half and works out. He just never wants to lose and tries to be the best all the time. I don't know if you could say [he is] limited talent-wise, but his style is very different, very unorthodox but he gets the job done. So you gotta like what he does with what he has, and I think that's his mindset, he wants to be the best. He's very intense…I sat beside Tony

[Esposito] for three years, and with Tony when he was playing, you couldn't talk to him because he was in a trance, and Eddie is the same way."

Teammate Jeremy Roenick also commented on the Eagle's intensity:

"You have to know [Eddie Belfour] to like him. He is a very personable person with his players. He is a very to himself person, he likes his privacy and he likes his stuff like he likes it, and if he doesn't have it that way, he can be pretty unbearable to live with. Probably the biggest, most intense competitor on our hockey club is Eddie Belfour. He demands perfection, he works for perfection, he won't accept anything else but perfection. If he lets one goal in a game he's not happy with himself. Eddie's got that fight in him, which is amazing. He doesn't talk during a game. He's a very intense person. You don't get on Eddie's bad side, because he's a guy that doesn't forget."

Teammate Joe Murphy feels much the same way, commenting:

"Eddie's a competitor. Fiery. A little on the edge. One of the best goalies in the League. Well prepared. Stay out of his way before the game. Eddie's a nut, but he's a good guy."

Sitting atop a career 2.64 GAA, (168-106-40 in 332 games with 28 shutouts) as of the close of the 1994-95 season, the Eagle's attributes have resulted in a myriad of achievements in the NHL. In 1990-91, he received the Calder (outstanding rookie), Vezina (best goaltender), and William M. Jennings Trophy (goaltender(s) for team with fewest G.A.). That season, he was named a First-Team All-Star and was dubbed *The Hockey News* NHL Rookie of the Year and Goalie of the Year. *The Hockey News* also named him to their 1991 All-Star team. To top off that season, he also took home the Trico Award (NHL goalie with best save percentage).

In 1992-93, he once again took home the Vezina and the William M. Jennings Trophies, sharing the latter award with Jimmy Waite. That season, he helped Chicago to a 2.70 GAA, posting a personal GAA of 2.59, leading the league in games played with 71. He helped the Hawks to a team GAA of 2.37 in 1994-95, again winning the Jennings Trophy and tying for the NHL lead in shutouts, with five.

Belfour has also made two Campbell Conference All-Star game appearances, first in 1991-92, and then in 1992-93. In addition to that, he played very well for Team Canada in 1989-90. Belfour holds the NHL record for most consecutive wins by a goaltender, with 11 in 1991-92. He also holds several Blackhawks club records as well. In 1990-91, he became the first net-minder in club history to win over 40 games in a season, breaking Tony Esposito's record (38) by recording 43. That same season, he also broke Esposito's record for games played in a single season by a Blackhawk goaltender (71), when he appeared in 74. Then, in 1992-93, he posted a second season of 40-plus wins by recording 41, making him only one of five goalies in NHL history to have a repeat 40+ season, next to Ken Dryden, Jacques Plante, Bernie Parent, and Terry Sawchuck. Finally, in 1991-92, the Eagle set a new record for penalty minutes in a season by a goaltender, when he recorded 40.

During the 1993-94 season, Belfour tied his career-high for shutouts, when he recorded seven. Two of them (March 8th vs. Anaheim, [3-0] and March 9th vs. Los Angeles [4-0]) were back-to-back. This marks the second time he accomplished such a feat, as he previously had back-to-back shutouts in 1991-92 (November 10th vs. Hartford [3-0] and November 14th vs. Toronto [3-0]).

Belfour gave stellar performances in the 1994-95 postseason, keeping his squad in the running, during which several games went into double overtime. In the final series against the Red Wings, Belfour faced 183 shots, compared to Mike Vernon's 99. "I don't think Eddie's human," said Jeremy Roenick after the series, in a June 13, 1995 *Chicago Sun Times* article by Brian Hanley. "I don't care what anybody says, I think he deserves the Vezina Trophy."

Belfour has also chosen an interesting hobby; collecting old hot rods, namely old Mopars (Chryslers). Among his collection are a '68 Roadrunner, '71 Cuda, '69 GTX, '70 Super Vee, a '67 and a '68 Charger, and two '70 Challengers.

CHRIS CHELIOS

Turning to the defensemen on Chicago's roster during this decade, several excellent athletes emerge. They are integral parts in the Blackhawks' defense-oriented system of play. The first and foremost Blackhawk blue-liner is Chris Chelios. Born in Evergreen Park, Illinois, on January 25, 1962, Chelios was acquired with a second-round pick in 1991 (Michael Pomichter) on June 29, 1990 from the Habs in exchange for Denis Savard. Chelios played hockey in San Diego, with the U.S. International University team. Eventually, he was cut from that team, and experienced bad luck playing forward for different Junior B teams in Canada at the age of 16. "Well, it goes back," said Cheli, reflecting upon the hardest setbacks on his road to the pros. "Not makin' it to junior teams or college teams. There were a few setbacks. It's just fortunate that I was in the right place at the right time. I've been lucky enough to be on good enough teams, and some winning teams that everybody got a little bit more successful."

After awhile, Chris finally found himself playing Junior Tier II hockey as a defenseman for the Moose Jaw Canucks in Moose Jaw, Saskatchewan, where he was the only American on that team. After earning a scholarship, he went on to play at the University of Wisconsin, under Badger Bob Johnson in 1982-83. From there, he spent the following season (1983-84), playing for both the U.S. National and the U.S. Olympic team.

Cheli broke into the NHL with the Montreal Canadiens in 1983-84, when he was chosen as their fifth choice (40th overall) in the entry draft. He played with the Habs until 1989-90. While there, he was Team Captain and helped the Canadiens secure a 1986 Stanley Cup victory.

Chelios has been a Blackhawk regular ever since 1990-91. As of the close of the 1994-95 season, he had racked up a career total of 129 goals for 600 points in 767 games. In addition to those numbers, he had also accumulated 1,786 minutes in penalties. Chelios has acquired a reputation around the league for his heavy-hitting, aggressive, and sometimes dirty style of play. He is an excel-

Chris Chelios—one of the best defensemen of the 90s.
(Photo courtesy of the Blackhawks.)

lent two-way player and penalty-killer, who plays very competitively. In the May, 1991 issue of *Hockey Digest*, in an article by Brian Cazenueve, Red Fisher, of the *Montreal Gazette*, described Chelios as "a mean, aggressive, dedicated, unflinching SOB who lives and loves the game, who plays with pain, and who is hated by anyone who has ever faced him."

After trading him away, Cheli's former coach Pat Burns explained…that he liked his intensity and the way he led by example. He commented that when the Habs traded Chelios to the Hawks, they gave up a junkyard dog who would not back down from anyone.

Chelios' defensive partner, Steve Smith, gave his impression of Chelios in the December, 1992 issue of *Beckett Hockey Monthly*, in an article by Tom Wheatley, commenting: "Cheli has this mean streak in him that adds to his game. That's a three-way combination that's unseen in this League:

offense, defense, and a mean streak. It just comes from a burning desire to win. That's the one thing I can say about Chris Chelios to sum up everything. And that is, he's a winner."

A winner he is indeed. Chelios's athletic talents have reaped him a considerable array of awards. In 1984-85, his first full NHL season, he was named to the NHL All Rookie Team. In both 1988-89 and 1992-93, he received the Norris Trophy as the league's most outstanding defenseman. Since his debut in the NHL, he has played in the NHL All-Star game six times (1985, 1990, 1991, 1992, 1993, and 1994). In addition to that, he has received All-Star honors three times (First Team: 1988-89, 1992-93, Second Team: 1990-91). Topping off all of his achievements was an appearance with Team U.S.A. in the 1991-92 Canada Cup.

Teammate Cam Russell commented on Chelios, saying:

"Well, my personal comments on someone like Chris Chelios, you know I'm being biased, but I feel he's probably the best all-around defenseman in the League. He's very underrated on his defensive play and it just amazes me because I've never seen the guy get beat one-on-one. Or, if he's ever put himself out of position, he always makes up for it. The guy does it all, and he plays 35, 40 minutes a game. He never has a bad thing to say about anybody and never complains about anything. So, I just think he's the ultimate defenseman, if you will. He's really personable. He's really down to earth. There's nothing pretentious about him at all. He's a great family person, and just an all around good guy."

For all of his achievements, Chelios gives a lot of credit to the athletes he's played with on the way, commenting: "I guess breakin' into the League it would be guys like Larry Robinson, Bob Gainey, and being able to play with guys like Guy Lafleur. It was a great advantage for me just learning from the best guys."

Chelios is involved in a noteworthy endeavor off the ice. He currently raises money for disabled children with teammate Jeremy Roenick through

J.R. and Cheli's Children. From the hockey camp they run during the summer, they have raised a lot of money that has been of great help to cocaine babies at Chicago's Maryville Academy.

One of Cheli's hobbies is collecting old hockey jerseys. Since he began collecting them, he has acquired sweaters from many different players, including Wayne Gretzky, Guy Lafleur, and Bob Gainey. Recently, he also opened Cheli's Chili Bar, which is located several blocks from the United Center on West Madison Street. There, one can eat Cheli's Chili.

The 1993-94 season was a mixed one for Chelios. A definite highlight was the new contract he agreed upon. At the time the biggest contract ever negotiated in team history, it is worth $12.275 million, and includes a $1.1 million exclusive marketing agreement.

The season also brought some disappointing moments as well. In an October 14, 1993, home game against Hartford, in which the Hawks lost 6-2, Chelios was penalized heavily and later given a four-game suspension. As it turned out, he was given a game misconduct after slugging Brian Propp. Then he was given a third-man-in penalty when he broke free of a linesman to jump into a fight between Adam Burt and Brian Noonan.

That game turned out to be quite eventful, and when it was over, Chelios had accrued two game misconducts, a 10-minute misconduct, a fighting major, as well as an instigator minor. He racked up a grand total of 51 penalty minutes, 37 of which came in the third period, both are Blackhawks club records. According to an article by Herb Gould in the November 11, 1993 issue of the *Chicago Sun Times*, the suspension without pay cost Cheli $45,833.

Chelios and Propp have been foes for some time. And while Cheli later commented that the incident was a lesson learned, he also said it wouldn't change his physical style of play. Both players had words for reporters after the incident occurred. In the October 17, 1993 issue of the *Chicago Sun Times*, in an article by Herb Gould, Chelios said "Propp is a gutless jerk. He has no [courage]. He punched me first the other night. I'll meet him on West Madison Street anytime. And tell him not to bring his shield." Propp also gave his feelings in an article appearing in the October 29, 1993 issue

of *The Hockey News*. Said Propp, "Chelios is just a lousy person. He's the kind of guy who will stick your eye out and not care."

Another disappointing moment for Cheli in the 1993-94 season last season occurred when he was handed a five-minute match penalty and an automatic ejection on February 2, resulting in a four-game suspension and a $500 fine. The reprimand was the result of Chelios' entanglement with Vancouver defenseman Dana Murzyn, in which he was accused of eye gouging.

Chelios felt he was the victim of officiating bias. In the February 4, 1994 issue of the *Chicago Sun Times*, he was quoted as saying: "Watch the tape. It's [bleeping] B.S. They call me for eye gouging just because their whole bench was screaming. I'm the one who has the cut under my eye. He [Murzyn] doesn't have a mark on him."

He then offered a few words about linesman Shane Heyer, saying: "When he was holding Dirk [Graham] and me by the jersey [during the fight], he said we start all the trouble. Those are his exact words, a direct quote…I know we are [held to a different standard of officiating], just by that comment [of Heyer's]. It's pretty obvious referees don't like us because we play more physical and more aggressive, which makes their jobs harder." Said Cam Russell about Chelios being a marked man: "Yeah, he seems to be a targeted guy. I'm not sure what the reason is for that. It could stem back to some incidence when he was younger, when he was playing against Philadelphia that year. But it just seems that he's always the topic or right in the middle of a problem somewhere. So, I don't know. I think he has a bad rap. He's just such a competitor. People are always goin' after him. Chelios is the kind of guy you either love or hate."

The 1993-94 season was not without its highlights, however. On October 14, in a game against the Jets, he recorded his 400th career assist, and later, on March 6th, he played his 700th career game against the Kings. These are hopefully only a small number of the milestones Chelios will reach during his career.

Prior to the 1994-95 season, during the lockout, Chelios was in the middle of a big problem when he made the following statement about NHL Commissioner Gary Bettman, taken from the September 30, 1994 *Chicago Sun Times*: "If I was Gary

Bettman, I'd be worried about my family, about my well being right now. Some crazed fan or even a player, who knows, might take it into his own hands and figure that if they get him out of the way, this might get settled. You'd hate to see something like that happen, but he took the job."

After making an apology to Bettman, Chelios was forgiven and allowed to play. In the same *Chicago Sun Times* article, he said: "I was emotional and flew off the handle. I'd just come off the ice after practice, I'd had a bad week, and you keep hearing all week, this guy says we're not going to play. I just got mad. In 11 years, I don't think I ever said anything like that."

During the 1994-95 season, Chelios scored five goals for 38 in 48 games, and led the team in +/- with 17. In the 1995 play-offs, Chelios tied a Hawk record held by Darryl Sutter when he scored two overtime goals in the same series during the division-finals sweep of Vancouver. His game changed a great deal as well, as he showed great restraint in getting into unnecessary entanglements with the opposition.

STEVE SMITH

Born in Glasgow, Scotland, on April 30, 1963, Smith was acquired by the Edmonton Oilers as their fifth choice (111th overall) in the 1981 Entry Draft. Before earning a regular seat in the League with the Oilers, Smith played for London of the OHL and both Moncton and Nova Scotia of the AHL. The Chicago Blackhawks acquired him in a trade for Dave Manson and future considerations on October 2, 1991.

Since that time, the 6'4", 215-pound blue-liner has fit in well in the Windy City. He is an excellent all-around defenseman who emphasizes a team game. He plays aggressively, and, according to former coach Darryl Sutter, one of his greatest assets is his consistent play, whether the team is winning or losing. Smith's philosophy as a player is: "The harder you work, the luckier you get," and Smith loves to work hard.

Smith's teammate Cam Russell said of Smith: "A guy such as Steve Smith is such a well-rounded defenseman. He plays the power play, he's a superb penalty killer, a great defensive player. It was three years ago when we played against Pittsburgh, it was very close between him and Chris [as to]

who was the best defenseman on our team because he just played incredible. The best thing you could probably say about Smitty is that he never plays a bad game. He shows up every single night and he's just a great professional. He just never plays a bad game."

When asked about his most unforgettable moment as a Blackhawk, Smith replies:

"Deep thought, I've never much thought about it. I guess it's yet to come. I guess the most unforgettable moment is probably the disappointment of the last time we walked off the ice against the Pittsburgh Penguins after losin' to 'em in the fourth game and knowing we had an opportunity to win the Stanley Cup and weren't able to follow through."

Steve Smith – an excellent all-around defenseman. (Photo courtesy of the Blackhawks.)

Smith lists his father as the most influential individual on his career. Said Smith: "I would say probably the work ethic of my father [has been most influential], showing me when I was young. Knowing that he had to get up every day and work hard for every penny he made, and everything he did for us as a growing family. It was very important to us."

Many feel that if Smith weren't on a team with a defenseman of Chelios' caliber, he would be a candidate for the Norris Trophy. Whatever the case, Smith's career has been a fruitful one. During his six seasons with Edmonton, he played on four Stanley Cup championship teams (1985, 1987, 1988, and 1990). In 1991, he played in the NHL All-Star game, and was one of the best players in the Canada Cup tournament. On August 31, 1992, he signed a five-year, $4.9 million contract, which at the time was the third-largest in club history. Then, in 1993, he made the WHL East First All-Star Team.

The 1993-94 season was not a good one for Smith. Early in the season, on November 20, 1993, he was involved in a stick swinging incident with Denis Savard. According to a November 27, 1993 *Chicago Sun Times* article by Herb Gould, Smith was chopped by Savvy late in the game, and Smith wanted to "warn Savard he'd be looking for him the next time the clubs meet," and got his message across with a shove. Savard responded with his stick, and then Smith. The incident was broken up after Savard chucked his stick at Smith. Both players were eventually suspended for four games. According to the Gould article, Smith's 11-day suspension ended up costing $54,427; an expensive lesson. Humorously, the two ended up becoming teammates when Savard rejoined the team late in the 1994-95 season.

To make matters worse, in a February 24, 1994 game against the Jets, Smith ended up with a compound fracture of his left leg when it got twisted and he fell to the ice during a fight. He also ruptured the nerve that controls the toes, affecting his skating. In a September 13, 1994 *Chicago Sun Times* article by Brian Hanley, Smith said of his injury: "The first day they took the cast off I wanted to cry. The doctors warned me the [muscle loss] would be substantial, but it was literally bone and skin on my quadriceps. I couldn't believe the body could do that."

Smith returned for the 1994-95 season, scoring one goal for 13 points and 128 penalty minutes (second only to Jim Cummins' 158) in 48 games.

GARY SUTER

Although the majority of his successful, 10-year hockey career has been spent with the Calgary Flames, the Blackhawks now have the pleasure of having a fine defenseman on their roster by the name of Gary Suter. In a complicated trade, Suter's rights were acquired by the Hartford Whalers with Paul Ranheim and Ted Drury for James Patrick, Zarley Zalapski, and Michael Nylander on March 10, 1994. The following day, Hartford traded Gary to the Blackhawks along with Randy Cunneyworth and a future draft choice for Frantisek Kucera and Jocelyn Lemieux.

Things weren't easy for Suter at first, in terms of the adjustment to his new home, but things improved quickly.

"The biggest challenge is just trying to be consistent and help out the team on a nightly basis. I think last year when I first got traded here it was a big adjustment for me, but I feel a lot more comfortable this year [1994-95].

"[Chicago's] a great sports town. I had a chance to play in the old Stadium last year before they knocked it down, and then this new building here [United Center], so I've had a part in the history of the Chicago Blackhawks here, and I feel real happy to be playing for the Hawks. It's close to my home town [Madison, Wisconsin], so in a lot of ways it's like getting traded home for me."

Born on June 24, 1964, in Madison, Wisconsin, Suter played for the University of Wisconsin from 1983-85, before breaking into the League as Calgary's ninth choice (180th overall) in the 1984 Entry Draft. Suter's teammate Chris Chelios also attended Wisconsin, but not at the same time. Chelios was on his way to the 1984 U.S. Olympic team just as Suter was coming in. However, he did play a role in helping the Badgers recruit Suter, and the two of them have been very close friends since those early days. Besides playing together in the

Windy City, the two have played on Canada Cup teams together.

In *The Chicago Blackhawks Yearbook — 1995*, in an article by Herb Gould, Chelios said of Suter: "When you get to know Gary, he has a real dry sense of humor. But he's basically a real quiet guy. He plays an aggressive game, a tough game, but he's not real chippy."

In a February 12, 1995 *Chicago Sun Times* article by Brian Hanley, coach Sutter said the following of Gary Suter: "He takes a lot of heat off Cheli. He's been the guy who pretty much gets the puck out [of the corners] and makes the plays. And as long as they play together, it saves a lot of wear and tear on both of them."

In addition to winning the Calder Trophy (outstanding rookie) in 1986 and being named to the NHL All-Rookie team, Suter was named to the NHL second All-Star Team in 1988, and has played in four All-Star games (1986, '88, '89, and '91). While play-ing for Team USA, he was named their co-MVP in 1985. Suter also played in the 1992 World Championships.

Suter still turns to his father for advice, and lists him as being most influential on him in his development as a player. "I would have to say my Dad [has been most influential], no question about it. He's coached me from the time I was a mite up until high school. He's still my biggest supporter, and every time I have any questions, or am going through a difficult time, why, I just talk things out with him."

During the 1994-95 season, Suter scored ten goals for 37 points in 48 games. During 681 career games, he has scored 140 goals and 607 points.

CAM RUSSELL

The man who has come to be known as Chicago's chief enforcer is defenseman Cam Russell. Born on January 12, 1969, in Halifax, Nova Scotia, and standing at 6'4", he ranks among the League leaders in penalty minutes. In a February 24, 1994 *Chicago Sun Times* article by Brian Hanley, former coach Darryl Sutter commented on Russell, saying: "He gets hit, but it doesn't affect him. And I'll guarantee you, when it's over the other guy knows he was in a fight that it wasn't one of those punch-and-grab things."

Before coming to the Chicago Blackhawks, who acquired him as their third choice (50th overall) in the 1987 Entry Draft, Russell played junior hockey with Hull of the QMJHL, where he was named to their Third All-Star team in 1988. Up until the 1992-93 season, he spent time teetering between the Indianapolis Ice and the Hawks. In his first full NHL season, he racked up 151 penalty minutes, which he surpassed in 1993-94 with a career-high 200.

Explaining the type of player he is, Russell comments: "The type of player I am, I'm a defensive-defenseman. I pride myself on hard work and giving 110% each night. Ya know, I'm not going to go out and score many goals a season or help the team that way [offensively], but you know, I'm going to play a physical game and stand up for my teammates if there's trouble."

Russell recently reflected upon his role as the Hawks' tough guy. When asked about the worst entanglement he's been in, he replied: "I'd say eas-

Gary Suter — veteran defenseman of quality. (Photo courtesy of the Blackhawks.)

ily the worst one was my first year when I was out trying to impress Mike Keenan. I dropped the gloves with Dave Brown. I don't think I'll ever forget that one. It was over pretty quick and I wasn't on top to say the least. I was seein' stars for awhile after that."

When asked about the things that go through a player's mind before a fight, he answered: "Those things happen so quick. I mean, you spend more time worrying about them before they actually happen. When they do happen, the adrenaline kicks in and you don't have any time to be scared, it's just react. Everything's done with reflexes and, like I said, the adrenaline kicks in and you don't feel any pain. You don't feel any bumps or bruises until the next day when you put your helmet and gloves on. It happens so fast, you don't have any time to think about it. The biggest problem with guys that play the type of role that I do in the League, we spend more time worrying about it and when you think about it, you don't even have to."

Russell claims that, despite his role, he has no personal enemies in the League:

"I wouldn't say anybody's really my personal enemy. I don't really try to pick guys out. I basically go out there and the only time I really get in a fight is if someone is taking liberties on one of our players, someone's roughing up one of our players. Or, if the team needs a bit of a boost to get going, if we're not playing very well, then I'll go out and maybe I'll go after one of their tougher guys. But, I really don't target anybody or try to get into any fisticuffs for no reason at all."

In terms of people being influential on his career, Russell points to former head coach Darryl Sutter, explaining: "I'd probably have to say Darryl Sutter [was most influential on me]. From coaching me in the minors in Indianapolis to my first year of pro, he gave me the opportunity and the trust that he instilled in me. He just really believed in me and gave me a lot of chances. [He] let me know that if I worked hard, it didn't matter if I made mistakes, as long as I gave it 100 percent every night."

The 1993-94 season wasn't a kind one for Russell, who suffered an injury to his neck in a

Cam Russell – "The Enforcer." (Photo courtesy of the Blackhawks.)

March game against the Nordiques. As it happened, Quebec left-wing Chris Simon blindsided him, resulting in a herniated disc that required surgery. Luckily, he returned healthy for the next season.

Aside from playing the game, Russell is part owner of a local team in his home town of Halifax, Nova Scotia. "They're an expansion team so they're doin' as well as you can expect," he said during the 1994-95 season." They started out strong and they've had a tough time lately. They've traded a lot of their older players for younger kids because they're making a bid for the Memorial Cup in '96, so we want to have a good team by then. These things take awhile and I think they're going to do well in the next couple of years. They've got a lot of young, talented kids comin' up, so they should be doin' pretty good. I really don't look at it as an investment. I haven't put a heck of a lot of money into it. Ya know, basically, it's just fun for me. For lack of anything better to say, it's giving me a chance to put something back into the community. It's just kind of fun. It gave me a place to skate when I was back home for the lockout, too."

JEREMY ROENICK

One of the Blackhawks' most talented forwards is Jeremy Roenick. Born in Boston, Massachusetts, on January 17, 1970, Roenick played high school hockey at Thayer Academy Prep, on their championship team. In 1988-89, he played for both the Hull Olympiques of the QMJHL, and the U.S. Jr. National team. While playing for the U.S. Jr. National Team, he was the leading scorer for Team U.S.A., and a first-team All-Star. While with Hull, he was named to the QMJHL's Second-All-Star-Team. In 1988-89, he was acquired by the Blackhawks as their number one pick (eighth overall) in the entry draft, and joined them late in the season. Today, he ranks among the very best players in the League.

Roenick plays center for Chicago, and is a talented, all-around player who plays a fast, hard-hitting game. He is intense and physical on the ice, possesses good ice vision, and isn't afraid of the corners. J.R. is also a very durable athlete. In the 1988-89 play-offs, he sacrificed a few teeth when Blues defenseman Glen Featherstone got him in the mouth with the shaft of his stick. In that same game, he was cut in the nose by a skate blade, taking eight stitches. Despite all of this, he still scored a goal, helping the Hawks beat St. Louis 4-2 and move on to the semifinals against the Flames.

Describing what kind of a player he is, Roenick explains:

"I'm a finesse hockey player. I like to go out and I like to make the hard play. I like to go out and make the low-chance, low-probability play. I'm an antagonist. I'm a pain-in-the-ass on the ice. I like to be, obviously, turning heads. I like the guys out there to realize when I'm on the ice and have to know when I'm on the ice. Ya know, if I go out there and I have [put] the fear in other people that I can make the good move, I can score a goal, I can hit you as hard as I can in the corner. There are many different dimensions of my game that I try to improve on.

That's how I think. I think I'm not really an old-style hockey player, but I do like to take my licks, give my licks, and get back in and do it again. It is old-fashioned, yeah, [but] I don't consider myself an old-fashioned player. I like new things. I'm up-to-date on all new things. Maybe the mentality of the way I play might be [old-fashioned], but I try to do a lot more fancy stuff than they did back then. I do like to go in and throw my body around and make that big hit, or get hit. I try to be an all-around player. I don't want to be one-dimensional."

Roenick also gave some insight into what his philosophy is on the ice, commenting:

"I'm sure it's the same philosophy as a lot of people. My number one thing is you've got to go have fun. If you don't have fun playing the game...obviously it's a game that should be loved. It takes a lot of intensity [and] a lot of hard work. My first thing is, make sure you have fun at it. Whether that be fooling around or, ya know, making jokes here and there, or fooling around on the ice. Little things like that, just make sure you keep the game fun. Still have that competitiveness where you can go out and lay out one of your buddies with a good physical hit and still go out and have a beer with him. It's a game you've got to play for your team and your teammates. There are no real friends on the ice, but there's a happy medium where you can have fun and still have that competitive edge, where you'll knock somebody's head off. I'm a competitive person. I want to be consistent, I want to be good every game. Each game, I go into another game trying to play better than I have the game before. Obviously, you have good games, you have bad games, but I want to continue to be at the top of the game. So I go into every game as an opportunity that I can have the best game of my career tonight, so it keeps that adrenaline flowing."

Teammate Joe Murphy described Roenick, commenting: "J.R. is a real giving guy. He's flamboyant. I mean, he loves to have a good time off the ice and on the ice. He's a good guy. He cares about all his teammates. Personally, I think he's the best player in the League at this point right now [1994-95 preseason]. He does it all. Sometimes people and other players get mad because of some of the things he says but, ya know, that's the person he is. He says things from the heart. I'm just glad he's with Chicago. I mean, he's such a valuable player to the team."

Defenseman Steve Smith also gave a good description of Roenick in an article by Tim Sassone that appeared in the February 14, 1992 issue of *The Hockey News*. "The only guy I can compare him to is a young Mark Messier. He's so fast. And when Jeremy hits people, believe me, he hurts them. The only thing is maybe he doesn't have the mean streak of Mess."

A perfect example of a Roenick hit can be seen by looking at one he dealt Vladimir Kostantinov of the Detroit Red Wings on January 27, 1994. It was pay back for when Kostantinov slashed him in the head with his stick in a game two days prior. Early in the game, J.R. boarded him so hard, that the plexiglas partition ended up in the crowd.

Much has been said in the press about the fact that Roenick feels restrained by the defensive style of hockey Chicago plays. Commenting on this situation prior to the 1994-95 season, Roenick discussed his role, and what he'd like it to be:

"Well, obviously I'd like to have free reign," he said. "I'd like to do what's gotten me to the NHL. I want to go out on the ice and do what I feel I'm best at. So when I feel that I'm being held back from doing that, obviously I'm going to shout out and disagree. That's just my personality and I'm always going to speak up with that. The Hawks' style is very defensive-oriented, which is why we've won so many hockey games in the past five, six years. By playing smart, defensive hockey. A good defense leads to a good offense. But, you know, I like to take chances and at times it does disable my defensive play a little bit. The big part of

my game is read-and-react to anticipate a lot of things. And sometimes I could get caught, but that's all right. I just go out and play. When I don't have the puck I try to play as good defense as possible and when I do have the puck I try to be as creative and offensive as possible."

Roenick lists his father as being most influential on him early in his development.

"[The biggest influence] was probably my dad, no doubt," he said, looking back. "My dad was my coach from the time I started skating until I was a Bantam. He coached me at every level up to Bantam [in] many, many different towns. We moved around a lot. I never stayed in one place more than a couple of years. My dad was my biggest [influence]. He was always there for me. He always supported me. Obviously, he was very tough on me, which helped me to be a competitive person."

Before Jeremy became involved in hockey, his father had no real experience with the game. "He never played," Roenick explains. "He was a football and soccer player. He never played hockey, he just got into it when I started. We learned together as we went. He really didn't know the game that much, so he couldn't teach it. But he did learn it and he did study it as I went along, so it was kind of like we learned together, so it was a lot of fun."

Many other people have been influential on Roenick in his development into a pro. "Coming into the NHL it was guys like Mike Keenan, Doug Wilson," he said. "Obviously, Michel Goulet and Steve Larmer had a lot to do with my career. Guys like Denis Savard who were really there for me in the beginning of my career. These guys are tremendous role players and they taught me a lot about what it took to make it in the game."

Although he has yet to help his teammates skate away with Lord Stanley's Cup, Roenick was fortunate to come close, which has been one of several highlights in his career with the Blackhawks.

"The Stanley Cup finals against Pittsburgh were phenomenal," he said. "It didn't finish up the way I wanted it to, but the experience was great.

Jeremy Roenick – one of the Blackhawks' most talented forwards getting some game action against the Red Wings. (Photo courtesy of the Blackhawks.)

You know, you get a taste of it that makes you want it back even more. Just to think that I made it to the finals is a mouthful for me and just to get the chance to get back there again is something that I can't stress enough that I want. That was impressive for me."

Losing never sits well with a true champion, and that goes double for Roenick. "I never take losing lightly," he said. "I do not accept losing. I don't appreciate losing. As a matter of fact, I [really] hate losing. So, whenever I get in those situations, especially the play-offs, and we fail, it's nothing that stands very tall with me and I don't accept it very well. But, I think about it and I take the positives out of it, I learn from my negatives and I throw it away."

The highlights don't end with his appearance in the Stanley Cup finals, however. "Obviously, my first All-Star game in Chicago Stadium was a phe-

nomenal thing," he continued. "It was amazing. It was the most amazing thing for me to have my first All-Star game in my home rink with my home fans and during the time of the [Gulf] War. There was talk that it was going to be cancelled, this and that, and the fans came out and gave the best ovation of the National Anthem that I ever heard. Then to have my 50 goals in Boston, and my 50th goal in Chicago, of two places that I've lived the past 15 years of my life. I scored my first 50th goal in Boston and I scored my second 50th goal in Chicago, it's pretty weird."

Due to his status as one of the Hawks' key offensive players, one might think that the pressures would be intensive. However, Roenick said that there really is not any pressure, explaining: "There is no pressure, I don't think. I don't feel pressure most of the time. Obviously, when you have big games [you do]. But, to me, I just go out and do the best I can. If I come out and say that I've worked as hard as I can, I have nothin' else I can give. So, pressure is what you make it. To me, I just go out and I play hockey. Ya know, if I play as hard as I can and I do everything possible and I succeed, that's great. At least I say that I did everything that I could."

As of the close of the 1994-95 season, Roenick has scored a career total 235 goals for 529 points in 458 games. Among his accomplishments are six career hat tricks, an appearance with Team U.S.A. in the 1991 Canada Cup, and All-Star game appearances in 1991-94. In 1989-90, he was named Rookie of the Year, as voted on by NHL players in *The Sporting News*. Among the many Blackhawk Club records he holds are several large accomplishments. In 1991-92, Roenick joined Bobby Hull and Al Secord as the third player in club history to score more than 50 goals in one season. Besides Hull, he is the only Hawk to have back-to-back 50-goal seasons (1992 and 1993). He is the first player in club history to have three consecutive 100-point seasons (1992, 1993, 1994). Roenick also notched his 500th career point on January 29, 1995, against Los Angeles.

After a knee-to-knee collision with Dallas Stars' defenseman Derian Hatcher on April 2, 1995, Roenick suffered an injury that was originally believed to put him out of the game for at least a year. Doctors feared that he had torn his anterior cruciate ligament, which prevents the knee from hyperextending. Luckily, the injury was not as serious as believed, and Roenick was able to rejoin the team during the play-offs wearing a brace. As it turned out, he severely bruised his tibia and hyperextended his knee. Many felt the hit to be dirty. However, with the hard-hitting style of hockey that Roenick plays, such incidents are likely to happen by chance. "It's part of the game," said Hawks Pro Scout Jim Pappin. "I don't blame the kid that hit him, if that's what you mean. I mean, sure he stuck his leg out, but everybody sticks their leg out. That's part of the game. When you take your stick and hit somebody over the head, then you're trying to injure him. But that was just a bang-bang play, and it happened."

After the 1994-95 season came to a close, Roenick expressed his opinion regarding his injury in a June 14, 1995 *Chicago Sun Times* article by Brian Hanley, saying:

> *"I didn't come back under the terms I wanted. The whole injury wasn't treated right by everybody…But I wanted to go with my heart and I wanted to do what's best for the team. I figured 80 percent of J.R. is better than no J.R. Now that the season's over, I probably made the wrong decision.*
>
> *By returning I might have hurt myself publicly, with the team or stats-wise. But people have to realize what kind of condition I was in, or how I felt. People have to realize I was really playing on one leg. I had a lot of stiffness, a lot of pain and not a lot of mobility. Plus, I had a brace on to boot, and I'd never played with a brace."*

In the same article, Roenick publicly criticized coach Sutter's defensive system and the fact that he did not get enough ice time during the play-offs: "With Darryl, everything is a struggle, everything is a project, and it doesn't have to be that way. But the Sutters have a fighting personality—they're intense people, which is why they've succeeded so long in the National Hockey League. I think you have to be able to communicate and talk to your players—not only be the coach, but also be a friend. He has to remember what it's like to be a player."

Besides his on-ice duties, Roenick is also involved with the National Hockey League Player's Association as his team's representative. Discussing his involvement in detail during the NHL lockout, Roenick said:

> *"Well, ya know, I'm the rookie at it this year [1994-95]. This is my first year as player rep. Bob Goodenow and our team really thought it would be a good idea to have someone who was more visible and more outspoken like myself to be a part of it. I feel that everybody has to stick up for everybody in the League. Just because you're an upper-echelon player doesn't mean that you can't get in there and defend the guys that are the 20th and the 19th guys. I mean, they're just as important to a hockey club as anyone else. It's very important to show people that it's just not the 17th, 18th, and 19th guys who care about everybody's future. Obviously, I care about everybody's future tremendously, and I'm in there supporting it in every way, regardless of how much money I'm losin' or how much money they're losin'. I think it's all in the same aspect. We have to think for each other and work for each other. That's what we do when we go on the ice; we play for each other. There's no reason why off the ice we can't do the same thing. It's been very uplifting to me. I've learned a lot of things. Obviously, I'm learning a lot of things. I'm becoming more knowledgeable of union things, being, the different pensions, the different insurances, all the ins and outs, the CBA. Things I had no clue about before that I understand much greater now. I think it's going to be good for me when I bring on other kids that are comin' up in the League. I can teach them, and maybe they can get interested in it. Obviously, a big part of my job is to be a leader, and to take kids that are comin' on and lead them in the right direction."*

During the off-season, J.R. enjoys golfing and plays on the Celebrity Golf Association tour.

BERNIE NICHOLLS

A recent addition to the Blackhawks' roster has been Bernie Nicholls. Born in Haliburton, Ontario, on June 24, 1961, Nicholls was drafted sixth by the Los Angeles Kings (73rd overall) in the 1980 Entry Draft. Before being signed by the Kings, Nicholls played for Kingston of the OHL.

Nicholls had a very successful career with the Kings. During two of his seasons, he scored more than 100 points, with 100 (46 goals and 54 assists) in 1984-85, and 150 (70 goals and 80 assists) in 1988-89. He also had 95 and 97-point seasons in 1983-84 and 1985-86, respectively.

Over the course of his 14-season, NHL career, Nicholls has been named to the Second All-Star Team once (1989), and has played in three All-Star games (1984, 1989, and 1990).

Nicholls was with the Kings until 1989-90, when he was traded to the New York Rangers for Tomas Sandstrom and Tony Granato on January 20, 1990. He has since had stints with both the Edmonton Oilers and New Jersey Devils before being signed by the Blackhawks as a free agent on July 14, 1994.

A free-spirited individual, former head coach Darryl Sutter described Nicholls in a March 2, 1995 *Chicago Sun Times* article by Brian Hanley, saying: "He plays with a lot of enthusiasm for an older player. He looks like he is still having fun out there. And after having him here, I can tell why he's a great play-off player—he finds the balance between being cool and being a great competitor, so he's always loose enough to handle [tough] situations."

Hawks Pro Scout Jim Pappin said the following of Nicholls:

"The reason we picked him up this year is because we watched the play-offs last year and New Jersey almost beat New York out to win the Stanley Cup and Nicholls was New Jersey's best player in that play-off series. He's been on three or four different teams because he has a different personality. Chicago's the type of city that his personality probably fits, because he's easy goin' and he doesn't have to impress New York people or California people - the Hollywood types. Sure, he's sort of in the middle and, he's got a few

Bernie Nicholls has several 4-goal games under his belt, putting him in the ranks of Bobby Hull. (Photo courtesy of the Blackhawks.)

good friends on the team in Joe Murphy. Ysebart was a good friend of his too. So, he's relaxed here and he's a good player."

In his first season with the Blackhawks, Nicholls showed management he was worth every penny of his near $1.2 million salary, by leading the team in points with 51 (22 goals and 29 assists). This puts his career numbers at 438 goals and 1,074 points in 933 games. He also has two 4-goal games, joining Bobby Hull (1965-66) as the only other Chicago Blackhawk to accomplish this feat.

TONY AMONTE

Born in Hingham, Massachusetts, on August 2, 1970, Tony Amonte is one of Chicago's key right-wingers. The Ranger's third choice (68th overall) in the 1988 Entry Draft, Amonte played for Boston University in 1989-90 and 1990-91 before breaking

Tony Amonte is one of Chicago's key right-wingers.
(Photo courtesy of the Blackhawks.)

has is a good vision of the ice. He sees the ice and he knows the game. When you match that with the speed and the shot, it makes a pretty talented hockey player."

During the 1994-95 season, Amonte scored 15 goals for 35 points in 48 games.

JOE MURPHY

The Blackhawks also have offensive talent in left-wing Joe Murphy. Born in London, Ontario, on October 16, 1967, Murphy was acquired to give the Hawks some scoring punch. He came to the Windy City on February 24, 1993, in a trade with the Edmonton Oilers for forward Dean McAmmond and defenseman Igor Kravchuk.

Before breaking into the NHL, Murphy played for the Canadian Olympic Team in 1985-86. That same season, he also played for Michigan State University, and was named the CCHA Rookie of the Year, scoring 24 goals in 35 games. Said Murphy: "With the Canadian Olympic Team, [the best thing] was probably just heading overseas and just experiencing [things] ... ya know, it was really my first time travelin' a lot, and just seein' the different cultures and the cities and how people lived. We were in Finland and Germany and just the experience of the hockey was intense. It was a lot of fun. Craig Mactavish was over there. He was practicing with the Olympic Team there because Edmonton was signin' him comin' out of Boston. I really hung around with him and he was a big help and a good influence on me."

Commenting on his game philosophy, Murphy said: "I think you've got to believe that you can win. You've got to believe in yourself and believe in your teammates around you. You have to be a family and think that's a big thing. Confidence and belief is my philosophy on being a player."

The Red Wings picked Murphy as their first choice (first overall) in the 1986 Entry Draft. While with Detroit, he struggled to earn a regular seat in the League, teetering back and forth between Adirondack of the AHL and the Red Wings. Eventually, Detroit sent Murphy to Edmonton with Petr Klima, Adam Graves, and Jeff Sharples in exchange for Jimmy Carson, Kevin McClelland, and the Oiler's fifth-round draft choice in the 1991 Entry Draft (later traded to the Habs, who selected Brad Layzell). While an Oiler, he performed very respectably under influential coach Ted Green in his two full sea-

into the NHL. While there, he was named to the Hockey East Second All-Star Team and the NCAA Final Four All-Tournament Team in 1991.

Before being acquired with the rights to Matt Oates by Chicago in a trade for Stephane Matteau and Brian Noonan on March 21, 1994, Amonte spent three seasons playing for the New York Rangers, and was named to the NHL/Upper Deck All-Rookie Team in 1992.

Amonte grew up with teammate Jeremy Roenick, with whom he played hockey at Thayer Academy Prep school. Said Roenick of his fellow teammate: "Me and Tony [Amonte] are very, very knowledgeable of each other. We played together growin' up. We went to high school together. We grew up together, so obviously we feel very comfortable together. Tony's a tremendously fast skater. He's got great hands. He's got a booming shot, which is why he scores so many goals. What Tony

sons there, with a 27-goal, 62-point season in 1991, and a 35-goal, 82-point season in 1992.

Teammate Jeremy Roenick gave his feelings on Murphy, commenting: "Murph is an unbelievable hockey player. He's a guy who loves to have the puck all the time, kind of like myself. That's where we didn't hit it off exactly like we wanted to, but Murph and I did play very well together. We were a good pair for each other [in the 1993-94 season] and I'm sure you'll probably see a lot more to come."

Since coming to the Blackhawks, Murphy played his first full season in 1993-94, filling the void left by the departure of Steve Larmer. The previous season, he played in only 19 regular season games, due to contract woes with the Oilers. In 1993-94, however, Murphy did very well, posting a 70-point season (31 goals and 39 assists), equal to Larmer's last season as a Hawk.

Joe Murphy being checked by a Tampa Bay Lightning player.
(Photo courtesy of the Blackhawks.)

When asked if he felt as though he felt obligated to fill the void left by Larmer's departure, he said: "Well, a lot of people maybe expected or looked at me to [take] his place but, ya know, personally I wasn't trying to replace Steve Larmer. I mean, he's a great hockey player and he's done a lot in his career. I just tried to come in and separate the two and just come in and try to play my game and do the best I can, just work as hard as I could. I mean, there's always gonna be pressure and expectations. I just came and tried to play up to my ability."

Former Hawks' head coach Darryl Sutter also gave a description of Murphy in an April 10, 1994 *Chicago Sun Times* article by Brian Hanley, saying: "Murph gets a lot of ice time, so he has to contribute. If he plays with a high level of intensity and focus, he's a top-notch player. If not, he's an average player." As of the close of the 1994-95 season, Murphy had a career total 144 goals for 329 points in 452 games. During the 1994-95 season, he led the Hawks in goals with 23.

When asked about playing for the Blackhawks, Murphy replies: "I love playing in Chicago. I feel that with the defensive team we have, we're gonna have a shot, we're always gonna be in games, we're always gonna give ourselves a chance to win. Just gettin' traded to Chicago [has been great]. I love it. I think it's just a great, great city, great organization, new rink, I mean, I think just gettin' traded there was probably the most unforgettable thing to happen."

BRENT SUTTER

Born June 10, 1962, in Viking, Alberta, Brent Sutter is a member of the well-known Sutter clan. Sutter was the New York Islander's first choice (17th overall) in the 1980 Entry Draft. Before breaking into the NHL, he played for Red Deer of the AJHL and Lethbridge of the WHL. After playing eight games for the Islanders in 1991-92, Sutter came to the Blackhawks with Brad Lauer in a trade for Adam Creighton and Steve Thomas on October 25, 1991. So far, his best season point-wise was in 1984-85, when he scored 42 goals for 102 points in 72 games.

Said Jeremy Roenick of his teammate:

> *"Guys like Brent Sutter are tremendous role players. Brent has a job that he does on this hockey club and he ac-*

cepts it well and he does the job extremely well. He's a great guy with the players. Brent gets along with everybody. He's put in a very sticky situation with his brother being a coach and stuff like that. But, he just wants to be one of the guys. He doesn't want to be thought of as the coach's brother. He doesn't want to be thought of as another guy on the team's brother. He wants to be known as Brent Sutter. He helps kids, he helps the young kids. He helps the older guys, he's a friend with all the older guys. He's really a guy that you love to have on your hockey club because he's genuine, he's personable, and he'll go out and give you 150 percent every single night."

"Brent [has a good] work ethic," said Joe Murphy. "He's one of the hardest workers. I think last year [1993-94] he was the best-conditioned player on the team. He's definitely a leader. He's won two Stanley Cups and he's an important piece to our puzzle. He comes to play hard every night, night in and night out. I know that it's not showin' up on the score sheet, last year, but the intangibles that he brings to the hockey club are as important as any goals he can get. He's a real leader and a good guy to have in the dressing room."

One area of controversy has been that surrounding the fact that Brent's older brother Darryl was also his coach. Jeremy Roenick said the following of the situation: "Everything's been great. I mean, us as players, we don't even think about them being brothers. It's not even an issue and all the time, you don't even think of it. You don't see them and say, 'Hey, they're brothers, you get special treatment.' You almost forget that they're brothers because they all do their own thing."

One highlight of Brent's career with the Blackhawks occurred when he snapped a 42-year-old team record for the fastest goal from the start of a game when he did so in eight seconds in a February 5, 1995 game against the Vancouver Canucks. The record was formerly nine seconds, held by Gus Bodnar (2-19-53 vs. Rangers) and Bobby Hull (12-6-70 vs. Maple Leafs).

In 1994-95, Sutter scored seven goals for 15 points in 47 games. This put his career numbers at 341 goals and 767 points in 940 games.

Brent Sutter broke the team's 9-second 42-year old record for the fastest goal from the start of the game in 8 seconds. (Photo courtesy of the Blackhawks.)

DIRK GRAHAM

When one thinks about team leadership, another one of Chicago's recently retired forwards immediately comes to mind. Born on July 29, 1959, in Regina, Saskatchewan, Dirk Graham was a long-time hockey veteran, and Captain of the Chicago Blackhawks, until his retirement in the summer of '95. A tough, defensive player, he possessed an excellent knowledge of the game and was a good checker and penalty killer.

In his home town of Regina, Graham played junior hockey with the Pats of the WCHL from 1976 to 1979, scoring 218 points in his last two seasons there. But before making it to the NHL, Graham struggled for a long time in the minor leagues. In June of 1979, he was the Vancouver Canucks' fifth choice (89th overall) in the Entry Draft. However, in that season, after appearing in only two exhibition games with them, he was sent to their farm team, the Dallas Blackhawks, of the now nonexistent Central League. His contract there wasn't renewed the following season, as the Canucks weren't impressed with his performance.

After that let down, Graham found his way to the IHL, which at the time wasn't really affiliated with many NHL clubs. Playing for the Fort Wayne Komets in only six games, he was quickly acquired by the Toledo Goaldiggers, where he scored 70 goals in 1982-83, and secured First Team IHL All-Star honors. Toledo's coach, Bill Inglis, was very impressed with Graham and became a positive influence on him. It was he who got the Minnesota North Stars interested in Duke, as his teammates now call him.

After signing as a free agent with the North Stars on August 17, 1983, Dirk spent more time in the minor leagues during his first two seasons there, first with Salt Lake City of the CHL, and then with Springfield of the AHL in 1984-85 for half of the season. While playing for Salt Lake, he was a First Team CHL All-Star, racking up a season total of 94 points. After that time, he became a sturdy, consistent performer in the NHL. On January 2, 1988, the Blackhawks acquired him in a trade for Curt Fraser, and he spent the remainder of his professional career with Chicago.

"He's a consummate leader. A perfect captain," said former Hawk Billy Gardner. "He plays under stress. [Dirk is] a guy who struggled for about five years in the minors, finally got a chance, and he's still playing. He can do it all. He can score, he's a great penalty killer, and you know you're going to get your money's worth every time he's on the ice. I think he's one of best captains probably ever in a Blackhawk uniform."

Said teammate Jeremy Roenick:

"Dirk Graham, [and] I've said [it] many times, Dirk Graham is the captain of captains. He is a man that has gone through so much adversity, who has paid his dues well beyond anybody's expectations. He knows the game, he's a tremendously, tremendously caring person. He is a team guy of amazing proportions. He is somebody that you have to know personally to really get a grip of. You can talk about Dirk Graham as much as you want, but until you actually see the per-son that he is and the things that he brings to a hockey club, you can't really imagine. You can explain as much as you can, but he's a person that you actually have to come in contact with to grasp."

Teammate Joe Murphy also views Duke in a positive light, commenting: "I think Dirk Graham is probably the most important player on our team, being the captain right now. He holds the group together. There are different egos in sports and on different teams and, ya know, he's our captain, he's the guy the guys look up to. His work ethic [makes him a great leader]. He's a quiet leader, but when he has something to say, the guys listen to him. He just goes out and plays hard. When you see Dirk Graham out there workin' hard, there's your leader. Night in and night out he does it. He's one of the

Dirk Graham retired in the summer of 1995.
(Photo courtesy of the Blackhawks.)

best in-shape guys on the team. Everybody has a lot of respect for Dirk."

While with the Blackhawks, Graham experienced several high points. First, in 1990-91, he was awarded the Frank J. Selke Trophy as the League's best defensive forward. Then, in 1991-92, he set the club record for most goals by one player in one play-off period, when he scored three times in game four of the finals against Pittsburgh.

In 1993-94, Graham missed 17 games after suffering a separated shoulder in a February 18, game against the Winnipeg Jets. The injury occurred after former Hawk Mike Eagles knocked him to the ice during the second period, also causing a cut to his head that required ten stitches to close. After the season's end, the 35-year-old veteran hinted about retiring, as he had done in the past. However, he returned for the 1994-95 season, and continued contributing valuable leadership, along with four goals and 13 points. This placed his career totals at 219 goals and 488 points in 772 games, with 912 penalty minutes. After the 94-95 season, Graham retired from playing and joined Lorne Henning as an assistant coach.

MICHEL GOULET

Another one of the Blackhawks' best forwards during the nineties was future Hall-of-Famer Michel Goulet. Born in Peribonka, Quebec, on April 21, 1960, Gou, as he was called, played left-wing for the Hawks, just as his childhood idol Bobby Hull did.

Before breaking in with Birmingham of the WHA in 1978-79, Michel played junior hockey for Quebec of the QMJHL for two seasons. After Birmingham, Goulet earned a regular seat with the Nordiques, who picked him as their first choice (20th overall) in the 1979 Entry Draft. He spent 11 seasons with Quebec, posting a career-high, 106-point season in 1987-88. He was acquired by the Chicago Blackhawks on March 5, 1990, in a trade that sent himself, Greg Millen, and the Nordiques' sixth-round choice (Kevin Jacques) in the 1991 Entry Draft to the Windy City for Mario Doyon, Everett Sanipass, and Dan Vincelette.

While in Quebec, where he spent the best years of his career, Goulet experienced several career highlights. He was named to the NHL First All-Star Team in 1984, 1986, and 1987, and to the NHL Second All-Star Team in 1983 and 1988. In addition to that, he appeared in the NHL All-Star Game five times (1983-86, and 1988).

Goulet, who was excellent around the net, had 16 career hat tricks and two four-goal games during his career. In Chicago, his longevity was recognized as he became one of a select few to appear in over 1,000 games on January 10, 1993, in a game against Los Angeles. He is a member of an even more elite group of NHL players to score over 1,000 career points, reaching the milestone with a hat trick against the Minnesota North Stars on February 23, 1991. Even more distinguishing is the fact that he is one of very few players to score over 500 career goals, when he reached the milestone in a February 17, 1992 game against the Calgary Flames.

Jeremy Roenick commented on the easy-going Goulet in a November 26, 1993 *Chicago Sun Times* article by Herb Gould, saying: "Michel is just so smart. He knows everything about the game, where to be in every situation. That's why he's going to be a Hall-of-Famer. It's one thing to play the game well. It's another to know it well."

The 1993-94 season wasn't a good one for Gou. Because he was playing inconsistently, Sutter benched him at several points during the regular season. Then, to make things even worse, Michel suffered a career-ending concussion in a March 17th game against the Habs when the puck got tangled up in his skates, causing him to slip and hit his head on the endboard and ice. The incident resulted in a stretcher ride off the ice, and a stay at Montreal General Hospital in the intensive care unit for observation.

In a January 27, 1995 *Chicago Sun Times* article by Brian Hanley, Goulet reflected on his retirement from the game, saying: "Today is a big day, looking back on a career in which I'm very satisfied and very proud. I always wanted to give 100 percent on the ice…And the day I couldn't play my best hockey, [I decided] I would not."

In the same article, Goulet's teammate Dirk Graham said the following of Goulet: "Obviously, Michel will be known for his scoring. He's probably the best left-wing scorer in all of hockey [history]. But what is lost is the leadership Michel brought to the team. That's what I'll probably miss most—his invaluable leadership and knowledge of the game."

Said Darryl Sutter in an April 14, 1995 *Chicago Sun Times* article by Brian Hanley: "He is probably the quietest superstar, in terms of people talking about him, who has ever played the game. I'm sure Michel hasn't even thought about [coaching] but we have a lot of French prospects in our organization and he would be a hell of an example for them."

Goulet scored 16 goals for 30 points in 56 games in 1993-94, putting his career total at an impressive 548 goals for 1,152 points in 1,089 games. He still assists the Hawks as a "roving instructor" on a part-time basis and periodically participates in radio broadcasts.

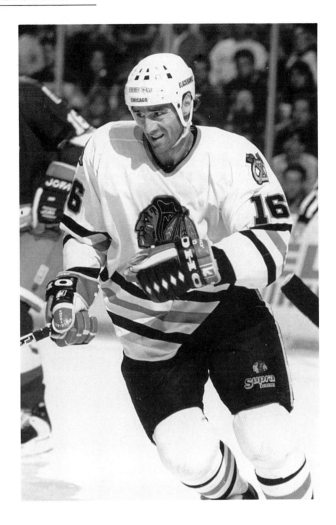

Michel Goulet played left-wing just like his childhood hero Bobby Hull. (Photo courtesy of the Blackhawks.)

1995-96 Chicago Blackhawks – top row, l to r: Rob Pulford, Phil Thibodeau, Mark King, Troy Parchman, Mike Gapski, Lou Varga, Pawel Prylinski, Jim DeMaria. Third row, l to r: Sergei Krivokrasov, Jim Cummins, Brent Grieve, Patrick Poulin, Cam Russell, Tony Horacek, Bob Probert, Greg Smyth, Roger Johansson, Darin Kimble, Eric Weinrich, Keith Carney, Jeff Shantz, Steve Dubinsky. Second row, l to r: Jeff Hackett, Tony Amonte, Bernie Nicholls, Gerald Diduck, Gary Suter, Ed Belfour, Jim Pappin, Rich Preston, Paul Baxter, Phil Myre, Michel Goulet, Murray Craven, Jeremy Roenick, Joe Murphy, Denis Savard, Jimmy Waite. Front row, l to r: Steve Smith, Dirk Graham, Bob Murray, Tommy Ivan, Bob Pulford, Michael Wirtz, William W. Wirtz, W. Rockwell Wirtz, Peter Wirtz, Jack Davison, Brent Sutter, Chris Chelios.